Poisons and Poisoners

Poisons and Poisoners

*An Encyclopedia of
Homicidal Poisonings*

Michael Farrell

ROBERT HALE · LONDON

ISBN 0 7090 4714 2

Robert Hale Limited
Clerkenwell House
Clerkenwell Green
London EC1R 0HT

Photoset in Times Roman by
Derek Doyle & Associates, Mold, Clwyd.
Printed in Great Britain by
St Edmundsbury Press Ltd, Bury St Edmunds, Suffolk.
Bound by WBC Bookbinders Ltd, Bridgend, Glamorgan.

Acknowledgements

I am grateful to many people who helped me in preparing this book.

The staff of the British Library were always efficient and helpful, as were the staff of the Library of the Royal College of Physicians.

His Honour Judge Brian Clapham kindly commented on some of the cases and made helpful suggestions about the range of cases to be covered.

Tricia Farley of Epsom District Hospital made many useful suggestions on the sections concerning particular poisons while Dr David Reaveley of Charing Cross Hospital spent an enormous amount of time with me commenting on both poisons and related issues such as forensic tests. Home Office Pathologist Professor Bernard Knight generously read the sections which concerned poisons and related issues and made many helpful comments.

The manuscript was word processed with great speed, efficiency and good humour by Yvonne Webster.

Everyone who helped did so with enormous enthusiasm for their area of knowledge and I hope I have been able to convey some of that in the text.

M.F.

To my dear friend
David Wells

A to Z

Aconite

Aconite (*Aconitum napellus*) is a poisonous plant also known as wolf's bane or monk's hood found in Europe and North America. Aconite or aconitine is also a poisonous alkaloid extract from the plant in the form of a white crystalline powder. Ancient Greeks are thought to have given the plant its name because it was found growing on rocks which they called 'aconas'.

Such is the potency of aconite that Pope Clement VII charged the physician Matthiolus to find an antidote. Using criminals condemned to death, Matthiolus set up an experiment. He split the prisoners into two groups, giving the poison to both but the particular antidote he wished to test to only one group. Oil and water was found to be the most successful 'treatment', simply because, being an emetic, it caused the sufferer to vomit out the poison.

Aconite, applied to the skin as a liniment has been used as a counter irritant to relieve pain such as that from rheumatism. In times past, tinctures of aconite were used in the early onset of fevers, partly because they promote sweating.

Aconite is absorbed by the gastro-intestinal tract if taken internally but can also be absorbed through the skin. There was real danger of over liberal use of aconite liniment in the past, especially if the skin was broken.

A fatal dose of aconite can be as little as 5 ml to 10 ml of tincture or about 1 mg. Large doses kill almost instantly.

The action of aconite on the skin explains its past use as a pain reliever. Because it stimulates nerve endings it is able to relieve pain in muscles served by the same nerve root. One theory of how such a counter irritant might work is that the substance sets up pain impulses from the skin which alter the effect of the original pain from other sites 'connected' to the same nerve route. This 'vasodilation' (dilation of blood vessels) has the effect of easing the original pain.

Taken internally, aconite affects the CNS and paralyses the muscles. Death may be caused by paralysis of the heart or the respiratory centre. The heart is first slowed through the vagus centre and is also affected directly. Heart co-ordination is disturbed so that the blood ebbs and flows rather than circulating properly. Eventually the heart stops often suddenly.

Taken by mouth, aconite causes a sensation of warmth or tingling in the throat, mouth, stomach and skin. Later the skin feels cold, giddiness and restlessness arise and the sufferer experiences breathing difficulties. Vomiting and diarrhoea occur, convulsions take effect and breathing problems increase as the muscles controlling respiration become paralysed. Death ensues some eight minutes to four hours after the poison has been taken.

Stimulants such as atropine are sometimes given by injection to try to counteract aconite poisoning.

Action of Poisons

Two of the major ways in which poisons act are by attacking enzymes and/or by affecting the nervous system.

An enzyme is a chemical ferment manufactured by living cells. The first enzyme to be isolated in a fairly pure state was identified in 1926 and subsequently hundreds more have been obtained. All the enzymes so far discovered have been proteins and they are found in many bodily tissues and in digestive fluids. Essentially enzymes are catalysts which although they are produced by living cells operate independently from them. Being more delicate than inorganic catalysts, enzymes are easily destroyed for example by heat. Acids or alkalis also destroy them because enzymes are active only within a certain range of acidity or alkalinity.

Thrombin in the blood is an enzyme which causes coagulation. Pepsin in the gastric juice and trypsin of the pancreatic juice are two further enzymes. Both split up food proteins into simpler molecules and ultimately break them down into amino-acids which the body uses to build back its own protein materials.

Enzymes are essential to the proper functioning of the body. In small amounts, they can produce large-scale transformations of various compounds. Each enzyme has a specialized function and affects a particular chemical reaction in the body. Some enzymes are present in large amounts while others occur in comparatively tiny quantities. Some are not so important; others are so called 'key' enzymes. Their structure is a complex network of atoms of carbon, oxygen, nitrogen, hydrogen, sulphur and others. Enzymes may be globe shaped and have loops and twists which are easily destroyed by poison.

When a poison inhibits enzyme activity, this can cause

enormous damage. A poison which attacks an enzyme which is both present in tiny amounts and a 'key' enzyme, is particularly destructive. If sufficient molecules of a poison are present, the vital enzyme is destroyed. Cyanide (q.v.) attacks a vital enzyme in the blood. Some poisons attack enzymes in the nervous system, so there is no rigid distinction between poisons acting on the nervous system and those acting on enzymes. Among other poisons which effect enzymes are lead, antimony, arsenic and mercury.

Turning to poisons which effect the nervous system, these can be further subdivided into those influencing the central nervous system (CNS), those affecting the peripheral nerves and those working on the autonomic nervous system.

Poisons influencing the CNS (the brain and spinal cord) may depress or stimulate it. Among drugs which depress the CNS are barbiturates of which Seconal is an example, an overdose of Seconal causing death by this depressant action. Strychnine by contrast stimulates the CNS, although it has other ways of acting too.

In considering poisons which affect the peripheral nervous system, it will first be necessary to outline the nature of that system. The peripheral (or cerebro-spinal) nerves stem from the CNS, there being forty-three on each side.

The system activates voluntary muscles via a nerve-muscle junction. This is essentially a gap which is alternately filled by two fluids; one which allows the nerve impulse to pass and another which destroys the first fluid. At nerve endings are stored tiny clusters of acetylcholine. An impulse travelling down the nerve releases some of these clusters allowing acetylcholine to bridge the gap and touch the membrane on the other side. At rest, this membrane is 'polarized' that is, it has a negative electrical charge inside and a positive charge outside. The acetylcholine changes the membrane's electrical condition (depolarizes it) and thereby sends an impulse to the muscle. To prevent continual stimulation of the muscle, the second fluid, cholinesterase, is released, destroying the acetylcholine and breaking the connection. The whole process takes only one five hundredth of a second. In the case of voluntary muscles, the junction is between a motor nerve and a motor end plate of the muscle.

Curare based drugs are among those which act by competing with acetylcholine. They combine with the receptors on the muscle's motor end plate and block them. This prevents the end plate from being depolarized by acetylcholine. The muscles become paralysed and flaccid.

Other substances act by depolarization, and succinylcholine chloride is one of these. It mimics the action of acetylcholine at the motor end plate causing the voluntary muscle to contract. Unlike acetylcholine, however, the drug is not destroyed straight away. Consequently depolarization continues. This does not lead, as might be first thought to continued contraction of the muscles, and it may be that this is because the drug at the same time decreases the excitability of the end plate. So although depolarization of the end plate continues, it does not contract the muscle. Possibly the neuromuscular block may be due to reduction in the excitability of the muscle as much as to depolarization. The two effects may also be interrelated.

Again, before looking at poisons working on the autonomic nervous system, we need to look briefly at that system. The autonomic system is concerned with the internal organs, blood vessels, and glands which secrete. It functions mainly independently of will. The system is situated in the neck, chest and abdomen and comprises ganglia (clusters of nerve cells) connected by nerve fibres. The autonomic system consists of a sympathetic and a parasympathetic system. The sympathetic system augments heart action and inhibits intestine action. The parasympathetic system is connected with the CNS through nerve centres in the mid-brain, medulla and lower end of the spinal cord. It inhibits heart action and augments intestine action.

Nerve cells put out or receive impulses. Outgoing impulses are conveyed by efferent nerves to muscles and blood vessels. Incoming impulses are conveyed to the nerve cells by afferent nerves which carry messages from sense organs, skin, joints and so on. Acetylcholine is involved in transmitting nerve impulses not just from motor nerve to voluntary muscle, but is particularly important in the autonomic system. In the parasympathetic system, it transmits nerve impulses to the brain. It mediates transmission from nerve to nerve and from nerve to organs.

Atropine is a poison which blocks the effect of acetylcholine and thereby disturbs the action of the parasympathetic aspect of the autonomic nervous system.

As well as categorizing poisons as those attacking enzymes and those affecting the nervous system, there are other ways in which poisons can be grouped in relation to their mode of action. Among these is the subdivision into corrosives, irritants and narcotics.

Corrosives burn and destroy tissues on contact, acting directly. Among well known corrosive poisons are strong mineral acids like nitric acid; alkalis such as caustic soda or ammonia; and some strong salts such as corrosive sublimate.

Irritants or acrid poisons produce inflammation or irritation often in the stomach and intestines and can cause vomiting, diarrhoea and abdominal pain, collapse, unconsciousness and death. Among better known irritants are white arsenic (arsenious acid), yellow arsenic (orpiment), acetate of lead, sulphate of copper, subacetate of copper, arsenate of copper (Scheele's green), tartrated antimony (tartar emetic) and phosphorus.

Narcotics affect the CNS causing a stuporous state, although many narcotics also have an irritant effect and are sometimes further sub-classified as acronarcotics or narcotico-irritants. Substances which are predominantly narcotic include opium and its derivatives, prussic acid (hydrocyanic acid), potassium cyanide and chloroform. Poisonous gases such as carbon monoxide are included as narcotics. Generally, the symptoms produced by narcotic poisoning include headache, giddiness, visual problems, convulsions, stupor, unconsciousness, coma and death.

Narcotico-irritants comprise substances which cause symptoms of irritation such as sickness, vomiting, convulsions, delirium or excitement. Included in this group is strychnine, foxglove (*Digitalis purpurea*), monk's hood (*Aconitum napellus*), henbane (*Hyoscyamus niger*), deadly nightshade (*Atropa belladonna*), tobacco (*Nicotiana tabacum*), spotted hemlock (*Conium maculatum*) and some types of poisonous fungi. Symptoms begin with vomiting, diarrhoea and stomach pains and progress to delirium and convulsions, stupor and death.

Administration of Poisons

Administering poison in food or drink is the most common murder method and a great variety of fare has been used. The poison menu includes tea with arsenic (Mary Blandy, Kitty Ogilvy) and with cyanide (Brian Burdett). Coffee has been doctored with strychnine (Eva Rablen), while beer or stout has been laced with cyanide (Richard Brinkley), arsenic (Henrietta Robinson) and prussic acid (John Tawell). Charlotte Bryant used Oxo drink with arsenic and milk was laced with arsenic by Mary Creighton and Everett Appelgate. Mineral drink (and fruit pie) was mixed with arsenic by Frederick Radford.

As well as poisoning her father's tea, Mary Blandy also stirred arsenic into his gruel. Other foods which have been used include steak and kidney pie with paraquat (Susan Barber), corned beef with strychnine (Ethel Major) and game and tarts mixed with mercuric sublimate (Frances Howard).

Cake has been spiked with arsenic (Marie Lafarge) and aconite (Dr George Lamson), while arsenic impregnated chocolates have been employed by Cordelia Botkin and possibly by Herbert Armstrong. Arthur Ford impregnated chocolate covered sweets with cantharidin.

A particularly calculating way of administering poison is in tonics or medicines expected to benefit the victim. In this category falls the cyanide contaminated tonic sent to fellow soldiers by Adolph Hofrichter. Jean Vaquier similarly doctored Bromo salts with strychnine knowing they were to be taken by his lover's husband. Mary Blandy convinced a gullible couple they were in danger and must take a packet of special powder each day for a week as protection. One of the packets contained mercuric chloride, while the extra antidote given was honey mixed with arsenic.

Mass murderer Sadamichi Hirasawa administered cyanide pills to bank employees convincing them it was a treatment for dysentery. Captain John Donellan switched his brother-in-law's medicine for cherry laurel water while Carlysle Harris changed the contents of capsules compounded for insomnia so they contained a lethal dose of morphine. In the course of his wife's treatment Dr William King administered arsenic to her. William Waite similarly tampered with capsules of medicine prescribed for his wife, filling one with arsenic.

Injections have included diphtheria bacteria masquerading as cholera vaccine (O'Brien), arsenic (Marie Hilley), succinylcholine chlorine (Dr Carl Coppolino), insulin (Kenneth Barlow), cyanide (Dr Pierre Bougrat) and bacteria taking the place of camphorated camomile (Henry Girrard).

Inhalation of poison fumes as a form of homicidal poisoning is something of a rarity but was used by Reginald Hinks (carbon monoxide) and Dr Etienne Deschamps (chloroform).

Animal Poisons (Zootoxins)

When reviewing criminal cases of poisoning, it is unusual to come across animal poisons although strictly speaking poisoning by insulin (q.v.) constitutes using a substance with an animal origin. Kenneth Barlow (q.v.) injected his wife with insulin to murder her, but such cases are comparatively rare, when compared with, for example, the number of cases in which plant poisons were used. Also Arthur Ford was convicted of manslaughter using cantharides (q.v.).

But animal poisons constitute an area of great intrinsic interest. When considering zootoxins, snake venom is perhaps the first example to spring to mind. Snake poisons are an example of paranteral poison or venom which is produced by a special gland and administered by a poison apparatus. Generally speaking, snake venom works on the nerves. It digests and destroys tissue enabling the poison to be dispensed more effectively and causes copious bleeding. Particular kinds of snake carry with them their own particular legends and inspire their own brand of fear.

Rattlesnakes move only slowly on land, at most about five kilometres per hour but are good at swimming and climbing trees. Their sight is limited to about four and a half metres but they have a temperature sensitive eye between their light sensitive eye and their nose. This special 'eye' picks up temperature differences as small as 0.02°C. While rattlers cannot hear sounds, they are very sensitive to vibrations carried through the ground. The fangs are hinged back into the upper jaw but come down as the snake strikes and venom is pushed through them.

Rattlesnake venom has about twenty-five ingredients, and contains large proportions of the chemicals causing bleeding. Blood vessels perforate and blood leaks so much that the heart cannot circulate enough blood to maintain the necessary oxygen supply. Death is then by suffocation.

Cobras can be as long as 5.4 metres (eighteen feet) and may carry enough venom to kill thirty people at once. The Egyptian Cobra or Asp grows to about 1.8 metres (six feet) in length and is used by snake charmers. It was the Asp which Queen Cleopatra used to help her commit suicide in 30 BC after Augustus Caesar had made clear his intention to parade her as a spoil of the war between Rome and Egypt. Symptoms of cobra venom poisoning are blurred vision, giddiness and general slowed reflexes after about three hours. An hour or so later breathing becomes laboured and death may ensue. In some cases death can follow fifteen minutes after the cobra bite. Shakespeare in his play *Antony and Cleopatra* of course had to call on poetic licence to have the heroine die after a few minutes.

Cobra venom contains several lethal components: a powerful nerve poison, a substance called lecithinase which kills red blood cells, and another component which acts directly on the muscles to paralyse them.

Northern Australia and New Guinea is home to the taipan (*Oxyuranus Scutellatus*). Like all snakes, it 'smells' by tasting the air with its tongue so that odour particles are transferred from the tongue to an organ in the roof of the creature's mouth. In the case of the taipan, however, the sense of smell is particularly acute, as is its eyesight. Striking repeatedly, the taipan causes death to man almost immediately. Its venom paralyses the central nervous system causing breathing to cease. At the same time it destroys red blood cells.

Venomous insects and spiders, like snakes, loom large in the popular imagination as creatures of fear and myth. Scorpions may be universally feared but not all are deadly. However, the deadliest ones inject a venom every bit as lethal as snake poison. At the bottom of the Grand Canyon, lives the Arizona scorpion (*Centruroides sculpturatus*), a creature some twenty centimetres long. Stinging from two poison glands in the tip of its tail, it injects a poison which attacks nerves, deadens sensation and disturbs the heart. Anyone unfortunate enough to be stung will experience choking, convulsions, disturbed sight and a raging fever before death occurs.

The female 'black widow' spider, notorious for sometimes making a meal of her mate after courtship is only about the size of a pea. But one bite from the spider can be fatal. Its venom contains four main poisons, one of which wreaks particular havoc on man. This poison effects nerve endings by keeping the nerve transmission fluid, acetylcholine, in action until the supply is depleted. Paralysis and death result.

Venomous fish, while perhaps less well known, can be just as deadly. Among the deadliest fish is the stone fish found in the Indian Ocean, the Western Pacific Ocean and the Red Sea. On its back, it has thirteen or fourteen spines each with little sacs of nerve poison on each side of them just beneath the skin. If anyone treads on the stone fish or even touches it, the poison flows up grooves in the sharp spines. Should the poison enter the system the results are convulsions, paralysis, unconsciousness and death which occurs some two to four hours after the sting.

But a venom administered by special apparatus like fangs or a tail sting are not the only form of animal poison. Other creatures are poisonous when eaten. Among these are the Asiatic horse shoe crab whose poison is unknown, and the puffer fish which is more often than not fatal to any person who consumes it unprepared. The Japanese puffer fish harbours in its ovaries fugu poison (tetrodoxin) which may act as a protection to its eggs which would be poisonous if eaten. Minus its internal organs, the fish is a great delicacy in Japan but not surprisingly its preparation requires special training for only ten milligrams of tetrodoxin is lethal.

The plankton *Gonyaulaux catenella* are consumed by shellfish such as oysters but during the warm part of the year the plankton secrete a poison, saxitoxin, which is also eaten by the shellfish.

Saxitoxin was originally isolated by scientists to test whether it was present in shellfish intended for human consumption and to create new drugs. Saxitoxin was carried as a sort of alternative suicide pill by fighter pilot Gary Powers in his 1960 flight over the Soviet Union. Discovering it on a little pin hidden in a silver dollar the Russians tried the poison out on a guard dog which died within seconds.

Another form of animal poison is one produced by a poison gland but released into the atmosphere. These crinotoxins are released by certain tree frogs including some species of Hyla and Phyllobates found in South and Central America. It is such secretions that are used by Indians as arrow poisons.

Antidote

An antidote is a substance which acts immediately or quickly on a poison to counteract its effects. It also prevents the poison being absorbed or if the poison has been absorbed, the antidote counteracts its damaging action.

The history of antidotes begins in the shadows of superstition. From the days of Hippocrates (460–377 BC) to those of Paracelsus (AD 1526) it was believed that certain universally effective antidotes existed which could counteract any poison in the body. These might be swallowed or worn as an amulet. Elk hoof and various plants were among these wonderful substances.

Also, it was thought that particular antidotes existed for specific poisons. The bite of a mad dog could be cured with the ashes from a dog's head according to this view. Intermingled with such superstitions were practices with a more rational basis.

Dioscorides recognized the use of emetics and the Islamic scientist Avicenna (AD 980–1077) recommend 'ambulatory treatment' for some poisons. (Holmstedt, B. and Liljestrand, G., 1963). The physician Matthiolus tested antidotes to aconite and arsenic by order of Pope Clement VII. Orfila and others pursued the notion of chemical antidotes. These included substances thought to work antagonistically against the poison and cancel out its effects.

Other substances are closely related to the antidote, among them the talisman, amulet, fetish, charm and potion. A talisman was originally a symbol. Metal or stone was often the material on which the symbol was engraved, but it could also be written on paper or parchment. The talisman inspired love in those seeing it, but it also defended the owner against evils including poisons. An amulet kept away evil and poisons while a fetish offered a more general form of protection to its owner. Whereas a charm drew its potency from spells and witchcraft, a potion claimed only to be a liquid medicine for physical and mental afflictions.

Mineral stones were used to fend off poison. Pliny, the Roman scholar of the first century, believed that certain rocks, including sapphire and ruby, could counteract poison. The diamond, he believed, could ward off all poisons.

Agate was supposed to offer protection from scorpion stings while bloodstone was a popular 'cure' for snake bites. An amulet of serpentine, a speckled green stone like serpent skin, was thought to protect against poisons including serpent bites. The Arabian physician Zoar, is said to have swallowed a poison herb then counteracted its effects by placing an emerald on his stomach and putting another in his mouth. Golden topaz is supposed to 'sense' when poison is near and darken in colour.

So-called animal stones have long had connections with poison. The term is rather loose and can mean stone-like material found in animals or stone shaped like an animal.

Bezoar stones were thought to be a universal antidote. A hard particle of food lodges in an animal's stomach or intestines. Calcareous materials gather round the irritant forming a 'stone' which may be as big as a hen's egg and is usually yellow in colour. Bezoar stones were probably first used about AD 1100 in Arabia and their mystery soon spread. Cows, goats, horses and certain llamas and ape species yielded the bezoar stones.

Such was their mystique, that even stories which demonstrated dramatically their failure did nothing to dent their popularity. A Spanish aristocrat attempted to sell a bezoar stone to King Charles IX who sought the opinion of the court physician Ambrose Paré as to its value. Paré told the King plainly that such stones were worthless. Charles then decided to try the stone on the palace cook who happened to be imprisoned at that time, condemned to death for stealing. The cook was offered a free pardon if he agreed to take a poison then allowed the bezoar stone to be administered. Within a few hours of consuming the poison the cook expired.

A toadstone is a stone either thought to have been formed in the body of a toad, or more commonly is shaped like a toad. It was thought to be an antidote to poisons and could be held over a bite to draw out the venom. A snakestone, shaped like a snake was thought to draw out the poison of a snake bite. In America in the 1800s, madstones were held to have similar powers, including being a treatment for the bite of a mad dog (hence the name).

Certain related terms have been used in the past to denote particular types of antidotes or similar substances. A theriac was an antidote to the bites of venomous creatures. (The Greek derivation *thériaki* meaning antidote draws on the term *thér* and therion which means 'wild beast'). A catholicon was simply a panacea, the expression deriving from the Greek root '*holou*' meaning 'universally'. Medicine prepared by the person recommending it was often called a nostrum (from the Latin '*noster*' meaning 'my').

A modern general antidote for poisons, which are still in the stomach, is activated charcoal, perhaps the closest it is possible to get to the universal antidote of folklore.

A dramatic demonstration of the effectiveness of activated charcoal was given in 1830 by Parisian pharmacist P.F. Touery. In front of the French Academy, he swallowed ten times the fatal dose of strychnine immediately followed by fifteen grams of activated charcoal and was unharmed.

Activated charcoal is made by the controlled heating of burned wood, peat or similar substances at 540°C in an atmosphere of water vapour, air or carbon dioxide. This causes numerous tiny pores to be formed in the charcoal which are able to absorb liquids or gases or substances dissolved in fluid. It is not effective against all poisons, being powerless against cyanide for example. But among the poisons it can absorb are arsenic, digitalis, morphine, nicotine, opium, phosphorus and of course strychnine.

Even when some poisons are absorbed into the blood activated charcoal can still be used to soak them up. An instrument called a B-D Hemodetoxifier allows blood from the body to pass through it and absorbs the poison before the blood is pumped back into the body.

To take a more recent example, the preferred antidote against arsenic poisoning was developed by R.A. Peters, professor of biochemistry at Oxford (1923–54). Devised as an antidote to the arsenical war gas Lewisite, the substance came to be called British Anti-Lewisite (BAL) and also as dimercaptopropanol. It is also an effective antidote for some other metal compounds including those containing antimony or mercury.

Antimony

Antimony is a brittle, bluish-white, semi-metal with a flaky, crystalline texture. In organic antimony compounds, the antimony may be trivalent (having three electrons available for bonding with other substances) or pentavalent (with five electrons available for bonding). Trivalent antimony compounds include antimony potassium tartrate which is also known as tartar emetic (q.v.). This takes the form of colourless crystals or white powder which is odourless but sweet tasting. Pentavalent antimony compounds include sodium antimony gluconate.

Antimony has been known since about 4000 BC and was one of the components of ancient bronze. Antimony sulphide or Kohl has been used as an eye cosmetic for 3,000 years. Pliny the Elder, the Latin naturalist and Pedanius Dioscorides, the Greek physician who served Emperor Nero, both wrote of antimony being used as a medicine and a cosmetic.

Its effectiveness as an emetic is illustrated by the Roman practice of using a goblet made of antimony alloy as a 'calices vomitorum'. Wine left standing in the goblet and then consumed, readily induced vomiting. (Much later up to the twentieth century, tartar emetic and other salts of antimony were being used as powerful emetics.)

Paracelsus, in the sixteenth century, prescribed antimony compounds for various diseases. It was even thought that Louis XIV was cured of typhoid with antimony treatment. Certainly in the sixteenth century, it was used for dropsy, ague and smallpox.

In more recent times antimony was used in cough medicines but is now considered too toxic for this purpose.

Trivalent organic antimony was used to treat the tropical disease bilharzia. Pentavalent organic antimony was a treatment for another group of tropical diseases – leishmaniasis. Modern uses of antimony include parasiticides and uses in paint, lacquer, enamel and in the glass and rubber industries.

Antimony is absorbed slowly from the gastro-intestinal tract. Little is known about its distribution although high concentrations of antimony have been found in the liver and thyroid. It is mainly excreted by the kidneys in the urine. Pentavalent antimony is passed out rather more quickly than trivalent antimony because it is not linked up with red blood cells. Trivalent antimony compounds are more toxic than pentavalent. Death has occurred following the intravenous injection of two grains of tartar emetic.

Trivalent antimony links itself to sulphydril groups of atoms in bodily cells to form so called thioantimonates. Notably it binds to red blood cells. All this breaks down key elements of cell structure.

Small doses of antimony cause nausea and act as an expectorant, that is it helps clear secretions from the air passages, because salivary glands and bronchial glands are stimulated. Other symptoms of acute and chronic antimony poisoning are similar to those of arsenic and of lead. Calcium hydroxide or magnesium oxide precipitates antimony which is still in the stomach. Dimercaprol is the antidote.

Archer-Gilligan, Amy

James Archer died suddenly in 1910. Three years earlier, with his wife Amy, he had founded the Archer Home for Elderly People in Hartford, Connecticut. After James's death his widow continued to manage the home alone. Amy remarried in 1913, but her new husband, Michael Gilligan, passed away after a brief illness.

On 30 May 1944, Franklin Andrews, a resident at the home died quite unexpectedly. Normally in good health, he complained of feeling unwell after dinner and expired the same night. Nurse Archer-Gilligan refused to let the deceased's sister view the body, saying it was being embalmed.

Although the doctor who was called to certify death diagnosed the cause as gastric ulcers, Franklin Andrews' sister was not happy and turned to the local paper, the *Hartford Courant* to investigate. Their reporter uncovered some disturbing facts which had been worrying some members of the local community.

Deaths at the home seemed far too frequent, the death rate being six times the regional average. Between 1910 and 1914, an average of twelve people a year died under Archer-Gilligan's care while another old people's home in the area averaged about two deaths a year over the same period. It emerged that Archer-Gilligan's patients each had to pay as much as $1,500 according to their age and finances. For this they received life care. Where life was short, the home's profits under this arrangement were substantial.

Ominously, it also appeared that patients would occasionally be sent out to buy arsenic supposedly to get rid of rats. Police were discreetly called in and a woman detective was placed in the home as a patient, paying $1,500 for 'life care'.

In December 1914, Alice Gowdy, a resident of the Archer

Home fell ill and her doctor Emma Thompson was summoned. Alice died the same night, but Dr Thompson noticed an unusual stiffness in the limbs of the corpse which was not rigor mortis. She informed the police.

Alice Gowdy's funeral went ahead, but no sooner had the body been buried than it was secretly disinterred and examined. Arsenic was found. Four more cadavers were exhumed, one being Michael Gilligan, Nurse Gilligan's second husband, the other three being past residents of the home. In the case of all four bodies, cause of death was judged to be due to arsenic poisoning.

Amy stood trial at Hartford in June 1917 accused on five counts of murder and entered a plea of not guilty. Instructed by the judge that wilful poisoning constituted first-degree premeditated murder, the jury delivered a verdict of guilty. At appeal, Amy won a retrial in June 1919 but finally she confessed all. Imprisoned for life at Wethersfield, Amy Archer-Gilligan was judged insane in 1923 and five years later died at the age of fifty-nine.

Armstrong, Herbert

The suspicions of Dr Hinks, a GP in the Welsh border town of Hay in Brecon, played a great part in bringing a wife murderer to justice. For in October 1921, Oswald Martin, a local solicitor, suffered vomiting and diarrhoea and felt extremely weak. When Dr Hinks was called, encouraged by Martin's father-in-law a local chemist, he had a sample of vomit analysed. In it one thirty-third of a grain of arsenic was found. It emerged that shortly before his illness, Martin had been invited to tea with Major Herbert Armstrong, a solicitor in a rival firm.

This discovery started Dr Hinks thinking about Major Armstrong. A retired British Army major, Armstrong had also become a part-time officer in the Territorial Army with the rank of major. Yet he was short, mild-mannered and had been dominated by his wife Katherine.

In 1905, at the age of 36, Armstrong had become managing clerk to Mr Cheese, a local solicitor and soon afterwards had bought a partnership in the firm. Later Cheese died leaving Armstrong as sole owner. A year later, Armstrong married Katherine Friend and as time passed, the couple had three children.

In July 1920 Mrs Armstrong made a will leaving everything to her husband. But on 22 August Katherine was taken into

Barnwood Private Asylum, Gloucestershire, after suffering bouts
of depression and delusions. In January 1921, however, she was
well enough to return home. There, her health began to fail again.
She died on 22 February 1921 and was buried in Cusop
churchyard. Cause of death was thought to be a heart condition.

Armstrong's diary entry for that day was a curt, 'K. died' and
after his wife's burial he took a long philandering holiday.

As Dr Hinks considered Katherine Armstrong's death in the
light of Oswald Martin's illness and Major Armstrong's possible
connection with it, he began to see Mrs Armstrong's symptoms in
a new light.

She had suffered neuritis which he had assumed to be a
functional disorder. Now he thought the condition might have had
an organic origin related to arsenic poisoning and could have been
peripheral neuritis. The theory also fitted Mrs Armstrong's other
symptoms: vomiting, a high stepping gait and discolouration of the
skin.

Dr Hinks wrote to Barnwood Asylum where staff remembered
that Mrs Armstrong's symptoms had diminished while she was in
the asylum but had reappeared after she went home.

The Home Office were put in the picture and the Director of
Public Prosecutions instigated low-key inquiries. On the last day of
1921, Major Armstrong was placed under arrest on a charge of
attempting to murder Oswald Martin. In one of Armstrong's
pockets when he was arrested, was a small packet of arsenic. He
claimed that he had bought an ounce of arsenic to kill dandelions
in his garden. There being twenty dandelions, he had divided the
arsenic into twenty packets, one for each weed.

Mrs Armstrong's body was exhumed and viewed by Dr Hinks
and Dr Bernard Spilsbury, the Home Office pathologist. Both
recognized evidence of possible arsenic poisoning from the good
state of preservation of the remains. Autopsy results confirmed the
presence of arsenic and on 19 January 1922 Armstrong was
charged with the murder of his wife.

Armstrong's trial began on 3 April at Hereford Assizes where
the prosecution was led by Attorney General Sir Ernest Pollock
KC. The defence led by Sir Henry Curtis Bennett KC argued that
Mrs Armstrong committed suicide in February 1921 with one fatal
dose of arsenic. But there was a discrepancy between the single
dose theory and the time it should have taken for the poison to
reach parts of the body where it was detected in the autopsy. To
try to meet this difficulty, Dr F. Toogood was called by the defence
to state that most of the arsenic had become encysted on the

stomach wall. Reference was made to the 1846 case of the Duc de Praslin in which a similar claim was made. The prosecution scored, and Major Armstrong's moral reputation was damaged when his doctor testified that he had venereal disease.

Mr Justice Darling in his summing up returned to the earlier references to the Duc de Praslin case, pointing out that it had involved falsified evidence. Armstrong, found guilty and sentenced to death, unsuccessfully appealed at the Court of Criminal Appeal and was hanged on 31 May 1922 at Gloucester Prison.

Armstrong, John

On the evening of 22 July 1955, Sergeant Bulley visited the home of 24-year-old John Armstrong and his 19-year-old wife Janet and found them watching television. This quite normal pastime struck Sergeant Bulley as surprising in this case because at lunchtime on the same day the Armstrongs' 5-month-old baby Terence had died suddenly.

Earlier that day, Portsmouth GP Dr Ian Buchanan had visited the child and found him apparently well. At 1.20 p.m., however, John Armstrong, a sick-berth attendant at a Royal Navy hospital at Haslar, telephoned urgently and Buchanan's partner Dr Bernard Johnson rushed to the house. Arriving at 1.30 p.m., he found that the infant had just died. Unable to establish the cause of death, Dr Johnson could not issue a certificate and reported the case to the coroner.

Dr Harold Miller, a local hospital pathologist conducted an autopsy at 5 p.m. and discovered a disintegrating substance in the infant's throat. It looked like red skin, possibly from poisonous berries.

That evening, when Sergeant Bulley visited the Armstrongs' house, they told him that Terence had been tired and wheezing the evening before.

John Armstrong had given the baby artificial respiration and had then telephoned Dr Buchanan who called at 8.40 a.m. Later, John had gone to work four miles away and returned for lunch at 12.15 p.m. The baby was very ill and the father applied artificial respiration again. Incredibly, John Armstrong had not called the doctor from home but had cycled back to work before making the emergency call.

Bulley took the baby's last feed-bottle and a vomit-stained

pillow to Dr Miller who informed him of the suspicion that Terence could have eaten poisonous berries.

Bulley returned to the Armstrong house and discovered that in the garden grew a bush of poisonous red daphne mezereum berries. It was possible that Terence's 3-year-old sister Pamela could have innocently given the baby some of the berries.

Dr Miller next sent the infant's stomach contents to the County Analyst with a note saying that daphne berries were suspected. The 'skins' by now had completely disintegrated. The analyst found no evidence of berries of any kind, but some 'uncooked maize starch and the synthetic dye eosin'.

Burial was authorized by the coroner but Hampshire CID pursued investigations. Three weeks after the death Dr Miller suggested to Detective Inspector Gates a possible explanation for the analyst's findings in the stomach contents. Eosin is a pink synthetic dye used to colour certain drug capsules, particularly Seconal. The barbiturate Seconal would not be expected to be prescribed for a 5-month-old infant. The maize starch could have also come from Seconal capsules.

Gates reported this to his superior Superintendent Walter Jones and the remains of the stomach contents were sent to the forensic laboratories at Scotland Yard. About one third grain of Seconal was found in the stomach contents and another one-fiftieth grain in the vomit stain on the baby's pillow.

The Armstrongs denied ever having had Seconal in the house, but it emerged that five months before Terence's death, at the Royal Naval Hospital where John Armstrong was working, a dangerous drugs cupboard had been rifled. Among the drugs stolen were fifty Seconal capsules tinted bright pink with eosin.

The infant's body was exhumed and a second autopsy carried out. A further one-twentieth grain of Seconal was extracted from the organs. It was estimated that the baby had swallowed between three and five one-and-a-half grain capsules. Professor Keith Simpson, the eminent pathologist told Superintendent Jones that such a dose would be lethal to a child within an hour.

The baby had died just before 1.30 p.m. The father had got home for lunch at 12.15 p.m. and returned to work at 1 p.m. Mother was present the whole time. Either parent could have administered the lethal dose.

Mr and Mrs Armstrong separated. Then on 24 July 1956, the dead infant's mother told the police that the drug Seconal had been kept in the house at the time of her son's death. Her husband had been taking the capsules to aid sleep. After the baby's death when police had earlier questioned the couple John Armstrong had told his wife to get rid of the capsules. Mrs Armstrong complied.

Having made the statement, Janet Armstrong said that if action was taken against her husband, she was ready to give evidence. All this, however, did not remove police suspicion of Janet Armstrong herself. On 1 September 1956, husband and wife were arrested and charged with murder.

At the trial, held at Winchester, John Armstrong was defended by Malcolm Wright QC and Janet by Norman Skelhorn QC. Sir Reginald Manningham-Buller, the Attorney General, led the prosecution.

John Armstrong claimed to have no notion of how baby Terence came to be poisoned. But Janet said that on the day the infant died, her husband had returned home from lunch and had had the opportunity to be on his own with Terence. Also there was Seconal in the house on that day.

John Armstrong was found guilty. Janet was acquitted. Subsequently, however, the husband was reprieved. A month later, Mrs Armstrong claimed that she had administered the Seconal to the baby to help him get to sleep.

Arsenic

The element arsenic is classified in chemistry as a 'semi-metal'. Along with antimony and bismuth it occupies this division of substances lying between metals and non-metals. In nature, while it may be found uncombined with other materials, it is usually coupled with antimony and silver. Rather than being mined, the element is normally recovered when certain ores including lead, copper and gold are smelted. Being inert, elemental arsenic is not toxic when swallowed because it is not absorbed into the system. Compounds of arsenic are quite a different matter, however.

Arsenic compounds were known long before the substance was recognized as a chemical element. Among the ancients, Greeks, Romans and Arabs used compounds of arsenic both as medicines and as poisons. Albertus Magnus is credited with the first observation of the element arsenic in AD 1250 when he noted the appearance of a metal-like substance when orpiment, an arsenic compound, was heated with soap. It is well known that arsenic compounds were favoured by Medieval and Renaissance poisoners. Producing symptoms similar to those of cholera, arsenic poisoning must have often gone undetected during that period. By the eighteenth century, the element and many of its compounds were widely known. As late as the 1950s, the medical uses of arsenic ranged from the treatment of leukaemia to its external application as a paste to destroy the nerves of carious teeth. Caution was beginning to be more widespread, however, and the results of using arsenic as a tonic were recognized as 'unpredictable and uncontrollable' (Martindale, W.A., 1958). Practically the only use of arsenicals in twentieth-century medicine is that of Melarsoprol in the treatment of the tropical disease African trypanosomiasis, better known as sleeping sickness.

Compounds of arsenic may be inorganic or organic. Inorganic arsenicals are either trivalent (having three electrons available for bonding with other substances) or pentavalent (with five electrons for bonding).

Among trivalent arsenicals, perhaps the best known is arsenic trioxide also called white arsenic. Resembling sugar in appearance, it is almost tasteless and was in the past easily available making it a common choice for criminal poisoning. White arsenic is used as a rodent poison, in insecticides and herbicides. It also finds uses in the textile industry and in glass and enamel manufacture. Even as late as the early twentieth century, white arsenic was thought to make the figure curvaceous and improve the complexion. Apparently peasants in the province of Styria ate small doses with food for just those reasons. They also thought the substance improved the 'wind' for climbing hills (Christie, T.L., 1968). Another trivalent arsenical is the arsenate, cupric arsenate or Scheele's Green which is an ingredient in paint and dye manufacture.

Turning to pentavalent forms, potassium arsenate is a constituent of sheep dips and insect poisons. Soil may be sterilized using lead arsenate which is also used in paint. The United States ambassador in Rome suffered chronic arsenic poisoning when over a period of two or three years, lead arsenate dust gradually fell from the paint in her bedroom ceiling.

Up to the 1820s, the distinction between inorganic and organic substances hinged on the supposition that organic materials contained some vital force which inorganic ones lacked. This distinction was discredited when in 1828, the chemist Wöhler demonstrated that inorganic ammonium cyonate could form urea (an organic substance excreted in urine) when heated. By the end of the nineteenth century, the term 'organic substance' had come to mean simply a carbon compound.

Cacodylate, the first known organic arsenical was identified in 1842. Paul Ehrlich's pioneering work, including in 1907 his discovery of Arsphenamine (606), laid the foundations of chemotherapy. The painstaking nature of Ehrlich's work becomes apparent when we note that Arsphenamine (606) derives its full title from being the six hundred and sixth compound which he tested for activity. The scientist altered the molecules to give slightly different formulas and then tested each one. In the present day, chemists design the molecules which they judge will have a specific action and then test the substance. Organic arsenicals were found to be less toxic than inorganic forms and were more easily absorbed into the body. Yet they still had a toxic effect on certain bodily cells. These findings led to the discovery that certain toxic substances could be 'attracted' to sites of infection or disease. There they could work on diseased aspects of the body without major harm to the bodily functions. Around 1911, Ehrlich discovered the arsenic compound Salvarsan which became the first cure for syphilis. Subsequent to Ehrlich's work, organic arsenicals became used in treating syphilis until the advent of penicillin. Melarsoprol, mentioned earlier, is still used to treat sleeping sickness.

Some arsenicals such as arsenic trioxide dissolve only slowly in water. So when they enter the body, the speed at which they are absorbed depends on how finely or coarsely the substance is powdered. The coarser the powder, the less toxic it tends to be because coarse powder can be passed out in the faeces before it has the chance to dissolve. By comparison with oxides or arsenic, arsenates such as potassium arsenate are more water soluble and therefore better absorbed.

The distribution of arsenic in the body is influenced by the particular arsenical administered and by the length of time over which the doses have been taken. Arsenic is predominantly stored in heart, lung, liver and kidney tissue while neural tissue and muscle hold smaller amounts.

Keratin, a natural substance found in hair and nails, contains a high proportion of the sulphydril group of atoms. Because arsenic binds particularly to sulphur atoms, a high concentration of arsenic is found in the hair, nails, bones and teeth. Within a few hours of administration arsenic begins to be laid down in the hair where signs of it remain for some years. Arsenic is excreted mainly in urine although faeces, milk, sweat, hair, lungs and skin also excrete the poison from the system.

All else being equal, trivalent arsenicals tend to be most toxic followed by pentavalent arsenicals and organic arsenicals. The trivalent arsenical arsenic trioxide demands particular attention because of its extensive use in criminal poisoning. Factors like the fineness of powdering influence bodily absorption and therefore toxicity, but estimates are possible. The minimal recorded lethal dose of arsenic is about one grain. As a rough guide, a teaspoonful of arsenic would be seven times this dose.

Trivalent arsenicals primarily bind to sulphur atoms in the body's enzymes. They inhibit sulphydril containing enzyme systems which are essential to normal cellular metabolism. Pentavalent arsenicals compete in the cells for inorganic phosphate. Substituting themselves for phosphate, they combine with an organic compound to form a derivative that is quickly broken down. The process is known as arseniolysis.

Early signs of acute arsenic poisoning may include burning lips, a tightening of the throat and problems with swallowing. Severe gastric pains, violent vomiting and excessive watery diarrhoea follow. Kidneys become inflamed and proteins and blood appear in the urine which is passed only in very small amounts. Indeed, in time no urine may be expelled at all. A raging thirst and muscular cramps develop. With the ongoing loss of fluid from vomiting and diarrhoea, symptoms of 'shock' emerge. Coma and death follow. Where poisoning is very severe, death can ensue in an hour. More commonly severe poisoning leads to death in about twenty-four hours.

In chronic arsenic poisoning, an abnormal amount of fluid accumulates under the skin, with face and eyelids being particularly affected. In the past, this was mistaken for a healthy gain in weight and gave arsenic its reputation as a tonic.

Other signs are loss of appetite, nausea, vomiting and diarrhoea. Inflammation and itchiness arise in the membrane covering the front of the eye (the conjuctiva) and the mucus membranes of the nose. Soreness affects the mouth.

Low doses of arsenic give a healthy looking 'peaches and cream' complexion and indeed, arsenic was at one time widely used as a cosmetic. What was not realized, however, was that this 'healthy' complexion was simply caused by dilated blood vessels. Continued use of small doses of arsenic over an extended period can damage the skin. It becomes pigmented, dry (causing dermatitis) and grows thicker assuming a horny quality. Hair and nails may fall out.

Later symptoms are anaemia and cirrhosis of the liver. Jaundice appears as bile pigment deposited in the deep layers of the skin turns the skin's surface yellow. Peripheral neuritis develops, which is a form of nerve inflammation. Numbness and tingling occurs in the limbs, particularly in the feet sometimes causing a high-stepping gait.

Dimercaprol is the best known antidote and is administered by an intra-muscular injection. It works by competing with the sulphur atoms in the bodily cells for the arsenic thus soaking up the arsenic to form a stable, soluble compound which can be excreted.

Atropine (Belladonna)

Belladonna (*Atropa belladonna*) is the plant whose name translates from Italian as 'beautiful woman'. Indeed, for centuries women used eye drops of the deadly nightshade to widen the pupils and so enhance their attractiveness. Its history is intertwined with folklore and superstition. Witches were thought to use belladonna as a principal ingredient of flying ointment used to levitate broomsticks.

Atropine, an alkaloid extracted from belladonna, is named after Atropos one of the three fates who cuts the thread of life spun by her two sisters.

Belladonna liniment is applied externally to treat neuralgia (nerve pain). Atropine eye drops were used to dilate pupils so the interior of the eye could be examined and for related purposes. Belladonna is a constituent of cough mixtures for bronchitis and whooping cough. It helps control coughing and dry up mucus. Atropine has been used to counter the effects of poisoning by opium and muscarine, the poisonous component of some toadstools.

Atropine is absorbed by the gastro-intestinal tract and is also given intravenously. Toxic effects have been known from the absorption of atropine eye drops. It is partly oxidized in the liver. Atropine is excreted in urine.

Death has been reported after doses of less than 10 mg for children and less than 100 mg for adults.

Atropine blocks the effect of acetylcholine (the neuromuscular transmitter). This affects the action of the parasympathetic nervous system. This system is that aspect of the autonomic nervous system which inhibits heart action and encourages digestive action. In antagonizing this system, atropine tends to augment heart action and inhibit digestive action.

In small doses atropine relieves spasm because it paralyses the nerves of the muscles of digestion such as the stomach and intestine. It increases the rate of heart beats. In general terms it has an excitor effect followed by a depressor effect on motor areas of the brain.

The symptoms of atropine poisoning are in a sense extremes of the effects of small doses. Mouth and throat become extremely dry. Pupils dilate. Heart rate increases. Excitement and delirium is paradoxically accompanied by weakness. Later cerebral depression occurs, paralysis, coma and the gradual stopping of breathing and heart beat. In treating atropine poisoning, barbiturates are used to help control the excitement stage of the poisoning.

Autopsy (Post-Mortem Examination)

A forensic autopsy fits into the framework of more common autopsies. Autopsies may be hospital (clinical) or coroner's. In some of the coroner's post-mortems death may have been caused (or suspected of being caused) by crime.

A specialist 'Home Office' pathologist may be called in. In England and Wales there are some fifty such pathologists. About twenty are drawn from departments of forensic medicine at university teaching hospitals. Some thirty are National Health Service hospital pathologists.

It is important to the police Criminal Investigation Department that the body is examined as soon as possible after it has been discovered. This helps forensic investigation and establishes cause of death before anyone is charged.

The body is visually examined at the scene of crime and then transported carefully in a body bag to the mortuary to avoid evidence being lost.

Many people may be present at a modern forensic autopsy; pathologist, mortuary technicians, detectives, scene of crime officers, fingerprint specialists, forensic scientists and police photographers. Most police forces use a video TV team to record proceedings.

Identification of the body is established. In criminal cases relatives may identify the body, or if the body is badly damaged identification may be made by distant relatives or from items of clothing to avoid unnecessary distress to next of kin.

Clothing is examined and then removed. The external appearance of the body is studied, and nail clippings and samples of hair may be taken. The body is then cleaned up and incisions are made to enable the internal organs to be scrutinized and samples stored in various containers for laboratory examination. In suspected poisoning cases, samples are taken for later analysis by the toxicology laboratory. Particularly important are the stomach and its contents, liver, urine, blood and intestines. Samples are transferred to separate labelled chemically clean plastic containers. A variety of containers are used, including fluoride tubs for the estimation of alcohol. When the stomach is opened, signs of poisoning can sometimes be seen on the stomach lining. Tablets or capsules or powder may be stuck to it for instance.

Often in poisoning cases, the poison is stored or concentrated in the liver. The organ is sliced to be examined visually then the whole liver, or a sample is placed in a container for laboratory analysis. The small intestine may be sent for laboratory analysis in poison cases. It is rarer for the large intestine to be sent for analysis but in cases of heavy-metal poisoning this may also be necessary.

The forensic laboratory may need other specimens. Bile would be needed for suspected morphine poisoning for example. Also, vitreous humor from the eye, skin and subcutaneous fat and muscle is sampled where narcotic or insulin poisoning is suspected. Nasal swabs are taken where cocaine sniffing may be involved.

A defence post-mortem is often conducted later involving a second pathologist employed by the defence lawyers. This is always by arrangement with the first pathologist who often attends also.

Bacterial Poisons

Bacterial poisons are a sub-group of biotoxins along with plant poisons (q.v.) and animal poisons (q.v.).

The term bacteria is used here synonymously with micro-organisms, that is microscopic kinds of plant life, although specifically bacteria are simple, primitive forms of micro-organism.

Leeuwenhoek about 1687 was among the first to observe bacteria after the microscope had been developed. In 1842, Goodsir conclusively linked bacteria with disease, describing sarcinae in the stomach. This work came to fruition in the hands of Louis Pasteur who in the 1860s extensively studied how micro-organisms multiply and produce disease. Koch, a founding father of bacteriology, developed methods of getting pure cultures of different organisms.

Micro-organisms subsume moulds, yeasts, bacteria in the strict sense. Rickettsiae, and viruses.

Moulds include microscopic fungi which can grow in body tissue, ringworm being an example. One particular yeast produces alcohol. Bacteria proper include organisms of various shapes, round, curved or rod like. Rickettsiae, named after Ricketts, a bacteriologist, are disease causing micro-organisms larger than bacteria. (*Rickettsiae prowazekii* is the infecting agent of typhus, passed to man from infected lice.) Viruses are minute agents, causing diseases including poliomyelitis and influenza.

Simpler bacteria multiply by increasing in size and then dividing into two. This may occur twice every hour so that in theory one bacterium could in twenty-four hours create 300 million million bacteria.

Bacteria cause disease by producing toxins which are harmful to tissues. One group of toxins, endotoxins are retained in the bacterial cells and the bacteria can do damage wherever they are sited in the body. Another group, exotoxins, of which diphtheria is an example, pass from the bacteria and circulate throughout the body.

Tuberculosis is caused by one of two mycobacteria: the human type which usually causes tuberculosis of the lung, or the bovine type which causes abdominal tuberculosis. Typhoid fever and related diseases are brought about by Salmonella typhi, Salmonella paratyphi, and other similar organisms. Diphtheria is caused by the *Corynebacterium diphtheriae* which produces severe throat inflammation and other poisoning affects in the body. Influenza is caused by a virus, several specific ones of which have so far been identified.

To aid their identification, bacteria may be cultivated. First a nutrient such as gelatine or milk is placed on a Petri dish (a flat covered glass plate) or in a glass tube and then inoculated with the bacterial material. The apparatus is next incubated at body temperature for several days when the bacteria will have multiplied sufficiently to be visible to the naked eye. Samples are then removed, stained with special dye and studied under a microscope.

A notorious form of poisoning, shellfish poisoning, appears to be related to a virus infection. A poison, saxitoxin is present in certain planktons which under rare conditions multiply rapidly. When this happens, the saxitoxin accumulates in the shellfish which feed by filtering plankton. The virus may then in turn be passed to people eating the shellfish. Symptoms brought about in severe cases are numbness of the hands, weakness in the limbs, difficulty breathing and even paralysis and death.

In poison murders, bacteria have been used by Henry Girrard, Dr Arthur Waite and Patrick O'Brien, among others. Girrard poisoned an insurance broker by first introducing typhoid bacteria into a lunch-time water carafe and when this did not produce the desired results, injecting him with the bacteria.

Arthur Waite, dentist and bacteriologist, dispatched his mother-in-law using bacteria of influenza, diphtheria and tuberculosis. Diphtheria bacteria was also used by Patrick O'Brien, the fake Count de Lacy, to kill his brother-in-law who thought he was receiving a dose of cholera vaccine.

Barber, Susan

A classic betrayal scene greeted Michael Barber when he returned home unexpectedly early from a fishing trip in May 1981. His wife Susan and his best friend Richard Collins were in the bedroom together naked.

Barber beat his wife and threw Collins out. In fact, the lovers had been having an affair for eight months before the husband had found out.

The following day, after eating a steak and kidney pie, Michael Barber became ill. He was taken to hospital where doctors diagnosed first pneumonia and later a rare nervous condition Goodpasture's Syndrome. Barber was transferred to Hammersmith Hospital in West London but died there, a week after his illness had started. Cause of death was given as pneumonia and kidney failure.

An autopsy was carried out and the pathologist, Professor David Evans, was uncomfortable about the apparent cause of death.

Tests for Paraquat were requested at the National Poisons Unit at New Cross Hospital. When doctors later asked for the results, however, they were informed that the tests had excluded the presence of Paraquat.

Here Professor Evans might have left matters, but instead he suggested that the doctors involved in the case met together and studied the organs from Mr Barber's body. These had been earlier removed and preserved. Blood samples had also been kept and these were sent to two venues. The first was Imperial Chemical Industries (ICI) who manufactured Paraquat. The second was the National Poisons Unit. When the results came back, both places confirmed the presence of Paraquat.

But what about the earlier negative result from the National Poisons Unit? It became evident that the earlier tests had not been carried out. No samples had been sent to the National Poisons Unit. When doctors were told that the tests had excluded the presence of Paraquat this had been incorrect.

The police CID began enquiries in December 1981 under Detective Chief Inspector John Clarion of the Essex Police. It emerged that Susan Barber had put half a teaspoonful of Gramoxone (Paraquat) in the steak and kidney pie that her husband had eaten the day after discovering her infidelity. After her husband's death, Susan Barber had lived with Collins. She collected £15,000 from her husband's pension fund.

The couple were arrested in April 1982, nearly a year after the crime had taken place. Charged with conspiracy to murder, Collins was found guilty and sentenced to two years imprisonment. Susan Barber was found guilty of murder and given a life prison sentence.

Barlow, Kenneth

At 11.20 p.m. on 3 May 1957 in Bradford, Yorkshire, Kenneth Barlow beat on a neighbour's door and asked him to get a doctor for Mrs Barlow. On entering Barlow's house the neighbour saw

Mrs Barlow lying in the bath apparently dead. At 11.30 p.m. the doctor arrived and confirmed death and by 12.05 a.m. Detective Sergeant Naylor was at the scene.

Barlow, an unemployed nurse, had been married to Mrs Barlow for about a year. She was his second wife, and Barlow's son by his first marriage lived with them. He said that his wife had been ill after retiring to bed and about 9.20 p.m. had called him saying she had vomited. He lay beside her on the bed and at about 10 p.m. she got up to have a bath, while Barlow fell asleep. On waking, he discovered her lying in the bath with her head underwater and apparently dead. Draining the bath, Barlow said he had attempted artificial respiration while his wife remained in the bath because he was unable to lift her out.

Other pieces of evidence, however, pointed to a different course of events. Mrs Barlow had returned from her work in a laundry at midday on the day of her death and was seen at 3.45 p.m. apparently in good spirits. In the bathroom where the body was discovered, there were no signs of splashing and Detective Naylor was convinced that Barlow's pyjamas were dry.

Dr Price examined the body at 3.30 a.m. on 4 May when he noticed that water was trapped in the inner crease of the deceased's right elbow. When the body was found, the arms were folded over the chest. Had her arms been straightened to apply artificial respiration it was difficult to see how the water could have been trapped. Another clue emerged when Chief Inspector Coffey found hypodermic needles and syringes in the kitchen.

While autopsy indicated death by drowning, it was suspected that poison had been administered first. Time of death was estimated to be around 10 p.m. Analysis of forensic samples by Dr A.S. Curry excluded the common poisons and insulin came to be suspected. Dr Price re-examined the body finding four injection marks – two on each buttock. When tissues around the punctures were extracted, tests on them indicated the presence of insulin. Faced with this evidence, Barlow claimed that the injection marks were of ergometrine which he had administered to his wife who was pregnant to induce an abortion. Tests did not substantiate this claim however.

Proceedings opened at Leeds Assizes on 9 December 1957 before Mr Justice Diplock with Solicitor General Sir Harry Hylton-Foster standing for the Crown and Mr Bernard Gillis leading the defence. Barlow suggested that his wife might have injected herself with insulin and even that a third party may have entered the house and administered the injection. But former colleagues testified that the unemployed nurse had told them that insulin could be used for the perfect murder because it could not be detected in the body after death. (An inaccurate claim as events showed.) After the jury found Barlow guilty of murder, he was sentenced to life imprisonment.

What really happened on that May night may never be known but a likely course of events is that Barlow persuaded his wife to be injected. He may have assured her that he was using ergometrine to effect an abortion, while in reality he administered insulin rendering her unconscious. Taking her to the bathroom he then drowned her as part of his plan to pass off her death as an accident.

Bateman, Mary

Mary Bateman was forty-one years old and was nursing a baby when she was taken out to be hanged in 1809. After execution, her body was put on display and the money paid by the people who thronged to see it was given to charity. Finally the corpse was skinned and bits sold as charms. The events which had led to Mary Bateman's demise were as appalling as the end itself.

Born Mary Harker, a farmer's daughter from Thirsk, Yorkshire, she worked in York and Leeds as a domestic help and later married a wheelwright, John Bateman. From girlhood, she had become a rather ineffective petty thief. After marrying, she set up as a fortune teller and found this an effective way of separating gullible people from their cash.

The way in which she destroyed one family gives an insight into how she could play one person off against another and twist a situation to make money regardless of human suffering.

A certain Mr Stead was in debt and consulted Mary who told him to desert his wife and join the army. At first Stead was reluctant but Mary persuaded him with charms and deceit. She next turned her attentions to Mrs Stead, telling her that her husband was planning to run away with a mistress, and gaining money from her to magically avert this. Once Mr Stead had joined up and his wife had to live off charity, Mary often got her hands on the charitable payments and spent them herself.

Mary's own husband eventually joined the army and had to travel the country. Mary followed, making money as a fortune teller, swindler and robber.

The series of events that led to her execution began when Mary was consulted by Mrs Perigo, the aunt of Mrs Stead. Mrs Perigo was in pain and was convinced some enemy was using magic to harm her. Mary was called in to help. During late 1806 and early 1807 Mary managed to dupe Mr and Mrs Perigo out of food, clothes, alcohol and gold. She then decided to poison them.

To do this, she turned for help to an advisor she had invented and whom she had used in the past – a certain Miss Blythe. This mysterious advisor supposedly lived in Scarborough and wrote to Mary sharing her expertise in magic. Mary explained to the Perigos that Miss Blythe had foretold that the couple would be affected by great misfortunes. A way of avoiding these dangers was to stay at home for a week and each day eat a pudding mixed with powders that Miss Blythe would send. There would be a different powder each day. If during this time they fell ill, this would be due to enemies somewhere and they were to take honey as an antidote. This was also provided.

The couple ate the puddings and the powders from Monday to Friday without effect. But Saturday's powder contained mercuric chloride. Naturally the couple fell ill and turned to the honey antidote. This, however, contained arsenic. Mrs Perigo died but her husband pulled through.

Mary Bateman still managed to allay suspicion by explaining to the bereaved husband that Mrs Perigo must have done something to upset the magic. But Mr Perigo's gullibility was not infinite. He had some bags into which Mary had sewn guineas to act as charms before selling them to the Perigos. But Mary had used a trick she had often employed to swindle others in the past. For she only appeared to sew the guineas into the bags while in reality she sewed in worthless bits of paper. Mr Perigo opened his bags to extract the money and when he discovered the waste paper, his belief in Mary Bateman ended. Mary was arrested and tried and the scene set for her last walk – to the gallows.

Billik, Herman

Herman Billik, a married man with two children, traded from a tent at Riverside, Chicago, professing to be a sorcerer. In 1904 he was consulted by Martin Vzral a West Side milkman who was worried by the appearance of a rival milkman in the area. Vzral's family which was to figure importantly in what followed comprised his wife and seven children: Emma (25), Mary (22), Tilly (age not known), Rose (18), Ella (12), Bertha (an infant), and son Jersolobat (17) who was known as 'Jerry'.

To ward off the influence of the rival milk vendor, Herman Billik prepared a potion which was subsequently sprinkled on the competitor's door. Refusing direct payment, Billik asked only for a $20 loan but soon he had persuaded Vzral to loan him more and more until the debt stood at $2,000. As a further service, Billik provided Emma with love charms to give her a successful marriage – in fact she eloped with a local farmer.

Visiting California for a holiday alone in the winter of 1905 seems to be have been a time of taking stock and a turning point for Billik. Soon after he had returned to Chicago, Martin Vzral fell ill. Violent stomach pains, nausea, burning sensations along the alimentary tract and numb legs afflicted him until he died on 27 March 1905. Then followed a veritable catalogue of deaths in the Vzral family: Mary on 28 July, Tilly on 22 December 1905 and Rose on 26 August 1906 all experiencing symptoms similar to their father. When Ella died on 30 November there had been five deaths in under two years. All the children had life insurance which went to widow Vzral although sometimes the amounts were small. Neighbours began to talk about the powerful influence that Billik seemed to have over Mrs Vzral and these drove Mrs Vzral and the two remaining children, Jerry and Bertha, to move to another area of Chicago.

Police visited Mrs Vzral at her new home on 3 December 1906 and the following day interviewed Emma Vzral Neimann the daughter who had married a farmer. Emma was convinced that the deaths were at the hands of Billik and her mother, and the police set out to arrest the two suspects. By the time they arrived, Mrs Vzral was dead having poisoned herself. Billik was arrested at his home but later released.

When the five bodies were exhumed, arsenic was found in each one. Inspector George Shippey, Coroner Hoffman and State Attorney John Healy sifted the evidence, the state case being that Mrs Vzral had, with Billik, killed her children and had committed suicide to save Billik. Emma could give some support to this view, for she stated that Billik had given her father a white powder two weeks before Martin died and given Mary a potion of couple of days prior to her death. Jerry for his part told police that Billik had 'predicted' Mary's death and that he had seen his mother give Billik money.

Billik's trial was only the beginning of a further unexpected series of events which unfolded when the trial was called on 3 July 1907. Billik entered a plea of not guilty but was found guilty by the jury and sentenced to be hanged. Incarcerated in the county prison, he convinced prisoners of his innocence.

Sister Rose, a visiting nun and Father Peter O'Callaghan, the head of a Paulist brotherhood were also sure there had been a miscarriage of justice. O'Callaghan held street meetings with Vzral's children, Jerry and Bertha, claiming that Jerry had perjured himself, incited by Inspector Shippey and State Attorney Healy's assistant.

After such scenes Judge Barnes granted a stay of execution (the hanging was scheduled for 12 October 1907) and the case was reviewed by the Supreme Court of Illinois who eventually upheld the jury's decision. But Healy was not re-elected and another prosecutor was placed in office. An appeal was heard before Judge Landis in the US circuit court as the 12 October drew nearer. Just half an hour before Billik was to die a further stay of execution was granted. An appeal on a technicality was then taken to the US Supreme Court who rejected it and a new date of 11 December 1908 was fixed for the hanging.

Father O'Callaghan next pressed for the exhumation of the body of farmer Neimann's father. Traces of arsenic were found in the cadaver and Billik's supporters argued that as the accused could not have been involved in that particular death, someone else must have been. That same person may have also perpetrated the deaths for which Billik stood accused.

Governor Deneek granted a further reprieve after which Billik was sentenced to face execution in January 1909. However, on 22 January the Governor of the State Board of Pardons commuted the sentence to one of life imprisonment in the State prison in Joliet.

Black, Edward

Police bursting into a hotel room in Liverpool on 21 November 1921 found Edward Black, the man they were seeking, with blood streaming from a self-inflicted throat wound.

The injured man was a 36-year-old insurance salesman who lived in the little village of Tregonissey, St Austell in Cornwall. His 50-year-old wife had run the village sweet shop until she became ill. Doctors diagnosed gastro-enteritis, and Mrs Black's condition continued to deteriorate. A further problem was that Edward Black was in debt. On 8 November 1921 Edward left home not to return leaving his wife at death's door. Three days later she expired. The local doctor was uneasy about the circumstances surrounding Mrs Black's death and referred the case to the coroner who ordered an autopsy. Arsenic was traced in the body tissues.

This and the sudden disappearance of Edward Black set police on his trail until they tracked him down to the Liverpool hotel room. Recovering from his self-inflicted injuries, Black attended the coroner's inquest into his wife's death.

At the inquest, a particularly vital piece of evidence was given by a St Austell chemist. He testified that a purchaser buying two ounces of arsenic had signed his poison register 'E.E. Black' (Black's middle name was Ernest). The inquest jury delivered a verdict of arsenic poisoning administered by Edward Black.

Black's criminal trial opened at Bodmin on 1st February 1922 and lasted just two days. Retiring for forty minutes, the jury found Black guilty. A subsequent appeal proved unsuccessful and Edward Black was hanged on 24 March 1922.

Blandy, Mary

In the eighteenth century when a woman's only prospects were to marry well, there was a danger of being left on the shelf if she was not spoken for by her mid twenties. Mary Blandy was 26 and unmarried, despite being attractive and pleasant. Her father, a lawyer had perhaps set his sights too high for his daughter and had discouraged many acceptable suitors.

At this watershed in her life, Mary fell in love with the Honourable William Cranstoun. While he was well connected, being the son of a Scottish peer, he was penniless, in debt and physically unattractive. Mary's mother approved of her daughter's choice, however, and Cranstoun stayed with the family for six months in 1748 at their house at Henley-on-Thames.

It emerged that Cranstoun was already married, although he claimed the woman involved had only been his mistress. While this news incensed Mr Blandy, it did not put Cranstoun out of favour with Mrs Blandy or Mary. Indeed, Mrs Blandy became ill, and insisted Cranstoun stay close by. So he stayed at the house until 1749 when Mrs Blandy died of natural causes.

Cranstoun's debtors were closing in and Mr Blandy made no secret of his disapproval of his daughter's suitor. To further complicate matters, Mary discovered that Cranstoun had a mistress in London although she chose to overlook this setback.

Cranstoun, perhaps stung by Mr Blandy's views of him, persuaded Mary to administer a powder to her father. He had already earlier managed to get her to add some 'love powder' to her father's tea to try to make him better inclined towards Cranstoun. In June 1751 Cranstoun sent Mary a box of ornamental Scotch pebbles accompanied by a powder supposedly to clean them. It was this powder which Mary was to secretly administer and she knew by this time it was poison – in fact arsenic.

Mary added the powder to her father's gruel and he promptly became ill. The cook who also ate some was stricken as well. Susan, the housemaid became suspicious as she had seen Mary putting something in the oatmeal. Trying a little of the gruel, Susan made herself sick for two days. Confirmed in her suspicions, she handed the offending food to a chemist for analysis.

The housemaid also reported her suspicions to Mr Blandy who in turn confronted Mary. Next, Mary tried to burn some letters and the powder on the kitchen fire but did not stay to see everything burn. Once she had left the kitchen, the cook grabbed the packets of powder from the flames.

Mr Blandy was now gravely ill and a doctor was called who examined the powder and diagnosed poisoning. The physician lectured Mary on the seriousness of her role in it all. Mary wrote to Cranstoun telling him to burn all their letters and deeply implicating herself in poisoning her father. She gave the letter to someone else to post, but it was given to a clerk who in turn passed it to the chemist who had examined the powder. Mr Blandy died on 14 August 1751 and Mary was arrested and charged with poisoning her father. She unsuccessfully tried to blame Cranstoun. Tried at Oxford Assizes, she claimed to have thought the powder was a love potion. A guilty verdict was returned and she was executed in 1752, aged 32.

Botkin, Cordelia

On the afternoon of the 9 August 1898, the young grandson of ex-congressman John Pennington of Delaware collected mail from the Dover post office. That evening after dinner, the family sat on the front porch to read the evening paper and open the mail. A package from San Francisco addressed to the little boy's aunt 'Mrs John P. Dunning' proved to be a box of chocolate creams covered with a handkerchief and a note reading 'Love to yourself and baby, Mrs C.'

Mary Dunning was puzzled, not knowing the identity of the sender. She and her husband had lived in San Francisco some years earlier but he was now in Puerto Rico working as a war correspondent for Associated Press. Thinking the donor must be someone who had known her in San Francisco but whom she had subsequently forgotten, Mary ate some of the confections and passed them round to her sister Mrs Joshua Deane and to the two Deane children. Two young women passed by, Miss Bateman and Miss Millington and accepted an offer of some of the chocolate creams before they continued on their way.

Later, when everyone had retired to bed, Mary woke up with stomach cramps and nausea. Struggling to the bathroom, she found her sister and the two children there also ill. A doctor was called who pumped out the stomach contents of the sufferers. Next morning, it was discovered that Misses Bateman and Millington had been ill with similar symptoms and the chocolates were immediately suspected.

Although the two young women passers-by and the two children recovered, Mrs Deane died on 11 August and Mary on the following day. Autopsies revealed arsenic in their viscera and an examination of the remaining chocolates confirmed that they were impregnated with the poison.

John Dunning was summoned from Puerto Rico and as they awaited his arrival, the father of the dead women and other relatives were mystified by the tragic events. Then ex-congressman Pennington remembered that several months before Mary had received an anonymous letter also from San Francisco and, he believed, in the same handwriting as the note in the chocolates. It warned Mary that her husband who was then working at the Golden Gate was having an affair.

When John Dunning arrived he recognized the handwriting on the note and, grief-stricken, told his father-in-law the identity of the killer. Dunning had married Mary Pennington in February 1891 in Dover and the couple soon moved to San Francisco where John worked. In 1892 the couple had a daughter but soon afterwards John met a woman who called herself Mrs Curtis and who claimed her husband was away in England. Later 'Mrs Curtis' told Dunning the truth, that her real name was Cordelia Botkin, previously Brown, and her husband lived in nearby Stockton with their nearly grown-up son. Cordelia was separated from her husband, enjoyed gambling and a good time and soon she and John Dunning were lovers.

Cordelia took an apartment in Geary Street and Dunning rented quarters in the same building to be close to her. A few months later, bored and neglected, Mary Dunning returned to her family home in Dover. On and off, John Dunning's affair with Cordelia Botkin lasted for five years. In 1896, John lost his job with Associated Press but two years later his past employer asked him to cover the Spanish-American War for them. Consequently, on 8 March 1898, John told Cordelia they were finished and that he was leaving for Puerto Rico and wanted to patch things up with his wife. Cordelia offered to join him but he refused. Once John Dunning had revealed this to his father-in-law, it became clear that the finger of suspicion pointed at a jealous Cordelia.

Detectives were sent to San Francisco where, working with California police, they established a case against Cordelia. Arrested in Stockton where she was once more living with her husband, Cordelia was locked in the county jail. The poisoned chocolates were traced to a shop owned by George Haas where two women clerks identified Cordelia as the purchaser. Frank Grey, a pharmacist at the Owl Drug Store identified Cordelia as having bought two ounces of white arsenic which she claimed was for cleaning a hat.

Cordelia's trial began on 9 December 1898. Convicted on 4 February 1899, she was sentenced to imprisonment for life but incarcerated initially in the county jail. A retrial beginning on 2 August 1904 only reconvicted the prisoner and in May 1906, Cordelia was transferred to San Quentin. Her second appeal was refused in the autumn of 1908 and two years later, Cordelia died in prison.

Bougrat, Dr Pierre

When Jacques Rumebe visited the surgery of Dr Pierre Bougrat in Marseilles on 14 March 1925 an incredible series of events was set in motion.

Dr Bougrat, at 37, had been divorced for about a year. His wife might have made an excellent companion for someone else, but Bougrat enjoyed the company of prostitutes rather too much, neglected his practice and was getting into debt. In fact after his divorce, Bougrat took a prostitute as his companion. Jacques Rumebe was a long-time friend of Bougrat, was suffering from syphilis and had called at the surgery for an injection of mercuric chloride. Unfortunately for Rumebe, he brought with him a bag of his firm's wages money, 20,000 francs. A short time later Rumebe lay dead in the consulting-room having received a fatal injection and been beaten. Bougrat now locked his surgery and ordered his housekeeper not to go into the consulting-room. The housekeeper and her husband looked through the consulting-room keyhole. Someone was lying on the examination couch. On the floor was a briefcase which was not Bougrat's.

Madame Rumebe became concerned about her husband's whereabouts and spoke to Bougrat who confirmed that he had treated his old friend. The worried wife then reported her husband missing.

But Rumebe's body had not left Bougrat's premises. The doctor had concealed it in a cupboard in his consulting room then wallpapered over the cupboard door. The weeks passed and warm weather arrived. The surgery began to smell unpleasantly and neighbours complained. The City Sanitation Department was called and they sprayed the premises with formalin. Dr Bougrat explained that a rat had died.

But Bougrat's time was running out. At the end of May he was arrested for writing fraudulent cheques and held in police custody. The police then searched the premises. The dreadful smell had not abated and soon they located the concealed cupboard and the cadaver of Jacques Rumebe by now decomposing. On the doctor's desk they found two passports one for Bougrat himself and one for the prostitute who was his companion. The documents clearly signalled Bougrat's plan to escape from the suspicion that was growing around him.

But just as Bougrat had had a ready explanation for the all-pervading smell, so he had an account of how Rumebe's body came to be in his cupboard.

Rumebe had arrived at Bougrat's surgery on 14 March 1925 distressed and asking for help. He had been beaten up and robbed. Dr Bougrat left the consulting-room for a moment and in the interim, Rumebe injected himself with cyanide and ended his life. Bougrat on discovering the body was afraid that he might be accused of theft. He decided not to report the death but to hide the corpse in his surgery temporarily until he could dispose of it.

Doctor Bougrat's account did not convince the police and he was tried for murder. But the strange story did not rest there. Found guilty and sentenced to hard labour on Devil's Island, where he arrived in 1927, Bougrat escaped to Venezuela.

Because of his medical skills, he was allowed to remain there. He married and continued as a doctor up to the age of 75 when he died in 1962.

Brinkley, Richard

Producing a piece of folded paper, carpenter Richard Brinkley asked Johanna Blume for her signature. He was, he said, collecting signatures for an outing to the seaside. The 77-year-old widow duly signed. Brinkley gained two further signatures in the same way, those of Henry Heard and Reginald Parker.

But the folded document was nothing to do with a seaside trip. It was a will which Brinkley had made out and which left Mrs Blume's property to him. This property included cash and the house in Fulham, London where the old woman lived with her granddaughter. Two days later Mrs Blume died and the doctor issued a certificate of death from natural causes.

Brinkley now revealed the will but he had not accounted for the reaction of the old woman's granddaughter. She was not happy about the terms of the will and consulted a solicitor. Brinkley was required to show that the will was valid and this he knew, would lead to the 'witnesses' Heard and Parker being questioned.

Brinkley decided to get rid of the two witnesses and began with Parker. Pretending he wished to buy a dog from him, Brinkley went to Parker's lodgings. He took with him a bottle of stout to oil the bargaining process, leaving it on the table while the pair went outside to take a close look at the animal.

As fate would have it, while the two men were out, Parker's landlord Mr Beck entered the lodgings accompanied by his wife and daughter. Seeing the bottle, they decided to each have a taste. All three collapsed, Mr and Mrs Beck never to recover. The daughter, however, did pull through some days later.

The stout had been doctored with prussic acid. When questioned by police, Brinkley mentioned the poison stout before they had even raised the matter thus immediately implicating himself. Brinkley was charged with the murder of Mr and Mrs Beck. Mrs Blume's body was exhumed and an autopsy conducted. An inspection of the body was made for traces of poison but without success.

Brinkley stood trial at Guildford Assizes, was found guilty and hanged at Wandsworth Prison on 13 August 1907.

Brinvilliers, Marie Madeleine de

Certain fated meetings change the course of people's lives and one such encounter was that of Baron Antoine de Brinvilliers and

Godin who was usually called Ste Croix. It was this meeting that was eventually circuitously to lead Marie Brinvilliers, the Baron's wife, towards a career as one of the most notorious poisoners in French criminal history.

Baron Brinvilliers was an officer of the Norman regiment. In 1615, he had married Marie D'Aubray, a very sexually experienced 21-year-old. Strikingly beautiful she was also well connected (her father was Councillor of State) and in possession of a handsome dowry. By 1659, the dowry had been frittered away. (Both the Baron and Marie enjoyed gambling).

It was at this time that the Baron met Ste Croix, a charming attractive man given to gambling and womanizing. Soon Marie and Ste Croix were lovers. Having himself had a succession of mistresses, the Baron was tolerant of the liaison. But the lovers were very indiscreet and Marie even told her father of the affair. He had Ste Croix imprisoned in the Bastille.

While incarcerated there in the spring of 1663, Ste Croix befriended a fellow prisoner a notorious Italian poisoner Exili. When both men were released, Exili stayed with Ste Croix in Paris for several months tutoring him in the craft of poisoning. In turn, Ste Croix passed this knowledge on to Marie.

The reunited lovers were in need of money and after their clash with Marie's father, decided to dispatch him so Marie would inherit a share of his wealth. Having obtained a poison powder from Glaser, a chemist who was Apothecary-in-ordinary to the King, Marie wanted confirmation that it would work. She was particularly concerned that the substance would not be detected by autopsy.

So having mixed the powder in wine and fruit, Marie visited patients in hospitals to try it out. Early in 1666, Marie's father invited her to stay with him on his Offémont estate and to bring her children, (two of whom were by Ste Croix). He became very ill and eventually returned to Paris for medical help. All this time Marie 'looked after' him until he died in September 1666.

The following year, Marie decided to poison her brothers who inhabited the same house, and paid Ste Croix to help. An assassin was hired to kill one brother but was unsuccessful. Jean Hamelin (called La Chausee) a poisoner was brought into the house and secretly set to work. The older brother died in June 1667. The second brother breathed his last in September. Although an autopsy established poisoning as the cause of death, no one was held responsible.

La Chausee blackmailed Marie and became her lover. Ste Croix also blackmailed her, having in his possession incriminating letters.

Next, Marie planned to poison her sister Mlle D'Aubray and her sister-in-law. But she told one of her lovers, Briancourt who was a tutor to her children and he got a message to Mlle D'Aubray to warn her. So Marie moved Briancourt himself to the top of her death list. Three attempts on his life failed, however, one of them being an effort to poison him.

Marie then tried to poison her spouse so she would be free to marry Ste Croix. But Ste Croix did not wish to marry her and kept administering counter poisons to the poor husband. Meanwhile Briancourt fled to Aubervilliers and took up another teaching post.

But it was Ste Croix who died next, of natural causes, in July 1672. His long estranged widow discovered among his possessions a box of letters and other documents incriminating Marie. La Chausee, the poisoner who had aided Marie by dispatching her two brothers, was arrested and tortured. Marie fled to England.

In February 1673 La Chausee confessed and was sentenced to be broken alive on the wheel. The French authorities sought to extradite Marie, who now fled to the Netherlands, then via other refuges finally to Liège where she entered a convent.

Ironically, she was arrested on 25 March 1676 in Liège, the day before the city fell under Spanish sway and the French King's authority ended.

After a trial lasting from April to July 1676, Marie was sentenced to death. She was tortured by having a funnel forced into her mouth and having large amounts of water poured into her stomach. At Notre Dame she made a public confession and was then decapitated in the Place de Grève by the executioner's sword.

Bryant, Charlotte

Charlotte Bryant died in Exeter Prison at the end of the hangman's noose on 15 July 1936 for the murder of her husband. She had lived with her farm labourer husband Frederick in a cottage in Over Compton, a little Dorset hamlet. Charlotte had five children and it was rumoured that not all of them were fathered by Frederick for Charlotte had had several lovers.

One of these was Leonard Parsons a gypsy who moved into the Bryant's cottage in 1933. Between 1933 and 1935 he stayed some of the time at the cottage and at other times he would rejoin his Gypsy wife Priscilla Loveridge and their children.

Parsons was staying at the Bryants in May 1935 and went out

with Charlotte who left a midday meal in the oven for her husband when he came in from work. When Frederick returned home, he was seized with intense stomach pains and his cries brought round a neighbour who gave him salt water to make him sick.

Dr McCarthy, the local physician was called and found Bryant pale and complaining of cramp in the legs. The doctor diagnosed a gastric attack and within a few days the patient was well again. A similar illness afflicted Frederick in August 1935, this time diagnosed as gastroenteritis, and once more Bryant recovered.

Parsons went to stay with Priscilla Loveridge in November 1935. A local widow, Lucy Ostler moved in with Charlotte to keep her company, sleeping at night on a chair in the couple's bedroom. On 21 December, Frederick fell ill yet again suffering stomach pains and vomiting. The next day he was taken to a Sherborne hospital where he died that afternoon.

The autopsy revealed four grains of arsenic in the body and heavy traces in the deceased's finger nails. The Bryants' cottage and garden were searched and traces of arsenic were found. Further traces were discovered in the pocket of one of Charlotte's coats.

Poison registers of chemists within a fifty-mile radius were checked. A pharmacist in Yeovil informed police that he had sold a tin of arsenical weedkiller to a woman who could not sign her name but made her mark of a cross. Because Charlotte was illiterate, it was possible she could have been the customer but the pharmacist could not pick her out in an identity parade.

What needs to be remembered is the availability of arsenic from other sources than pharmacists. Certainly the sale of weedkiller or rat poison would have been recorded but there was no evidence that Charlotte had made such a purchase. Also many people in the rural community would have been able to get arsenic in less controlled ways. Sheep-dips and insect poison contained potassium arsenate. Yeovil had a glove-making industry which would have used arsenic trisulphide to prepare skins. Arsenic disulphide was another ingredient used for dressing leather.

What appeared to be a key piece of evidence, a battered empty tin with traces of arsenic was found with a heap of rubbish at the rear of the Bryants' cottage. Remains of the tin were found among the ashes of a boiler. A firm of weedkiller manufacturers identified the tin as one of theirs.

On 10 February 1936, Charlotte Bryant was charged with the murder of her husband.

With Mr Justice MacKinnon presiding, the trial opened in May at Dorchester Assizes. Sir Terence O'Connor, the Solicitor General led the prosecution and elicited an important piece of information from Dr Gerald Roche Lynch, senior official analyst at the Home Office. Lynch stated that the ashes in the boiler where remains of the tin were found contained arsenic in a concentration of 149 parts per million. This was an unusually high concentration the analyst explained, the expected concentration being about 45 parts per million.

Charlotte Bryant was found guilty. But after the verdict her defence council David Caswell received a letter from Professor William Bone of Imperial College of Science and Technology. Bone explained that the normal content of arsenic in coal ash is 140 parts per million at least. Usually approaching 1,000 parts per million. Consequently, it appeared unlikely that the ashes in the boiler could have contained the tin with arsenic in it.

The Court of Criminal Appeal's refusal to hear this evidence meant that Charlotte Bryant kept her appointment with the executioner.

Buchanan, Dr Robert

Killing a cat with morphine in court was part of the prosecution case against Dr Robert Buchanan. They hoped to demonstrate that by introducing drops of belladonna into the animal's eyes, they could prevent the pupils contracting into tiny points, a decisive indicator of morphine administration.

The strange experiment was brought about because Dr Buchanan was on trial accused of poisoning his second wife Anna Sutherland with morphine. Her body had been exhumed and an autopsy indicated that morphine was present. But the tiny pupils were notably not evident. However, witnesses said that Buchanan had boasted that he could counteract the effect of morphine on the pupils by introducing drops of belladonna into the eyes.

Buchanan qualified in medicine at Edinburgh, Scotland and formed a successful New York practice in 1886. He married, but enjoyed visits to the city's brothels. Anna Sutherland was a brothel 'Madame' whom Buchanan persuaded to make a will favouring him. He then divorced his first wife and married Sutherland. His patients threatened to go elsewhere for their treatment in view of Buchanan's unseemly marriage partner.

In 1892 Buchanan announced that he was sailing for Edinburgh alone. Four days before the ship was due to sail, however, he cancelled his journey. The reason was that Anna Sutherland had suddenly fallen ill. She died of cerebral haemorrhage. The inheritance which as a result fell into the doctor's hands was $50,000.

When the *New York World* followed the story, it became clear that Buchanan had not intended to sail for Edinburgh at all. Before Anna Sutherland had been buried a month, Buchanan had remarried. The 'new' bride was his first wife. It was then that an order was made to exhume the body and the process was begun which led to Buchanan's trial and the experiment with the cat, morphine and belladonna.

The dramatic demonstration put on by the prosecution successfully showed that belladonna could counteract the effects of morphine on the eye pupils. Buchanan was found guilty. Appeals followed but did not prevent justice from taking its course. On 2 July 1895 at Sing Sing Prison, Dr Robert Buchanan was electrocuted.

Bulgarian Secret Service (Markov Murder)

What appeared to be an accidental injury with an umbrella inflicted by a passer-by signed the death warrant of Georgi Markov. In 1960, Markov, a Bulgarian dissident defected, first to Italy and later to England where in 1969, he was granted political asylum. He broadcast for the Bulgarian service of the BBC and for Radio Free Europe. In the early evening of 7 September 1978 he left his office in Bush House in central London and walked across Waterloo Bridge for a break from his work. Feeling a pain at the back of his right thigh, Markov thought that a man standing in a bus queue had inadvertently jabbed him. In fact, the man apologized for the accident in a noticeable foreign accent. Hailing a taxi, the man disappeared.

Markov returned to his office but noticing his leg beginning to stiffen, he recounted the story of his injury to a BBC colleague, showing the tiny wound. At 11 p.m., feeling feverish, Markov left the BBC and went home to rest.

The next day, he was ill and his wife Annabella took him to St James Hospital, Balham. He was running a temperature. The next day, Markov was in a worse condition. His white blood cell count shot up and the patient was given antibiotic injections to try to counteract this. But two days later the Bulgarian defector died.

On 2 January 1979 an inquest was held. Commander James

Neville, head of the Anti-Terrorist Squad, Scotland Yard was present. Dr David Gall from the Chemical Defence Establishment at Porton Down gave evidence. (This establishment supplies to MI5 antidotes to poisons used by KGB assassins.) Dr Gall testified that he had concluded that Markov had apparently died from poisoning and had considered various possible poisons. Eventually, ricin was identified as the possible killer.

Dr Robert Keeley, a forensic scientist recounted how a minute metal pellet had been found in Markov's thigh. The tiny ball made from a platinum and iridium alloy, though it measured only 1.52 millimetres in diameter was drilled with two minute holes which, where they met in the centre of the pellet, formed a reservoir for the poison. Annabella Markov, Georgi's wife, said that her husband feared assassination by the Bulgarian secret police. The coroner found that Markov had been killed unlawfully by poison administered in a metal pellet.

Annabella Markov, Georgi's widow visited Bulgaria several times trying to establish who killed her husband. In June 1991, the Bulgarian Interior Minister, Kristo Danov disclosed that the Bulgarian secret police had been responsible. Moves were made to bring to trial the former Communist leader and ex-president of Bulgaria, Todor Zhivkov, in connection with the Markov killing. Another key figure for investigation was Stoyan Savov the 'Black General' who was head of the secret police at the time the murder took place. He had taken out secret files on the case which had later vanished.

Cantharides

Cantharides is a powder made from the dried wings and body of a beetle, *Cantharis vesicatoria*, found in Southern Russia, Italy and Spain. The beetle's Spanish habitat gives the powder its common name of Spanish fly. In the East, the dried beetle *Mylabris sidea* (Chinese or Indian blistering beetle) is used as a source of cantharides. In the case of both sources, the active component is cantharidin.

Being an irritant, cantharides acts on the parts of the body which it contacts and when it passes out of the system it irritates the genital organs. For this reason, it was thought to be an aphrodisiac. Although its application as a love powder in humans appears to be the stuff of myth and fantasy, it has been used on tame animals by breeders, particularly rabbit breeders.

Its medical use was as a blistering agent when it was applied to the skin as a plaster or was painted on as blistering fluid (Liquor Epispasticus). This was meant to ease severe forms of pain such as sciatica or to encourage the fluid in thickened joints to be absorbed. Cantharidin solution was sometimes used in hair lotions to stimulate the scalp.

Death has been caused by as little as one and a half to three grains but in other cases people have recovered after much larger doses. If taken by mouth, cantharides causes a burning pain in the throat and stomach and difficulty in swallowing, Nausea, vomiting, colic, bloody diarrhoea and blood in the urine are further symptoms before the sufferer collapses and dies.

Carbon Monoxide

Carbon monoxide is a colourless, tasteless and odourless gas present in coal gas, town gas (fumes from burning buildings and furnishings) and car exhaust fumes. It is absorbed by the lungs into the bloodstream.

A fatal dose of carbon monoxide involves breathing an atmosphere of one-tenth of 1% of carbon monoxide for three hours, or higher concentrations for a shorter time. Within this period sufficient carbon monoxide molecules would be breathed in to outnumber the body's red blood cells by 400 billion to one. About half of the body's red blood cells would be affected and there would not be sufficient oxygen getting round the body to sustain life.

Haemoglobin of the red blood cells has about 250–300 times the affinity for carbon monoxide that oxygen has. Consequently, in the lungs, the haemoglobin combines with carbon monoxide to form carboxyhaemoglobin instead of combining with oxygen to form oxyhaemoglobin. All this effectively prevents the transport of oxygen around the body as oxyhaemoglobin and deprives the body tissues of oxygen.

Carbon monoxide effects the ganglia (clusters of nerve cells) at the base of the brain and can destroy parts of it. It impairs the mental faculties so the victim is unaware of anything being wrong.

Because of the large amounts of carboxyhaemoglobin in the blood, the skin may become cherry red. Headache, dizziness and weakness develop. Nausea occurs and an increased rate of breathing and heart beat. Collapse, coma, respiratory failure and death follow. A patient, suffering carbon monoxide poisoning is given a mixture of oxygen and 5% carbon dioxide to inhale as soon as possible. Otherwise artificial respiration is given in fresh air.

Carew, Edith

A doctor attending Walter Carew, an English expatriate working in Yokohama, Japan, received a strange note from which seven words stood out – 'Three bottles of arsenic in one week'.

Walter Carew, a businessman who lived in Yokohama with his wife Edith had fallen ill in late 1896 with what appeared to be violent stomach upsets. When the doctor received the note, which was sent to him by Maruya, a Japanese chemist, he began to revise his diagnosis. It became clear that the businessman was dying from poisoning, and Carew soon breathed his last.

An inquest was held at which Maruya claimed to have received written instructions from Mrs Carew to supply several bottles of arsenic solution. This was to relieve a secret illness which Walter suffered from, Mrs Carew claimed. Edith Carew was arrested and charged with the murder of her husband.

Her trial, which fell under the judicial authority of the British Consul in Yokohama, began in January 1897. Love letters from a young bank clerk to Mrs Carew were presented to the court, which mentioned the possibility of Edith leaving her husband.

Mrs Carew claimed that another woman had been having an affair with her husband and produced letters said to be from this supposed mistress. In court these missives were revealed as forgeries made by Edith herself. Mrs Carew was found guilty of murder and sentenced to death, but the sentence was commuted to penal servitude for life.

Castaing, Dr Edme

In an inn at Saint-Cloud, near Paris on 29 May 1823, Auguste Ballet was enjoying a drink of mulled wine with a doctor and partner in crime 27-year-old Edme Castaing.

The two had collaborated together in a successful fraud involving Hippolyte Ballet, Auguste's older brother. Hippolyte was a wealthy man but had left Auguste out of his will. Castaing proposed that he should steal Hippolyte's will and destroy it. Hippolyte was slowly dying of tuberculosis and when he died, Auguste would then inherit. For his part in benefiting Auguste, the doctor would be given a large reward to help him keep up his indulgent way of life.

Accordingly the will was destroyed and Hippolyte died, so as they drank together on that May day, both men had cause to be pleased by their improved financial circumstances. Auguste had even made Castaing the main beneficiary under his will. As they drank, Castaing amiably added a powder, apparently sugar, to his friend's wine. Suddenly, Auguste became ill. He was taken home and a local doctor, Pigache was called. He in turn later called in Dr Pellatan, a professor at the Paris School of Medicine. Both noticed that the pupils of Auguste's eyes were very tiny. All this time, Castaing was constantly beside the ailing man, the picture of friendly self-sacrifice. Auguste was vomiting violently during his illness and Castaing, instead of keeping the substance for examination, disposed of it promptly. Eventually the patient fell unconscious and died.

Pigache recognized that, in the sudden and mysterious circumstances of the death, it would have been most useful if Castaing had retained the vomit for analysis. An autopsy was carried out, to which Castaing happily agreed, to establish cause of death and extinguish the inevitable gossip. The autopsy, however, revealed that death was due to morphine poisoning.

When it emerged that Castaing stood to benefit substantially from Auguste's will, suspicion immediately fell on him.

Hippolyte's body was also exhumed but doctors could not agree whether his death had been hastened by morphine poisoning.

At the ensuing trial for murder held at the Paris Assize Court in November 1823, damning evidence was produced against Castaing. As Auguste lay ill, Castaing had visited a Paris pharmacy where he bought some morphine acetate. He gave his real name and explained that he required the poison to kill rats in laboratory work.

Morphine was a little known drug in those days and at the trial several doctors were called to testify to its properties. Acquitted of the murder of Hippolyte, Castaing was nevertheless found guilty of the murder of Auguste. Castaing, the first medical doctor to be convicted of murder using morphine, was guillotined in 1823, aged 27.

Chantrelle, Eugène

Elizabeth Dyer was only 15 years old when she was seduced and made pregnant by the man who years later was to murder her. Eugène Chantrelle had supported the Communist cause in France in 1851, then come to England in 1862 where he taught French at a school. Eventually securing a teaching post in Edinburgh at a private academy, he met Elizabeth who was a pupil there. Married in 1868, as time passed, the couple had four children. But while Elizabeth proved a good wife and mother, Eugène was far from being a model husband, ill treating his wife and displaying boorish behaviour which lost him pupils and consequently weakened their financial position.

When Eugène started boasting that he could kill his wife and get away with it, the writing was on the wall. In 1877, soon after the Frenchman had insured his wife's life against accident for £1,000, a servant entering Elizabeth's bedroom found her insensible. Chantrelle was called and stayed in the room to care for his wife while the servants withdrew. Servants next saw Elizabeth dead and the room held an overpowering smell of coal gas.

When the doctor was called, Eugène claimed that Elizabeth had been overcome and killed by gas from a leaking pipe in the bedroom. Autopsy did not support this but indicated that death may have been caused by the administration of a narcotic. Chantrelle was arrested on a murder charge and his trial revealed that he had purchased opium before Elizabeth's death and that vomit containing the narcotic had been found on the deceased's bed linen. Found guilty, Chantrelle was hanged on 31 May 1878.

Chapman, George

The Prince of Wales Tavern off the City Road in London may have appeared like many other pubs in the 1890s but dark happenings were taking place behind its walls. They stemmed from the owner, George Chapman whose real name was Severin Klosowski.

The son of a Polish carpenter, Klosowski had worked in his native Poland for some years as a barber-surgeon. He married a Polish woman and later served in the Russian Army. In 1888, Klosowski left for England, leaving his wife behind.

In the East End of London, he worked as a barber's assistant and in 1889 'married' another Polish woman Lucy Baderski. Not long after this, his real wife came over from Poland and the three lived in the same house for a while before his original wife departed.

Klosowski and Baderski went to live in the United States in 1890, but Baderski returned alone a year later after quarrelling with her 'husband'. Klosowski came back to England in 1892 and was reconciled with Baderski for a time before she finally left him for good, taking their two children with her. He then lived with a certain Annie Chapman for a year and when she left him he adopted her surname and thereafter liked to be known as George Chapman.

Then in 1895, Chapman met Isabella Spink, a married woman separated from her husband. Using her money, Chapman set up a hairdressing shop in Hastings in 1897. While there he bought a quantity of tartar emetic from a chemist. Six months later the couple moved back to London where they leased the Prince of Wales Tavern. The scene was set for murder.

Isabella began suffering abdominal pains and vomiting attacks. When she died on Christmas Day 1897, the doctor diagnosed cause of death as consumption.

In 1898, Chapman employed Bessie Taylor as a barmaid and soon after went through a marriage service with her. Bessie became ill and Chapman gave up the lease on the Prince of Wales and moved to Bishop's Stortford where he became landlord of 'The Grapes'. Soon after, he moved again, this time to manage the Monument Tavern in Union Street in the borough. Bessie's health continued to decline and was not helped by Chapman's ill treatment and bullying of her. Death took Bessie on 13 February 1901 and the cause was certified as exhaustion.

Maud Marsh was the next barmaid and a familiar pattern began to emerge. Chapman persuaded her to become his mistress, went through a marriage ceremony with her and soon Maud was suffering abdominal pains. Chapman moved to be landlord of the 'Crown' a pub on the same street as the Monument Tavern. By 1902, Maud was gravely ill. Chapman, however, had not accounted for Maud's mother who had distrusted Chapman from the beginning of her daughter's relationship with him.

Mrs Marsh came to stay with her daughter in order to look after her. During her stay, Chapman made a drink of brandy and soda for his wife. Both Mrs Marsh and a nurse who was tending Maud had a sip and were violently ill with vomiting and diarrhoea. Believing that Chapman was poisoning her daughter, Mrs Marsh shared her suspicions with Dr Stoker who was treating Maud. But he appears not to have agreed. So Mrs Marsh sought a second opinion from a Dr Grapel, who concurred that Maud appeared to be suffering from poisoning. Arsenic was suspected.

When Maud died on 22 October 1902, Dr Grapel informed Dr Stoker of his suspicion and Stoker refused to certify death. He conducted a private autopsy and found poison in the body which he thought to be arsenic. Three days after Maud's demise, Chapman was arrested and charged with her murder. A second autopsy revealed that death was caused by poisoning, not from arsenic but from antimony. The bodies of Isabella Spink and Bessie Taylor were exhumed and they too were found to contain antimony.

Chapman's trial opened at the Old Bailey on 16 March 1903. Mr Justice Grantham presided and Sir Edward Carson led the prosecution while Mr George Elliott KC stood for the defence. Found guilty after a four-day trial, Chapman was sentenced to death and was hanged on 7 April 1903.

A further cause of Chapman's notoriety is that his is one of the names put forward as a possible perpetrator of the Jack the Ripper killings. One theory is that Chapman carried out the Ripper murders but became increasingly convinced that he would be caught. He turned to poisoning women as a safer outlet for his sadistic impulses.

Chief Inspector Abberline investigated the Ripper murders. He is reported to have told the policeman who arrested Chapman, 'You've got Jack the Ripper at last!'

Cherry Laurel Water

Prunus laurocerasus, the cherry laurel was used to prepare a killing bottle used by entomologists for collecting insects. Crushed, fresh entire leaves were enclosed in a corked bottle where they released hydrocyanic acid.

Cherry Laurel Water was used to make soothing solutions, its effect being due to the hydrocyanic acid it releases. Smelling of bitter almonds and having a sharp, sour taste, it is not an obvious choice of homicidal poison. Its toxic principle being hydrocyanic acid, the toxic effects, action, symptoms and antidote are the same as for hydrocyanic acid (prussic acid).

Chloroform

Chloroform is a volatile, heavy, colourless liquid with a characteristic odour and was discovered by Liebig in 1831. A compound of chlorine, carbon and hydrogen, it mixes with alcohol or ether.

In 1847, Sir J.Y. Simpson first used chloroform vapour as an anaesthetic drawing on its property first to induce drowsiness then in higher doses to cause unconsciousness. In time, inhaling the vapour of chloroform was called on to ease pain during childbirth and to promote unconsciousness for surgery although it is now no longer used for either purpose.

Chloroform also found its uses. One or two drops were taken with sugar to ease seasickness. Applied to the skin, chloroform was used as a liniment for soothing rheumatic pains. In the present day it is used as a solvent for fatty substances in various chemical processes.

Turning to the body's absorption of chloroform, the vapour is absorbed by the lungs and distributed into the bloodstream. Taken by mouth, it is absorbed by the gastro-intestinal tract.

Chloroform can sometimes kill quickly and suddenly after a very small dose by stopping the heart. One of the actions of chloroform is to make the heart particularly sensitive to the bodily hormone adrenalin. Too much chloroform can therefore lead to heart failure brought about by the body's own secretion of adrenalin. It can also cause respiratory arrest.

Death can sometimes occur a few days after the chloroform was taken because of damage to the kidneys, liver and heart. Chloroform is particularly toxic to the liver.

Oxygen and 5% carbon dioxide inhaled, helps clear chloroform from the bloodstream and was therefore used to treat a chloroform overdose.

Clark, Dr Henry and Fulham, Augusta

The eternal quadrangle might describe the motive for the double murder by Clark and Fulham. In 1911, the 42-year-old Dr Clark, was serving in the Indian Subordinate Medical Service in Agra, India. Unhappily married, he became the lover of Augusta Fulham, the 35-year-old wife of a military accounts examiner.

The pair decided to dispatch Augusta's husband Edward. Augusta Fulham suggested they should administer a poison which would mirror the symptoms of heat stroke. Dr Clark proposed arsenic which was easy to obtain in India at that time. He sent the poison to Mrs Fulham to give to her husband.

Edward Fulham was subsequently attended by Dr Clark, treated for heat stroke and given an injection of gelsemine. He died on 10 October 1911 and Dr Clark signed the death certificate.

Mrs Clark's was the next death planned by the lovers. Dr Clark hired four killers who on 17 November 1912 entered Mrs Clark's home and dispatched her with a sword.

Clark admitted to police that he was dining with Mrs Fulham on the night of Mrs Clark's death. Police interviewed Mrs Fulham and, searching her house, found a tin box beneath the bed containing around 400 letters. Most of these were love letters from Mrs Fulham to Clark and initialled by him.

One such letter requested the doctor to send Augusta Fulham a 'powder'. Another missive, this time from Dr Clark to his wife declared his impatience with her 'low disgusting ways'.

Edward Fulham's body was exhumed and found to contain arsenic. The case against the lovers and the hiring of the four assassins also began to piece together.

Dr Clark and Mrs Fulham were put on trial twice at the Allahabad High Court. The first trial was for the murder of Edward Fulham, the second for the murder, with the four hired killers, of Mrs Clark.

Having confessed from the dock Dr Clark was sentenced to death and hanged on 26 March 1913. Mrs Fulham turned King's Evidence but because she was pregnant with Clark's child escaped the death penalty. Sentenced to life, she served only fifteen months of her prison term before she died on 29 May 1914.

Fate had a final trick to play. For Mrs Fulham died of the very condition that she had planned should be the apparent cause of her husband's death – heat stroke.

Clements, Dr Robert

In 1947, following the death of Mrs Clements, two doctors committed suicide. One was Dr James Houston who had diagnosed her fatal illness as myeloid leukaemia. The other was Dr Robert Clements, a Fellow of the Royal College of Surgeons who was the deceased's husband.

Dr and Mrs Clements, the surgeon's fourth wife, lived in Southport, England, where Mrs Clements suffered a long illness which included symptoms of tiredness and vomiting. Friends trying to telephone Mrs Clements could no longer contact the invalid because her husband had had the telephone taken out. At her death, Dr Houston certified the cause as myeloid leukaemia. An autopsy was carried out, however, and the tiny pupils of the deceased's eyes led doctors to suspect that death might have been caused by a morphine overdose. But the funeral was to go ahead, until it became known that Dr Clements had prescribed morphine for a patient who had not in fact been given any. The funeral was stopped.

A second autopsy showed that the deceased had died from morphine poisoning. Police called to question Dr Clements, but found him dead from a self-administered overdose of morphine. A Coroner's Inquiry judged that Dr Clements had murdered his wife. It emerged that Mrs Clements' death would have left the husband extremely wealthy.

The doctor's three previous wives had also been well off. The causes of their deaths had all been recorded on the death certificates by Dr Clements. When the third wife died, police called to take the body for an autopsy only to discover they were too late. The body had already been cremated.

Dr James Houston killed himself because he was shocked to have made such an incorrect diagnosis of the cause of Mrs Clements' death.

Colchicum (Seeds)

Colchicum autumnale (*Liliaceae*), better known as autumn crocus or meadow saffron contains an alkaloid colchine in its flowers, corm (roots) and seeds.

Used as a medicine in ancient Egypt, the plant or its extract has been since used as a treatment for gout, a disorder causing inflammation of the joints (and other symptoms) connected with an excess of uric acid in the blood.

The corms were dried and used as a tincture (that is mixed with alcohol), as colchicum wine, liquid extract, dry extract or in a mixture. Colchicum flowers were dried and used as a tincture and the seeds were dried and used as either tincture or liquid extract. In these forms their use was to relieve the pain of gout and reduce the inflammation.

Corm, seed and flower preparations have been replaced by colchine an alkaloid extract from the plant which may be given intravenously or by mouth as tablets. Colchine has also been used to treat a form of chronic leukaemia.

A dose of 7 mg has caused death but in other cases people have recovered from larger doses. While the action of colchine is not understood, the symptoms of poisoning are the same for the alkaloid or the plant corm or seeds. After some three to six hours symptoms appear including the effects of irritation; burning and a feeling of rawness in the mouth and throat and difficulty in swallowing. Nausea, abdominal pain, vomiting and diarrhoea occur and within seven to thirty-six hours, death may be caused by exhaustion or respiratory paralysis.

Conroy, Teresa

On the night of Friday 25 September 1953, Michael Conroy slept at home without his wife Teresa. She had telephoned him at work earlier that day explaining that she was to stay with her cousin in Muswell Hill for a couple of days. She was taking their 13-year-old son John who suffered from epilepsy with her.

Next morning, Michael was searching for some money which he had misplaced, and checked the bed in which he had slept. Feeling between the divan base and the mattress, he touched something rather odd. Pulling back the mattress to investigate he was faced with the corpse of his son. The divan base had been torn open and the body had been pushed into the opening. The child's hands were crossed on his chest and the face was carefully exposed by the lining which was neatly folded back.

Teresa Conroy was questioned by police and eventually confessed that she knew her son was dead. She claimed that on Tuesday 22 September, John had suffered an epileptic fit. On the morning of Wednesday 23 September, she had found the boy out of bed and crouched beside the gas oven. She had taken him back to bed but he choked and died. She said she had then 'buried' him in the divan before leaving for Muswell Hill.

The autopsy told quite a different story. A fifty-five per cent concentration of coal gas (carbon monoxide) was found in the body. But in addition the corpse contained sixty grains of methyl-pheris-barbitone, (a medication used for epilepsy). This represented twice the fatal dose. Teresa Conroy was accordingly charged with murder.

At her trial before Mr Justice Havers at the Old Bailey on 8 December 1953, Mr Christmas Humphreys prosecuted and Mr Elliot Gorst QC stood for the defence. A verdict of guilty but insane was returned and Teresa Conroy was detained for an indefinite period.

Copper

Copper is an element possessing qualities which have made it a useful and desirable metal from ancient times. It may have been worked as long as 8,000 years ago. Bronze, an alloy of copper with tin was invented around 2500 BC while brass, an alloy of copper, zinc and other metals was used in Roman times. Uses of copper continue to exploit its conductivity of heat (and more recently electricity) and its attractive sheen making it a choice for ornaments.

Salts of copper, such as copper sulphate have been employed from the days of ancient Egypt where they were used in the treatment of conjunctivitis. Once used as emetics, salts of copper are now employed as pigments in the manufacture of ceramics and textiles, as fungicides, germicides and insecticides. Copper sulphate was used as a homicidal poison in parts of Europe and copper salts have been used homicidally in areas of India predominantly by women.

Being an 'essential' element, copper exists in all organisms. It is necessary for blood formation, is contained in several enzymes and is present in all bodily tissue, particularly brain, heart, liver, kidney and hair.

Taken by mouth, copper sulphate is absorbed by the gastro-intestinal tract but is not one of the more poisonous substances, some ten grammes being a possible lethal dose. The sufferer from copper sulphate poisoning becomes confused and cramps, convulsions, coma and death may follow.

Potassium ferrocyanide may be used to treat copper poisoning as it combines with copper to produce copper ferrocyanide which is insoluble. Copper sulphate poisoning may be treated by white of egg, milk, tartaric acid or magnesia.

Coppolino, Dr Carl

When Dr Carl Coppolino appeared in court in Florida in April 1967 it was his second trial for murder.

Coppolino had pulled himself out of a poor family background to qualify in medicine and become an anaesthiologist. He married Carmela Musetto who was also a doctor.

But Coppolino had an eye for other women. In 1962, he was attracted to 48-year-old Marjorie Farber, a married woman. A year later, her husband, a retired army colonel, became ill and was attended by Coppolino. Colonel Farber died suddenly of coronary thrombosis.

Three years later Carl and Carmela moved to Florida. There Carl again noticed the attractions of another woman, a 38-year-old divorcee Mary Gibson. Also Marjorie Farber moved to Florida and became a neighbour.

In September 1965, Carmela Coppolino died of a heart attack. In less than three weeks, Carl had remarried. His new bride was not Marjorie Farber, but Mary Gibson.

Marjorie Farber now told police that Coppolino had murdered his wife Carmela. She also informed them that she had been encouraged by Carl to inject succinylcholine chloride into her husband. This had contributed to the colonel's death. It was clear that the use of succinylcholine chloride in anaesthiology meant that Carl Coppolino would have access to the drug. The body of Carmela Coppolino was exhumed. A mark was discovered on the cadaver that seemed to be a needle puncture. Colonel Farber's body was also exhumed. An autopsy revealed that the cricoid cartilage in the throat was broken. This indicated pressure on the throat.

Carl Coppolino was first tried for the murder of Colonel Farber by a New Jersey court. The jury acquitted him. Next in April 1967 he stood before a court in Florida charged with the murder of Carmela his wife. F. Lee Bailey for the defence, argued that there was no satisfactory evidence about the cause of Carmela's death. Experts in forensic science were cautious because the case was the first alleged poisoning by succinylcholine chloride.

Found guilty of second-degree murder, Dr Carl Coppolino, the poor boy who had made his way in life, was sentenced to life imprisonment.

Cotton, Mary

One-time nurse Mary Cotton is suspected of having committed about fourteen murders, motivated either by the desire to profit from insurance or the wish to be rid of one spouse or lover to make room for another.

In 1871, she accompanied her husband Frederick to West Auckland in County Durham, England. Theirs was a bigamous marriage and the couple took with them Frederick's two stepsons and Mary's own six-month-old baby. Less than eight weeks after their move, 39-year-old Frederick died of gastric fever, making room for Joseph Natrass a lover of Mary's to become her lodger. Between 10 March and 1 April 1872, Joseph Natrass, Mary's baby, and Frederick's elder son who was ten years old all died.

When, on 12 July the remaining stepson died, a neighbour informed the police and the doctor who had seen the boy on 11 July, refused to issue a death certificate. After an autopsy revealed the presence of arsenic in the child's stomach contents, Mary Cotton was charged with the murder of the stepson. Pregnant by Quick-Manning a local excise officer, Mary was remanded in Durham Prison where her baby was born.

At her trial at Durham Assizes in March 1873, Mary pleaded not guilty, claiming that the deceased boy had been accidentally poisoned from wallpaper in his home. It was shown, however, that the defendant had bought some arsenic supposedly for cleaning bedsteads and killing bedbugs. Found guilty and sentenced to death, Mary attracted public sympathy because of her baby, but the Home Secretary declined to commute the sentence.

On 19 March 1873 the baby was taken from her and five days later Mary was hanged.

Cream, Dr Thomas Neill

One night in October 1891 in London, Louisa Harvey, a prostitute picked up a man with a noticeable eye defect. He was Dr Thomas Cream and he duly spent the night with her. Louisa had some spots on her face and the doctor offered to give her some pills to help clear them up.

When they met later and Cream offered the pills, his concern that Louisa swallowed them whole made her worried and suspicious. She only pretended to take the pills and in reality dropped them. In doing so, she saved herself from death by poisoning at the hands of the notorious Lambeth Poisoner.

Although born in Glasgow, Cream had graduated in medicine at McGill University, Canada in 1876 at the age of 26. He then practised in Chicago. Having poisoned with strychnine a Mr Stott, the husband of his current mistress, Cream seemed to want to court danger. He wrote to the District Attorney, suggesting that Stott's body be exhumed. Eventually he was charged with the murder and in 1881 sent to Joliet Prison for life. Released in July 1891, he left for London where in October he found rooms at 103 Lambeth Palace Road.

Over the next few months, Cream murdered prostitutes by poisoning them with pills containing strychnine, just as he had tried to do with Louisa Harvey. His victims were Ellen Donworth, Matilda Clover, Emma Showell and Alice Marsh. Cream also found time to get engaged to a young dressmaker.

The same trait which had led to his imprisonment in America began to emerge again. He drew attention to himself by offering to reveal the identity of the Lambeth Poisoner for a £300,000 reward. He lodged a complaint with Scotland Yard that he was being followed. He wrote a letter headed 'Ellen Donworth's Death' to the guests of the Metropole Hotel telling them that the murderer of Ellen Donworth was 'in the employ' of the hotel and that their lives were endangered. It was dated April 1892 and signed 'W.H. Murray'.

On 3 June 1892 he was arrested and charged with acting under false pretences. Soon after, the charge became one of murder.

Cream went for trial in October 1892 and Louisa Harvey the prostitute gave evidence for the prosecution. A chemist testified to Cream purchasing gelatine capsules and nux vomica from him. In addition, seven bottles of strychnine had been discovered in Cream's rooms in Lambeth Palace Road. The jury retired for only twelve minutes before returning a guilty verdict.

On 15 November 1892, 42-year-old Cream was led to the scaffold. It was said that as the bolt was drawn, he cried, 'I am Jack the ...' and his last words were stopped by the noose. Speculation inevitably followed that Cream might have been claiming to be Jack the Ripper, the killer of prostitutes around Whitechapel in London's East End.

Creighton, Mary and Appelgate, Everett

In the 1920s John Creighton and his wife Mary were tried for murder, charged with poisoning Mary's younger brother, but were acquitted. Later, Mary Creighton alone faced another murder indictment. Accused of poisoning her mother-in-law with arsenic, Mary was again found not guilty.

Moving to Long Island, the Creightons became the friends of Everett and Ada Appelgate who in 1935 moved into the Creighton home. Some months later, apparently suffering a heart attack Ada Appelgate died. Whispers started concerning the past life of the Creighton couple and as suspicions grew, an enquiry opened into Ada's death. An autopsy revealed the cause to be arsenic poisoning.

Apart from the death, parallel events were developing, for it emerged that Everett Appelgate had been having sexual relations with the Creightons' daughter. As the girl was only 15-years-old, Everett was charged with rape and taken into custody. Mary Creighton accused Everett Appelgate not only of raping her daughter but also of involvement in killing Ada Appelgate.

In the event, both Mary Creighton and Everett Appelgate were charged with first-degree murder and at their trial in January 1936 it emerged that they had been lovers. (Everett had discovered Mary's past and had threatened to reveal it.) Mary admitted from the witness-box administering arsenic to Ada Appelgate in a drink of milk. Both Mary Creighton and Everett Appelgate were found guilty and died in the electric chair in Sing Sing prison on 16 July 1936.

Crippen, Dr Hawley

When human remains were discovered in the cellar during a police search of 39 Hilldrop Crescent, London, Dr Bernard Spilsbury was called in. It was the first important case for the Home Office pathologist who was to later become Sir Bernard Spilsbury and one of the great names in criminal investigation. There was no head, nor limbs nor indeed any skeleton at all. But among the bits that had once been a human being, a piece of tissue was found that was recognizable as a portion of scarred abdomen. This identified the remains as those of Mrs Crippen who had allegedly left England to visit a sick relative in the United States. The poison hyoscine was detected among the remains.

This dramatic find signalled the beginning of the end for Dr Crippen. Born in Michigan, United States, in 1862, Crippen qualified as a doctor in 1885 and worked for a patent medicine firm. He married twice, his second marriage being to Kunigunde Mackamotzki. She Americanized her name to Cora Turner and, as an entertainer, called herself Belle Elmore.

Hawley and his dominant wife Cora moved to England in 1900. However, the doctor's American qualifications were insufficient for him to practise in England and he took jobs involving selling patent medicines. Eventually, the couple moved into 39 Hilldrop Crescent where Cora let rooms to guests.

It was in early 1910 that Cora disappeared and Crippen spread the word that she had returned to the United States to be with a sick relation. Crippen acted rather too precipitately, however, when his secretary Ethel le Neve moved in with him. For Ethel was also Crippen's mistress. What got local tongues wagging even more was that Ethel began to wear Cora's furs and jewellery for all to see.

Cora's disappearance was reported to Scotland Yard. Chief Inspector Walter Dew called on Crippen and searched the premises but nothing suspicious was uncovered. At this point Crippen and his mistress decided to flee. At Antwerp, they set out for Canada on the SS *Montrose*. Their flight attracted further attention and a second search of Hilldrop Crescent revealed the remains of Cora Crippen.

As the SS *Montrose* ploughed the seas, Captain Kendall became suspicious of a mild-mannered man and the young boy who accompanied him. The pair were unduly affectionate and the boy's clothes rested rather oddly on him.

The captain radioed London and the suspicion that the man and boy were none other than Crippen and Ethel le Neve was confirmed. Chief Inspector Dew embarked on a speedier vessel and despite his later start reached the destination before them. When the *Montrose* reached harbour on 31 July 1910, Drew was waiting for the doctor and his mistress.

Back in England, the pair were tried separately at the Old Bailey. Ethel le Neve stood accused of being an accessory after the fact but was acquitted. Crippen was tried for the murder of his wife and on 18 October 1910, found guilty. He was hanged on 23 November at Pentonville Prison.

It was the first time in which Marconi's new invention, the wireless was used to aid the capture of a murderer.

Cross, Dr Philip

Dr Philip Cross, having been an army medical officer in India, retired to Shandy Hall, County Cork in Ireland with his wife Laura and their six children. There the 62-year-old doctor fell in love with Mary Skinner, the auburn haired 20-year-old who was employed by Laura as governess to her children. Becoming aware of this, Laura dismissed Mary. But Dr Cross went behind his wife's back and arranged for Mary to stay in Dublin at O'Donnell's Hotel where he later travelled to stay with her as frequently as he could.

Then Mrs Cross became ill with sickness and diarrhoea. Diagnosing typhoid, Dr Cross asked Dr Godfrey, his cousin for a second opinion. Young Dr Godfrey was newly qualified and must have found it difficult not to concur with the older doctor's diagnosis. Godfrey did ask for specimens of urine and vomit for laboratory tests but was told that the housemaid had flushed them down the toilet.

Mrs Cross died on 2 June 1887 and Dr Cross signed the certificate. Developments then drew attention to the death. Burial took place only two days later with such haste that relatives wishing to attend the funeral could not get there on time.

Then, fifteen days later Philip Cross married Mary Skinner at St James's Church, Piccadilly in London. Returning to Shandy Hall, the newly-weds found local tongues well and truly wagging.

Suspicion being aroused about Laura Cross's death, her body was exhumed after investigations by Inspector Tyack of the Gardai. A coroner's inquest was under way and the initial hearing had been adjourned pending autopsy results.

The day before the inquest resumed, Dr Cross was arrested and charged with murder. When the inquest did continue, the pathologist testified that Laura had died from arsenic poisoning.

Dr Cross's trial opened on 14 December 1887. It was pointed out that with his experience in India, Cross would be very unlikely to misdiagnose typhoid. A chemist testified that he had sold arsenic to a man fitting Cross's description and signing the poisons register 'C. Osborne, Farmer, of Sligo' saying the arsenic was for sheep dip. The pathologist found 3.2 grains of arsenic in the body and considered this to be a residual amount left as a result of doses administered over several months. Cross's infatuation with Mary Skinner was evident from his hasty remarriage constituting a motive for murder.

After a trial lasting four days, Cross was found guilty and on 10 January 1888 he was hanged.

Curare (and Curacit)

Curare is an extract from certain trees of the strychnos family. One source is the stem of the *Chondodendron tomentosum*. Variations of the substance derive their name from the vessels in which South American Indians stored it, 'calabash', 'pot' and 'tube' curare.

The history and uses of curare are intertwined. For centuries, South American Indians have used curare as an arrow poison because it paralyses and kills the unfortunate victim.

The nineteenth century saw European interest in the properties of this strange poison. In 1811, it is said that Sir Benjamin Brodie rubbed curare ('woorara paste') on wounds in guinea pigs and discovered that death could be delayed if the creature's lungs were artificially inflated by inserting a tube into the windpipe. Brodie suggested that the drug might be useful for tetanus because of its muscle-relaxing properties.

In 1812, Charles Waterton visited South America looking for the 'wourali' poison. Having found the poison and tried it on a sloth and an ox, he noted its effect of making the muscles flaccid. His next experiments on fowl were to seek possible antidotes. Although he tried the less promising supposed antidotes, he did not attempt the most promising. This was to artificially introduce air into the lungs through using small bellows. On returning to England, he resumed his experiments, this time using a donkey which appeared to die. Waterton cut the windpipe, however, and inflated the lungs with bellows for two hours. The donkey recovered and was to live for another twenty-five years under the name Wouralia cared for by a peer of the realm.

Attempts were made to use curare for such conditions as rabies and epilepsy. But its usefulness was limited until 1942 when routine methods of artificial respiration became available.

The crystalline alkaloid d-tubocurarine chlorine is the active principle of curare and is used as a muscle relaxant while a patient is undergoing surgery. Introduced intravenously, it has its maximum effect after about four minutes. Immediately distributed in plasma, it is later excreted in urine and by the stomach while the body inactivates the remainder in several hours.

Its action is to compete with the neuromuscular transmitter acetylcholine. Curare molecules coat the muscle membrane side of the gap between nerve and muscle. This prevents acetylcholine attaching itself to the surface and stops any impulse being passed from nerve to muscle. This paralysis of muscle nerve endings paralyses the muscles and when the muscles of respiration are paralysed death ensues.

Cyanide

Cyanides are poisonous salts of hydrocyanic acid (prussic acid). They are found in nature in the seeds of various fruits and nuts including apples, plums, peaches, apricots, cherries and almonds all of which contain cyanide compounds. Leaves of the wild black cherry tree (*Prunus serotina*) produce lethal quantities of hydrogen cyanide in the stomach if swallowed. When the leaves are chewed and swallowed, amygdalin in them is broken down by enzymes in the stomach and turns into cyanide.

Compounds of cyanide include the salts potassium cyanide and sodium cyanide. Potassium cyanide is used to case harden steel, in electroplating, in photography and to extract gold and silver from its ores. Sodium cyanide is infamous for its use in prison gas chambers where a pellet of the compound is dropped into a container of dilute sulphuric acid to form hydrogen cyanide gas.

Sodium and potassium salts of hydrogen cyanide are inert. However, water or gastric acid immediately hydrolyses them into hydrogen cyanide. Therefore, if cyanide salts are taken by mouth, the hydrogen cyanide produced is absorbed by the gastro-intestinal tract and inhaled into the air passage also.

Estimates of the minimum lethal dose range from 0.7 mg to 3.5 mg per kilo of body weight. A fatal dose of 50 mg, weighing about the same as a postage stamp, contains ten billion billion molecules (in United States terminology) or ten milliard milliard molecules (using British measures). This would constitute around ten cyanide molecules to every body cell.

Cyanide inhibits the bodily enzyme cytochrome oxidase thereby preventing the body from using oxygen, even though oxygen is present in adequate amounts. Cause of death may be respiratory failure because the nerve cells in the respiratory centre of the brain are damaged by the lack of oxygen and the muscle walls of the heart are affected. Exposure to hydrogen cyanide gas can cause unconsciousness in ten seconds and death in one minute, due to cardiac arrhythmias and ventricular asystole (both conditions affecting control of the heart beat). Cyanide salts may also exert a corrosive action.

Once cyanide is administered, symptoms appear within a few minutes; giddiness, weakness in the limbs, slowing of breathing and blue colouration of the face and lips being pronounced. Heart action becomes slow and irregular and after about three minutes convulsions may occur before breathing and heart beat cease.

Antidotes for cyanide poisoning are nitrites (which convert the cyanide in the blood into a harmless substance cyanmethaemoglobin) and dicobalt EDTA, dicobalt ethylenediamine-tetra-acetate.

De Bocarme, The Comte Hippolyte

A servant at the Château Tournai, home of the Comte De Bocarme, a Belgian nobleman, came across a dramatic scene. Gustave Fougnies, the Comte's brother-in-law lay sprawled on the dining-room floor. Chairs were overturned. De Bocarme had blood on his face and said that Gustave had died of an apoplectic fit.

But things were not as they appeared. Young Hippolyte was thought of as a womanizer and as somewhat crooked, and had tried his hand unsuccessfully at business. His father died and Hippolyte succeeded to the title at the age of 24.

In 1843 he made what he thought was a marriage that would improve his financial position. Lydie Fougnies was the daughter of an apparently rich grocer in Mons. But when the grocer died he left only a few thousand francs, most of which went to his son Gustave.

It was against this background that Gustave was invited to the château and where he suffered his 'fit'. When Gustave's body was examined, it was thought poison might be involved. Acetic acid was discovered in the mouth and apparently splashed on the body. (Tardieu, A., 1895) De Bocarme's valet gave the police further useful information, stating that the Comte had a cellar laboratory where he performed experiments with perfumes and that he also grew poisonous plants. But it emerged that the apparent poisoning with acetic acid was a subterfuge.

In this laboratory was discovered a bottle containing nicotine, while hidden away under the cellar floor was the apparatus used to prepare the poison. A final piece of the jigsaw fell into place when Gustave's body was found to contain nicotine and the Belgian chemist Stas recovered nearly 0.4 grammes from the stomach contents. Autopsy also indicated signs of violence consistent with the deceased being restrained and having his cries stifled. For instance the face and nose were bruised and indented with nail marks. Comte and Comtesse De Bocarme stood trial at the Palais de Justice at Mons on 27 May 1851. Husband blamed wife and wife pointed the finger at husband, but the jury acquitted the Comtesse and found the Comte guilty. After unsuccessfully petitioning the King, the Comte De Bocarme was guillotined in July 1851.

73

Defences and Explanations in Poison Cases

Among explanations of prosecution evidence in poison cases, two features hold particular interest: explanations of the cause of death and, where poison is found in the accused's possession, the reason why.

Regarding cause of death, explanations of prosecution evidence in poison cases (whether legal pleas at a trial or a statement made to police or others by a suspect) can owe much to the particular qualities of murder by poison. If the weapon was a gun, axe or blunt instrument, then obvious signs of violence on the body make particular defences plausible, accidental shooting or self-defence for example. With poison, external signs are not always noticeable, except perhaps where the poison was injected or where it was so corrosive that burn marks effect the nose and mouth.

This absence of external violence allows the poisoner to suggest death was from other causes hoping that the real cause will not be established. Kenneth Barlow (q.v.) after injecting his wife with insulin tried to make it look as though she had drowned in the bath. After poisoning his wife with opium, Eugène Chantrelle (q.v.) claimed a gas leak was responsible.

Often, poison symptoms have been mistaken for symptoms of illness. When Major Armstrong (q.v.) killed his wife with arsenic, it was thought she had died of a wasting condition. Comte De Bocarme (q.v.) said his brother-in-law had suffered a fit when in reality the Comte had administered a dose of nicotine to him.

Confounding poison murder with death from illness was a feature of several cases in which medical doctors were the killers. Clements (q.v.) killed his wife with morphine and death was put down to myeloid leukaemia. (Both Clements and Doctor James Houston, who had misdiagnosed, later committed suicide). Coppolino (q.v.) poisoned Colonel Farber, the husband of his mistress with succinylcholine chloride and death was certified as coronary thrombosis. When Dr Philip Cross's (q.v.) wife was dying from the arsenic he was giving her, he diagnosed her symptoms as those of typhoid, being careful to get a second opinion from a young, newly qualified doctor who concurred. Similarly, Dr Henry Clark (q.v.) poisoned his lover's husband with arsenic and certified death as due to heatstroke.

Claiming that death was due to natural causes was a reasonable defence even if poison was found in the body in the days when potentially poisonous substances were freely available as medicines. Florence Maybrick (q.v.) claimed this was the case despite the evidence of arsenic in her husband's body, because he was a hypochondriac who took arsenic as a tonic.

Arguing that death was suicide was a defence in several notable cases. Knocking his father-in-law to the floor and bruising the old man's head, Reginald Hinks (q.v.) then put the victim's head in a gas oven to kill him. His defence was that the old man had killed himself and that the head bruise was inflicted as Hinks tried to revive the deceased. After injecting a patient with cyanide in order to kill and rob him, Dr Pierre Bougrat (q.v.) then hid the corpse. When the cadaver was discovered, Bougrat said that the patient had injected himself with cyanide.

Even where the accused admits having administered poison, there is room to claim that death was not the intended outcome. Maria Groesbeek (q.v.) claimed to have given her husband the ant poison which ended his life only to make him so ill that he would grant her a divorce. Dr Etienne Deschamps (q.v.) killed a 12-year-old girl with whom he had been periodically having sex. Having poisoned her with chloroform, his defence was that he had given the child an accidental overdose before he was to have sex with her.

Where it is futile to place a different interpretation on the cause of death, then insanity may be the only plea. Partial insanity was the defence when Sadamichi Hirasawa (q.v.) robbed a bank and killed the staff with cyanide pellets. In the appeal of Dr Arthur Waite (q.v.) against the charge of murdering his in-laws, the defence was insanity.

Reasons which murderers have given for possessing poisons often relate to the legitimate uses which some of the substances had. Doctors and other medical staff have the easiest explanation for possessing certain poisons as several potentially poisonous drugs form part of their medical supplies. Dr Robert Clements (q.v.) had just cause to be in possession of the morphine with which he murdered his wife. So did Dr Robert Buchanan (q.v.) who used morphine to kill his second wife. As a medical student, Carlysle Harris (q.v.) who got rid of his wife with the drug, had easy access to morphine. Manager of a nursing-home, Dorothea Waddingham (q.v.) used the morphine there to murder patients, claiming to have administered the drug on doctor's instructions. Dentist, Dr Etienne Deschamps (q.v.) used the chloroform which he employed in his dental practice, to kill his 12-year-old victim.

But explanations for possessing poisons go further than claiming medical usage. Major Armstrong (q.v.) explained having packets of arsenic by stating he intended to use it as weedkiller. His justification for having twenty little packets was less compelling – that each was to be used to make a dose to inject into twenty individual weeds. Attempting to poison her doctor's wife with strychnine, Christiana Edmunds claimed to have bought the poison to kill cats.

Another interesting feature of the Edmunds case was that she cooked the strychnine into cakes, and sent them to her intended victim by post. Edmunds in this way, sought to provide herself with the alibi of not being at the scene when death took place. Similarly, Adolph Hofrichter (q.v.) sent cyanide in a 'tonic' by post to officers whom he felt had been unfairly promoted above him. Arsenic laced cakes were sent by post from Marie Lafarge (q.v.) to her husband who was away from home on a business trip. When he returned home ill, she administered further doses which proved fatal. Cordelia Botkin (q.v.) sent chocolates dosed with arsenic through the mail to the wife of her lover. The confections were also eaten by the intended victim's sister. Major Armstrong (q.v.) may have also sent arsenic impregnated chocolates to Oswald Martin, a rural solicitor – a dinner guest ate some and was very ill.

Providing a plausible reason for possessing poison does not arise when the poison is part of everyday life as when Reginald Hinks (q.v.) gassed his father-in-law hoping to pass the death off as suicide. Florence Maybrick (q.v.) who murdered her husband, possessed arsenic which she claimed was for cosmetic use.

After killing his lover's husband with strychnine, Jean Pierre Vaquier (q.v.) claimed he had bought it to use in wireless experiments.

Among the more unusual cases is that in which Dr George Lamson (q.v.) poisoned his brother-in-law with Dundee cake laced with aconite. The brother-in-law was a school pupil and Lamson visited the school for tea with him and the headmaster. During the meal, Lamson acted out a strange and presumably distracting ritual of filling some harmless capsules and administering them to the victim. Johann Hoch (q.v.) having killed several wives, was found with a fountain pen in which was concealed arsenic. His claim was that this was a suicide pen meant for himself.

De la Pommerais, Dr Edmond

In marrying Mlle Dubisy in 1861, Dr de la Pommerais acquired a sizeable dowry. This was very welcome, for Edmond, the son of a country doctor, had a lifestyle above his means. Calling himself

Count de la Pommerais, he had got into debt and had been involved in several frauds. But the dowry was sufficient to help the bogus Count and even enough for him to keep a mistress.

His wife's mother, Madame Dubisy was also rich. She died suddenly with the young doctor de la Pommerais beside her and he became a wealthy man. But before two years had passed the doctor had frittered away the fortune. He now had to find money elsewhere. It was at this point that he turned to his mistress, Seraphine de Pawr. They conspired to insure her life for half a million francs. She was then to fake illness to frighten the insurance company. At this point Madame de Pawr would agree to cancelling the policy so long as the company paid her an annuity.

That was the plot as Madame de Pawr was led to see it. What in fact happened was that she became 'ill' and was attended by the young doctor. She died of cholera, however, before any arrangement could be struck with the insurance company about the life policy. The company were suspicious and began investigating. Madame de Pawr's body was exhumed and digitalis discovered.

De la Pommerais was arrested and charged with double murder, that of Madame Dubisy (his mother-in-law) and that of Madame de Pawr, his mistress. He was found not guilty of the murder of Madame Dubisy but guilty of murdering Madame de Pawr.

Public sympathy was with the doctor and pleas were made to Napoleon III that the only evidence was circumstantial. This did not prevent the law from taking its course and in 1864 'Count' de la Pommerais was guillotined.

De Melker, Daisy

Nurse Daisy de Melker embarked on a career as a serial poisoner which involved the deaths of two husbands and a son. In 1909, Nurse Daisy married William Cowle and over the years bore him five children, four dying in infancy. Rhodes Cowle was the only surviving child. The year 1923 saw William Cowle die apparently from cerebral haemorrhage. It also saw Daisy benefiting from the will and collecting £1,700 insurance.

Some three years later Daisy married again. Husband number two, Robert Sproat was persuaded by Daisy to change his will from benefiting his mother to favouring his wife. When Sproat died ostensibly from cerebral haemorrhage in October 1927, Daisy benefited by £4,500. Her husband's relatives were suspicious and had nothing more to do with her, but took their concerns no further. Daisy's third husband, Sydney Clarence de Melker, a well-known rugby player, married her in January 1931 and the couple settled near Johannesburg in the Transvaal.

Rhodes, Daisy's son by William Cowle, her first husband, had by this time grown into a troubled teenager. On 3 March 1932 he fell ill with what appeared to doctors to be malaria and died on 7 March.

By this time suspicions were well and truly aroused and police began to investigate. Daisy, it was discovered, had bought arsenic from a Johannesburg pharmacy intending to poison cats, or so she claimed. The body of Rhodes Cowle, her son, was exhumed and found to contain arsenic. The bodies of William Cowle and Robert Sproat were discovered to contain strychnine.

In October 1932, Daisy de Melker faced trial in Johannesburg on three charges of murder. It emerged in evidence that both husbands had shown signs of strychnine poisoning – that is opisthotonus (arched back) during their final illness. Found guilty, Nurse de Melker was hanged on 30 December 1932.

Deschamps, Dr Etienne

The story behind the seduction and killing of 12-year-old Juliette Deitsh vividly illustrates the gullibility of her father Jules and the unscrupulousness of her killer, Dr Etienne Deschamps.

Born in France in 1830, Deschamps fled his country in 1870 after becoming embroiled in revolutionary politics. By 1884, he had set up a dental practice in St Peters Street, New Orleans, USA. But he was also involved with paranormal activities and it was via these that he duped Jules Deitsh.

Jules, a local carpenter, was a widower with two daughters; Juliette aged 12 and Laurence aged 9. Deschamps convinced the naïve Jules that he was on the trail of the lost treasure of the pirate Jean Lafitte but needed a young virgin to act as a spirit medium to locate the exact whereabouts of the hoard. Juliette became that 'medium'.

In fact Deschamps used the girl for sex from June 1888 to early 1889, often dosing her with chloroform before intercourse. Then on 30 January 1889, Juliette's sister Laurence ran into her home in rue Chartres to fetch her father to Deschamps' house. Deschamps had sent her to tell her father that he (Deschamps) was dying. When the two arrived at the dentist's house, Juliette lay on the bed naked and dead. Deschamps was bloodstained from superficial self-inflicted stab wounds, and later recovered.

The dentist's story was that Juliette had agreed to sexual intercourse on many occasions but was given chloroform first. On the day of her death, Deschamps claimed he had accidentally overdosed the child. The police, however, saw the case differently, seeing an interpretation in which Deschamps had killed Juliette so she could not reveal his sexual assaults on her.

The trial opened on 29 April 1889 and a guilty verdict was delivered. An appeal on 28 March reached a similar conclusion and Deschamps was sentenced to death. Protests were made at the verdict, and a group of doctors pressed for Deschamps to be declared insane.

After two temporary reprieves, the 62-year-old dentist and charlatan occultist was hanged on 12 May 1892 still proclaiming his innocence.

De Scotiney, Sir Walter

During the period when a meeting of parliament was convened at Winchester by King Henry III around 1230, a group gathered for breakfast at the table of Lord Edward, the King's eldest son. Among those present were Lord Edward, the Earl of Gloucester, his brother William de Clare and Sir Walder de Scotiney, the chief counsellor and steward to the Earl of Gloucester.

Apparently as a result of the meal, William de Clare fell ill and died. Also the Earl of Gloucester suffered symptoms of what may have been the effects of chronic arsenic and perhaps lead poisoning around this time. His hair fell out, his fingernails came off, his skin flaked and his teeth were damaged.

Sir Walter was suspected of having administered poison at the meal and the Countess de l'Isle pressed for his arrest. In February 1230, he was apprehended in London along with William de Bussey, the principal counsellor of William de Valance, who was also thought to be implicated. Sir Walter was imprisoned and in 1231 was tried and convicted at Winchester and subsequently executed.

Deshayes, Catherine (La Voison)

Associated with several murders in French society, Catherine

Deshayes was eventually executed for attempting to kill King Louis XIV. While her husband Antoine Monvoison peddled jewellery, Catherine made a living telling fortunes, reading faces and passing herself off as a sorceress. Among a succession of lovers she could number Guillanime, the executioner of Paris and Blessis, an alchemist. She was able to call on Blessis's services in connection with another of her activities, selling poisons to wives who wanted to be rid of their husbands.

Catherine's clients for her poisons included the Duchesse de Bouillon and the Comtesse de Soissons. Another of her customers, Madame Leferon was investigated by the Chambre Ardente (Chamber of Poisons), a judicial commission appointed by Louis XIV to investigate the alarming number of poison deaths taking place. Such was the scale of their task that the commission sat from 1679 to 1682 some 210 times at the Arsenal near the Bastille.

Yet another client was Madame de Montespan who had been a favourite of the King but who had lost her privileged position to Mademoiselle Fontanges. In her jealousy, Madame de Montespan wanted both the King and his new lover killed and approached Catherine Deshayes and three accomplices, Romani, Bertrand and La Trianon who lived in the rue Beauregard.

It is said that in a first attempt on Louis XIV's life, Catherine gave Madame de Montespan some 'love powder' to administer to the King comprising cantharides, powder of dried moles, and bat's blood. When this plan proved impossible to put into effect, Romani and Bertrand conspired to kill Mademoiselle de Fontanges using gloves dusted with poison (possibly arsenic). Romani was to disguise himself as a pedlar and sell the lethal gloves to their victim but the plan never materialized and Mademoiselle de Fontanges lived until 1681 when she died of natural causes.

Next, Catherine Deshayes and La Trianon agreed to dispatch the King themselves for 100,000 crowns, using paper impregnated with a contact poison. It was the King's custom on certain days to receive open petitions from his subjects and it was on such a day that Catherine, armed with the poison paper approached him. The pressure of the crowd of other petitioners was so great, however that Catherine could not reach the King and so the plan failed. A few days later, Catherine was arrested along with her three accomplices.

At her trial, the long list of her clients was revealed and many figures holding privileged positions in society were compromised, in some cases being obliged to flee the country. On being found guilty, Catherine Deshayes was burnt at the stake.

Deveureux, Arthur

When Arthur Deveureux placed his eldest son, 6-year-old Stanley in a private school in London, he was pleased that he had done all he could to secure the boy a sound education.

However, the 24-year-old chemist's assistant had gone further in trying to give Stanley a good start than anyone should. He had removed the 'distractions' of his wife Beatrice aged 25 and their two twin boys Lawrence and Evelyn.

They had all lived in poverty in a squalid part of Kilburn in London. Arthur poisoned his wife and sons with morphine, placed the three corpses in a metal trunk and deposited it in a furniture repository in nearby Kensal Rise. He next moved to another area of London where he placed Stanley in private education.

But Beatrice's mother became concerned about the where-abouts of her daughter and two of her grandchildren. Arthur could give no satisfactory explanation, so the older woman asked questions at Beatrice's previous house in Kilburn. There she learned about the trunk deposited at Kensal Rise and got clearance to have it opened in April 1905.

Scotland Yard detectives tracked Deveureux to Coventry where he was working with a chemist, arrested him and charged him with the murder of his wife.

He claimed that Beatrice had poisoned the twins with morphine belonging to him and had then committed suicide by taking morphine. At his trial at the Old Bailey in July 1905 before Mr Justice Ridley, Deveureux tried to feign insanity, but was found guilty. On 15 August 1905 he was hanged at Pentonville Prison.

Digitalis

Digitalis is the extract from the leaves of the foxglove *Digitalis purpurea* an attractive purple and white plant. In German, the plant is called 'fingernüt' which means 'thimble'. *Digitalis*, its Latin name also alludes to the finger shape, digit being Latin for finger.

Dr William Withering was journeying from his home in Birmingham one day in 1775 on his way to see patients in Stafford Infirmary. Stopping for a change of carriage horses, he was asked to see an old woman suffering from dropsy, a condition in which fluid accumulates under the skin or body cavities. His prognosis was that the woman would soon die. A few weeks later, hearing that she had recovered, he was somewhat surprised. He discovered that her remarkable return to health seemed to be due to a herb tea, the principal ingredient of which was foxglove.

Withering was inspired to investigate the properties of the plant. He eventually discovered that extracts from its caused copious amounts of urine to be excreted by the kidneys in the case of some patients suffering from 'dropsy' (fluid accumulated beneath the skin).

Because of the potentially dangerous effects of digitalis, Withering counselled great caution in its use. Unfortunately, his wise words went unheeded and, after some physicians had poisoned their patients through misusing the drug, it fell into disfavour.

Digitalis continued to be used for tuberculosis and some other diseases, but it was to be another 150 years before it gained its rightful place. It then became the treatment for heart failure; for certain heart conditions characterized by rapid irregular beats and for 'dropsy'.

Digitalis is absorbed from the alimentary tract when taken by mouth. While about 20% of most digitalis preparations are absorbed by the gastro-intestinal tract, nearly all of the extracts digoxin and digitoxin are absorbed. This means that a lethal dose of digitalis is much greater (2.5 grammes) while that of digoxin is 5 to 25 milligrams and that of digitoxin is 3 to 5 milligrams.

Digitalis increases the activity of muscular tissue especially that of the heart and arterioles (small blood vessels). In therapeutic doses, it strengthens each heart beat and lengthens 'rest' beats. Increased blood flow leads to more urine being produced by the kidneys and so decreases 'dropsy' where it is due to heart failure. However, in toxic doses digitalis causes nausea, vomiting and blurred vision. Heart beat becomes irregular, breathing is laboured and the sufferer may become convulsed or unconscious. Eventually death may ensue.

Donellan, Captain John

On Saturday 9 September 1780 the body of Sir Theodorus Boughton was exhumed and placed in Newbold churchyard before a large crowd. An autopsy revealed that Sir Theodorus had died of poisoning and this finding marked the beginning of the end for Irishman Captain John Donellan.

Donellan's past life included service with the East India Company where, with other officers, he was commissioned to apportion treasure taken at the siege of Mazulipatan. Some shady dealings took place, however, and Donellan was court-martialled in 1759 and cashiered. He left for England, bringing with him from the East Indies a valuable diamond which he then sold. But through gambling and high living he became in need of yet more money.

In June 1777 he married the wealthy Theodasa, daughter of the late Sir Edward Boughton. In the summer of 1778 Captain Donellan and his wife lived in Lawford Hall, Newbold-on-Avon near Rugby. The residence was owned by the old Lady Boughton, the widow of Sir Edward and by her son, 18-year-old Sir Theodorus. Donellan soon came to dominate the place, but may have considered that when the young heir came to inherit the house he, Donellan, might have to leave. If the young Sir Theodorus died, however, then most of the property would go to Donellan's wife.

In August 1780, Sir Theodorus was twenty years old and in ill health mainly because of a debauched life. On 29 August, Mr Powell, a physician in Rugby prescribed some medicine to be taken the following morning. Theodorus left the draught in his dressing room which stood next to his bedroom and went fishing with some of the servants until 9 p.m. when he returned for bed. At 7 a.m. on Wednesday 30 August his mother went to his bedroom to give him the medicine. Theodorus complained of the bitter taste and asked for a little cheese to help it down. His mother got this then poured the medicine into a glass, noticing its smell of bitter almonds. Within two minutes of swallowing the 'medicine' the young man struggled and gurgling could be heard in his stomach for some ten minutes. He became sleepy and his mother left him for five minutes. When she returned, he was frothing at the mouth.

The old widow sent for Captain Donellan and for Mr Powell, the doctor. The Captain came to the room and Lady Boughton told him the ill effect the medicine was having. Donellan asked to see the medicine bottles (there were two). He took one, poured water into it and emptied the contents into a basin of dirty water. Ignoring Lady Boughton's protestations, he then took the other bottle poured water into it and tasted it. He then got the maid to take the bottles and basin away. Mr Powell arrived at 9 a.m. but the young man had been dead for nearly an hour.

Donellan wrote to Sir William Wheeler, the young man's guardian on Wednesday 30 August informing him of Sir Theodorus's death but hinting that the cause was a long-standing illness. But gossip about the death also reached Sir William in Leamington. On Monday 4 September, Wheeler wrote to Donellan saying rumour had reached him that Sir Theodorus had died of poison and requiring that the body be opened. He specified Dr Rattray and Mr Wilmer of Coventry and Mr Snow of Southam for the task. The Captain sent for them.

Rattray and Wilmer arrived together at Lawford Hall at 8 p.m. on the same day but Donellan did not disclose the circumstances of the death to them. They inspected the corpse which was quickly decomposing and neither were keen to open the body and so returned to Coventry having only viewed it.

On Tuesday 5 September, the Captain wrote to the guardian saying the doctors had been but carefully not saying that the body remained unopened. On Wednesday 6 September, however, Sir William Wheeler heard that this was the case and ordered the body to be opened by Mr Bucknill in the presence of Mr Snow. Both went to Lawford Hall the same day but at different times. Neither felt they could act without the other being present so again nothing was done. The body was interred in the family vault in Newbold church. But there was local uproar and this is what finally led to the coroner ordering the exhumation on Saturday 9 September. As the crowd pressed round, Mr Bucknill opened the cadaver. The autopsy was witnessed by Mr Powell (the doctor who had initially been called when Theodorus was dying) and by Dr Rattray and Mr Wilmer of Coventry and Mr Snow of Southam. Examining the viscera and stomach, they concluded that death was by poisoning. The inquest was adjourned for a week.

When it reopened, Lady Boughton revealed the damning evidence of how Donellan had rinsed the bottles. The coroner's verdict was that Donellan was guilty of murder and on Saturday 16 September he was taken to Warwick Gaol to await the Spring Assizes.

The trial opened on Friday 30 March 1781 in the old Shire Hall, Warwickshire, before Mr Justice Buller. Prosecution was led by Mr Howarth and the defence was led by Mr Newnham.

A book found in Donellan's room at Lawford Hall, included in it a description of preparing laurel water. The cook at Lawford said that a few days before Sir Theodorus had died, the Captain had given her a still which he owned and asked her to dry it in the oven. Phials of laurel water were produced in court for Lady Boughton to smell and she recognized the bitter almond smell that she had noticed from the 'medicine'. Evidence was given on the poisonous effect of laurel water.

After retiring for only nine minutes, the jury returned a guilty verdict. Donellan was executed at Warwick on 2 April 1781. He was taken to the scaffold in a mourning coach followed by a hearse. After hanging, the body was put in a black coffin, taken to the Town Hall and dissected.

E605 (Organic Phosphorus Compound)

At the Bayer works in Leverkusen, Germany, chemist Gerhard Schroeder developed organic phosphorus compounds which were used as powerful insecticides. After the Second World War, American troops seized the stocks and the insecticides were developed in the United States. The chemical name of the substance is diethyl p-nitrophenyl phosphorothionate. Its common name is Parathion and among its other names is DNTP, Etilon, Niran, Folidol, Thiophos 3422, Paraphos and SNP. By 1950 it was being extensively used in Florida citrus plantations and was being marketed around the globe. In 1948 when it was marketed back to Germany it took on its old name of E605. German chemists devised tests for detecting E605 in 1952 and 1953. To show the presence of E605 in the blood, for example, the material was treated with caustic soda and turned yellow if the test was positive.

Poisoning by E605 is similar to that by hydrogen cyanide, producing convulsions and paralysing the respiratory centres. Other symptoms include constriction of the pupils, salivation and bradycardia (slowed heartbeat).

Emetic Tartar or Tartar Emetic (Potassium Antimony Tartrate)

Tartar emetic is a salt of antimony (q.v.). Its history is bound up with that of antimony and its main use in the past is suggested by its name – in tiny doses it is a powerful emetic. Its absorption, distribution and excretion is similar to that of antimony as is its toxicity.

The action of tartar emetic is in particular to have an irritant effect on the mucous membranes of the stomach. Toxic doses also act on the CNS (specifically the medulla) to induce vomiting.

Symptoms of poisoning with tartar emetic are similar to those of lead or arsenic poisoning.

Exhumation

Exhumation, the digging up of a body that has been buried is sometimes necessary in suspected poisoning cases so an autopsy can be carried out.

Sometimes, crime was not suspected at the death and burial went ahead normally. Then at a later date suspicions developed necessitating an exhumation and autopsy. Such was the case when Herbert Armstrong (q.v.) poisoned his wife with arsenic. It was only later when Major Armstrong was suspected of poisoning a rival solicitor that the earlier death of Mrs Armstrong was reconsidered.

On other occasions several deaths may have occurred over a period which did not attract suspicion at the time. A further death may then occur which does point the finger of suspicion at someone and which suggests they may have been implicated in the previous deaths. One or more exhumations may then be required to explore this line of reasoning. This was a feature of the case of Amy Archer-Gillinghan (q.v.) who poisoned a former husband and several patients at her old people's home.

In Britain, the Home Secretary gives consent to an exhumation if there is a serious possibility that a crime was involved. Police and the coroner are also involved.

Canvas screens are set around the grave which is then opened and the coffin and grave carefully identified. If the body has been buried a long time, the coffin lid may be opened a little to allow gases associated with decomposition to escape. Samples of grave earth are taken where poisoning is suspected. These come from above, below and beside the coffin. Earth remote from the grave is taken as a 'control'. This is important because substances in the surrounding earth could be argued to have tainted the body giving a false impression of poisoning by say lead, or arsenic. By taking samples of earth this possibility can be checked and if necessary accounted for.

The coffin and body are transported to the mortuary for examination. As well as the pathologist, police, funeral director, scientists and possibly the coroner may be present.

The coffin is opened and samples of coffin wood, grave earth, coffin lining and shroud are taken in poison cases to assess the possibility of contamination of the body after death with some toxic substance. If the body is badly decomposed the pathologist must exercise all his skill to determine cause of death.

After exhumation the body is reburied and greatly decomposed bodies may be first wrapped in a plastic sheet before being placed in the original or a new coffin.

Fatal Dose/Toxicity

What constitutes a fatal dose of a poison? Many factors influence the outcome of poisoning. Snake bite, for instance, is not a single standard dose of poison. The effectiveness of the venom is influenced by the size of the snake, its age and how aroused it is and also by the exact components of the venom. With all poisons, factors to do with the person poisoned have an effect. Gender, age and physical and emotional health all play a part.

Previous exposures to the poison are also important. In some instances of arsenic ingestion, people have apparently been able to take doses which in normal circumstances may have proved lethal because their body seems to have developed a bogus tolerance to the substance. James Maybrick (q.v.) boasted of this. In other cases of chronic arsenic poisoning, the doses appear to have had a gradual cumulative effect leading inexorably to death. The poisoning of Major Armstrong's (q.v.) wife seems to have taken this course.

The way a poison is distributed after being absorbed by the body is important. Some latch on to blood, some to nerve tissue, some to proteins. Water soluble poisons would tend to have difficulty reaching the nervous system, including the central nervous system, because of the 'blood brain barrier'. This refers to the fatty substance around the capillaries of the nervous system which tends to repel water and consequently any water-borne material.

The effect of poison also depends on how it is ingested. It may be breathed in as with poisonous gases like carbon monoxide. It can be absorbed through the skin. Although arsenic is usually eaten (or drunk) there are instances of poisoners dusting gloves with arsenic. Poison can be eaten as was the case of Thomas Cream's murder of prostitutes by strychnine, or it can be injected as may be the case with digitalis. Some snake venoms which may be deadly when injected by the snake's fangs, can be swallowed without harm.

It will be clear from the above that the question 'What is a fatal dose of a particular poison?' is a complex one which cannot always be answered accurately, although estimates can be given. One attempt to standardize lethal doses is to record the percentage of deaths in animals administered the poison concerned. Hence

LD50 means a poison in a specified amount constituted a lethal
dose in 50% of the animals tested.

Fenning, Elizabeth

Although she was executed for attempting to poison her employer
and others, Elizabeth Fenning is thought by many people to have
been falsely accused. Her trial opened on 11 April 1815 at the Old
Bailey before the Recorder. The 24-year-old cook was charged
with poisoning her employer Olebar Turner, a law stationer in
Chancery Lane, his wife and his father Robert Turner.

Elizabeth had been in Olebar Turner's employ for some six
weeks when on 21 March she made some yeast dumplings for
dinner which were eaten by the three complainants. First Mrs
Turner suffered violent abdominal pains and vomiting, then the
two men experienced the same symptoms. Several hours later
John Marshall, a surgeon who had been called to the house arrived
but the three people were already recovering. Elizabeth and a
young apprentice who had both eaten dumplings were also ill with
the same symptoms as the others.

Olebar stated at the trial that he suspected that arsenic had been
put into the food. Searching the kitchen, he found the brown dish
in which the dumplings had been mixed and noticed it had some
food still adhering to it. He put a little water in the dish and a few
minutes later found a white powder had formed on the bottom of
the receptacle. This he gave to the surgeon.

Next, Olebar checked his office where he kept arsenic in an
unlocked drawer in two wrappers labelled 'Arsenick, Deadly
Poison'. He had last noticed the packets (which were kept for
killing mice) on 7 March, but on checking the drawer after the
mysterious illness, he discovered that the packets had been taken.
Finally, Olebar observed that the knives which the diners had used
to cut the dumplings had turned black. With this information to
hand, Olebar accused Elizabeth Fenning of putting 'something' in
the dumplings.

John Marshall, the surgeon, confirmed to the court that all the
dinner group showed symptoms characteristic of arsenic poisoning. Also the sediment given to him by Olebar was arsenic and
this poison would have turned the dinner knives black. Marshall
had examined the yeast and flour used to make the dumplings but
had found no arsenic.

Elizabeth Fenning pleaded her innocence, stating that the

poison must have been in the milk used to make the dumplings and which had been brought by Sarah Peer a fellow servant. Although the jury found Elizabeth guilty, popular feeling was aroused because it was felt there was insufficient evidence for conviction. Petitions delivered to the Prince Regent and the Lord Chancellor did not prevent the death sentence being carried out at Newgate Prison on 26 July 1815, with Elizabeth proclaiming with her last breath, 'I die innocent.'

It is said that in 1834, Olebar Turner died destitute in a workhouse where he confessed that he had put arsenic in the dumplings and falsely accused Elizabeth. What makes the circumstances particularly difficult to disentangle is an apparent lack of motive for Elizabeth to try and murder her employer and others or for him to poison his own food and then accuse the cook.

Ford, Arthur

Arthur Ford seemed to have a solid and reliable background. For thirty years, he had worked for a firm of wholesale and manufacturing chemists in Euston Road, London where he had become general manager of the office side of the operation. His career in the firm had been interrupted only by service in the Second World War and Ford was married with children.

In 1954, however, he developed a passionate attraction for one of the firm's secretaries, Betty Grant, an attractive 27-year-old. But Miss Grant was quite unresponsive to his interest and it was obvious that if events were left to themselves she would remain so. Around this time, Ford made a discovery that was to have disastrous consequences. Having been aware for some time that his firm stocked cantharidin, he realized that this was a derivative of cantharides or Spanish Fly. This was a revelation to him because Ford's role was that of an administrator and manager and he did not possess detailed knowledge of pharmacy.

On making this discovery, Ford's piecemeal knowledge (or lack of it) about Spanish Fly came into play. The war service that had interrupted his office work was as a member of the Royal Army Service Corps stationed in the Far East. Demobbed from Singapore in 1946, he heard rumours and myths from fellow soldiers concerning the aphrodisiac effects of Spanish Fly. He also knew it was used by breeders supposedly to encourage procreation in tame rabbits.

On the morning of 26 April 1954, Ford spoke to Mr Lushington, a chemist in the firm's stock room saying that he had a neighbour who needed cantharidin for rabbit breeding. On being told by Lushington that the substance was a 'number one poison', Ford stated that he had better not touch any. Once Lushington had left the stock room, however, Ford took a quantity of the poison.

Buying some coconut ice from a local sweet shop near the firm, Ford impregnated several pieces with cantharidin. On 27 April at 2.30 p.m. Ford appeared in the office with the bag of sweets before twenty-two women and four men sitting at three long tables. He picked out a piece for Betty Grant, one for Miss Glover and one for Miss Dobbs. He was not seen giving any to a June

91

Malins, a 21-year-old friend of Betty Grant, although a little later she was seen eating some. No suspicion was aroused by this. The staff noticed the bag was that of the nearby sweet shop and assumed Ford had gone out at lunch-time and bought the sweets.

But at 3.30 p.m. June Malins, complained of stomach pains and Betty Grant took her to the sickroom upstairs. Half an hour later Betty herself became ill with stomach pains and also went to rest in the sickroom. About the same time, Ford complained of a headache and looked to the other staff as though he was pale and sick.

A doctor was called and ordered all three into hospital. Taken to University College Hospital, the two girls grew worse and died while Ford recovered. Police interviewed Ford at the hospital on 28 April where he told them he suspected the coconut ice. But the autopsy on the two girls indicated a dose of cantharides of between one and two grains.

Detective Superintendent Jamieson who interviewed Ford told him he suspected cantharides poisoning and Ford was invited to the police station for interview. *En route*, Ford confessed and at the station made a full statement. It appeared that while he intended to give a doctored piece of coconut ice to Betty Grant, he mistakenly had given one to June Malins also.

Tried at the Old Bailey in June 1954 before Judge Lord Goddard, Ford pleaded guilty to a charge of manslaughter and was given a five-year prison sentence.

Forensic Tests for Poisons

Forensic tests have been developed not just to detect the presence of poisons but also the existence of numerous other substances that might have a bearing on criminal investigation: blood, semen and so on. Neither are the tests always the exclusive property of the forensic scientist. Rather forensic tests are scientific tests focused on the investigation of crime or suspected crime.

When poison was suspected in the nineteenth century certain chemical tests were available. The Marsh-Berzelius test for arsenic was introduced in 1836. It involved generating arsine, a deadly gaseous form of arsenic from an acidic solution. The gas was trapped on a mirrored surface where it left a black deposit.

Metals such as mercury, antimony and lead could be detected using the Reinsch test. A sample of gastric juices or urine was acidified. A coil of copper wire was inserted into the solution which was simmered. A black or brown deposit on the copper indicated the presence of one of the metals. Further tests were used to indicate the specific metal deposited.

Among modern methods are chromatography, immunoassays, atomic absorption spectroscopy and neutron activation analysis.

(i)   *Chromatography*

Various types of chromatography apply the same principle; they physically separate the components of a mixture by using the different distributions of each component between a 'stationary' phase and a 'mobile' phase. The stationary phase may be solid, or liquid coated on to an inert support material. The mobile phase may be gas or liquid. It is important that the two phases do not mix and the components of the mixture to be separated must not react with either phase.

Thin layer chromatography is a screening procedure, usually followed up by the more accurate gas chromatography or high performance liquid chromatrography. A thin layer of material such as silica has a spot of the target substance to be tested applied to it (the stationary phase). Solvent then flows past the spot separating the components of the target substance according to their affinity for the stationary or the mobile phase. Once the silica is dried, it is either sprayed with a stain or subjected to ultraviolet light so the spots of the components become visible. An 'Rf' value can be calculated by dividing:

(a) the distance travelled along the silica by the component by

(b) the distance travelled by the solvent

This helps identify the substance.

Gas chromatography uses an oven housing a separating column (a coil of tubing). When the oven increases temperature, it makes the compound to be separated more volatile. An inert gas (mobile phase) flows through the column. The stationary phase may be solid or liquid present on particles packing the column (packed columns) or coated on to the inner surface of the column (open tubular columns).

The target components have to be volatile so they can be separated. As the mixture proceeds through the separating columns, some components are borne along faster than others due to their affinity for the stationary or mobile phase. Consequently, the time it takes the components to reach the end of the column differs. A detector picks up the various components after they exit the column and this provides a trace showing the respective retention time of the components. This indicates the identity of the component. Alternatively a mass spectrometer may be used.

High performance liquid chromatography involves a separating column of finely divided particulate material through which a liquid mobile phase is pumped at high pressure. The target material to be separated is introduced on to the top of the column and distributes itself between the solid and the flowing liquid phase resulting in the separation of components of the mixture. Spectrophotometry is usually used to detect the separated components.

(ii)   *Immunoassays*
Immunoassays use the principle that antibodies 'recognize' and attach themselves to specific sites on antigens to make a complex. (Antigens are toxic bodies and antibodies are proteins in the blood which attack antigens).

Organic poisons of low molecular weight would not usually be antigenic. But bound to a larger carrier molecule, when injected into animals they would raise antibodies against themselves. Blood is then taken from the animal and serum is separated out. Using the original antigen as a detector, the serum is screened and the required antibodies are extracted. These antibodies are used in an immunoassay.

Immunoassays are often in the form of radioimmunassays. A known amount of antibody is mixed with a known excess of 'labelled' antigen molecules. Complexes are formed but about 50% of the spare labelled antigens are left over. A solution is then added (e.g. blood from the victim) which contains an unknown amount of unlabelled antigen molecules so as to establish how much unlabelled antigen there is in the blood. As the unlabelled antigens compete for binding sites on the antibodies they displace the labelled antigens in direct proportion to the concentration of unlabelled antigen added.

After incubation, the mix is separated into two 'fractions', one containing all the antibodies complexed to labelled or unlabelled antigen, the other containing all other molecules.

For each fraction, the amount of labelled antigen is estimated. The smaller the labelling response from the antibody complex fraction, the more unlabelled antigen was added. Calculations are then made to determine more accurately the concentration of antigen in the blood.

(iii) *Atomic Absorption Spectroscopy*
Atomic absorption spectroscopy is used to establish whether elements, especially metals, are present in a substance. It could be used to trace substances such as mercury, lead, arsenic and so on, perhaps in a blood sample. Atoms of metals absorb particular wavelengths of visible light when the atoms are 'free'. A solution containing a salt of the metal is sprayed into a flame so that it evaporates and the intense heat liberates the atoms of the metal. Once the sample is 'atomized' in this way a light of a wavelength at which the metal will absorb it is directed towards the sample. If the light is absorbed, this indicates the presence of that particular metal associated with that wavelength. The intensity of the light, which comes from a special lamp, is measured before and after it enters the sample. Any difference in intensity indicates how much metal is in the path of light.

(iv) *Neutron Activation Analysis*
In neutron activation analysis, a sample of material is placed in a cyclotron or experimental nuclear reactor and bombarded by a huge neutron beam. The poison, say mercury, is changed to isotopes (radioactive forms). The mercury isotope will emit radiation which will identify it as mercury. This radiation is detected by instruments. Parts as small as 1 per 1000,000,000,000 can be detected. Using this technique for detecting arsenic, strands of Napoleon Bonaparte's hair were analysed. The hair was from a locket which contained a sample cut shortly before the general's death. Arsenic was detected at fifteen times the normal level leading some researchers to suggest that Napoleon was poisoned in his last days on St Helena.

Gender of Poisoners

Poisoning has frequently been characterized as a predominantly female crime. Livy and Tacitus noted this. Reginald Scot in *The Discovery of Witchcraft* in 1584 wrote that 'women were the first inventors and the greatest practisers of poysoning and more materially addicted and given thereunto than men'. In the twentieth century C.J.S. Thompson (1935) claimed, 'there has always been a high percentage of women poisoners'.

But this view seems to have become orthodoxy on slender evidence. Certainly it is possible to compile a long list of female poisoners, such as Charlotte Bryant, Florence Maybrick, Frances Howard (the Countess of Somerset) and Marie Lafarge. Among these there are also certainly cases of serial murder such as those of Amy Archer-Gilligan, Daisy de Melker, Martha Marek, Mary Bateman and Mary Cotton. It is equally easy, however, to catalogue male poisoners from Dr William King to Edward Black and from Marcus Marymont to Pierre Moreau. Again there are instances of serial murder such as those involving Dr Thomas Cream, Johann Hoch, Dr Arthur Waite and Graham Young.

Reasonable sounding grounds can be made for thinking that women might be more likely to poison than men hinging on the assumption that males tend to be more overtly aggressive, extrovert and impulsive than females. For, whereas murders involving explicit violence might suggest an aggressive and impulsive nature, poisoning is seen as a method of quiet planning so as to avoid detection. Many poisoners have to decide on the particular poison and determine how to obtain it. They then plan how and when the substance is to be given so as to attract no attention. All this it can be argued fits the female approach. Even if this gender stereotyping were accepted, however, the view is not borne out by the numerous cases of male poison murderers. Nor can examples be drawn to demonstrate that women are more adept at poisoning or somehow have a particular capacity for this form of murder.

Against the deviousness of Amy Archer-Gilligan who murdered patients at her nursing-home for financial gain, can be set the cunning of Dr William Palmer, the mass poisoner executed for murdering a racing companion to acquire his gambling winnings.

Find a murderess like Cordelia Botkin who has the foresight to plan killing at a distance by sending arsenic impregnated chocolates through the post. At the same moment the case of Adolph Hofrichter springs to mind. Jealous of the promotion of army colleagues, he sent cyanide laced tonic by post to twelve of them.

Compile a list of husband murderers like Susan Barber, Charlotte Bryant, Edith Carew, Daisy de Melker (who murdered two husbands and a son), Maria Groesbeek, Marie Hilley, Marie Lafarge, Ethel Major, Martha Marek (who also killed a daughter and another relative), Florence Maybrick, Kitty Ogilvy and Eva Rablen. It is then just as easy to catalogue wife murderers: Major Herbert Armstrong, Kenneth Barlow, Ernest Black, Brian Burdett, Eugène Chantrelle, George Chapman (who also killed two barmaids), Dr Robert Clements, Dr Carl Coppolino, Dr Philip Cross, Johann Hoch (murderer of several wives), Dr William King, Marcus Marymont and Pierre Moreau.

It has frequently been pointed out that women traditionally prepare food and are therefore more likely to choose poison as a method of dispatch because it can often be mixed with food or drink and go unnoticed by the victim. Certainly Susan Barber added Paraquat to her husband's steak and kidney pie, and Mary Blandy mixed arsenic with her father's tea and gruel. Also it is thought that Charlotte Bryant poisoned her husband's food with arsenic and certainly added the poison to an Oxo drink. Marie Lafarge initially sent cakes mixed with arsenic to her husband by post when he was away from home and then when he returned, administered further doses to kill him. Corned beef was dosed with strychnine by Ethel Major to kill her lorry driver husband. While Kitty Ogilvy added arsenic to her husband's tea, Eva Rablen dosed her spouse's coffee with strychnine. Also, Henrietta Robinson added arsenic to the beer being drunk by her grocer and his sister-in-law. In most of these instances, the woman was preparing food in the home for her husband or a relative.

But while being a traditional preparer of food is probably a common feature of many cases where a woman murders by poisoning, there is no shortage of cases where men have poisoned food or drink. Richard Brinkley killed the landlord and landlady of an acquaintance with a drink of stout mixed with cyanide. Brian Burdett added cyanide to his wife's breakfast tea and claimed she had committed suicide. Adolph Hofrichter used cyanide laced tonic medicine, while Dr George Lamson murdered his brother-in-law with Dundee cake impregnated with aconite. John Tawell killed his mistress using prussic acid in a bottle of stout and Jean Pierre Vaquier left strychnine in the Bromo salts he knew would be taken by his lover's husband.

The characterizing of poison murder as in any way a specially female crime seems most difficult to justify.

Gilbert, Jeanne

A spate of deaths occurred in and around the village of Varennes near Amand-Montroud in France which seemed inexplicable. In April 1905, a wealthy farmer, Monsieur Gilbert died suddenly, while six months later his wife died without warning having previously been in good health. Then in September 1906, Monsieur Renaud, another local farmer died suddenly followed only one month later by his wife.

As well as these two couples, a farm labourer working for the Renauds died as did a young man, who was steward of a neighbouring château, and his daughter.

Some time later, a death occurred which seemed to shed light on the mysteries. Madame Pallot, a villager found a small cheese on her windowsill and thinking it was a gift from a kind neighbour she took it in and ate some for lunch. Three hours later she was dead. The cheese, which was impregnated with arsenic, was traced to Jeanne Gilbert, the daughter of the Renauds and daughter-in-law of the Gilberts all of whom had died.

Charged with the murder of Madame Pallot, Jeanne was sent to trial. One prosecution witness, Monsieur Bouillot, a pharmacist, produced his poison register showing signed purchases of arsenic by Jeanne Gilbert. These purchases, by the half pound, were stated in the register to be for killing rats on the Gilbert farm. Jeanne denied having made any such purchase, implying that the signatures were forgeries, but the judge asked her to write a sample signature and this matched the poison book entries. Jeanne now admitted having made the purchases but claimed they were purely for the purpose stated, that is, to use as rat poison. It was shown, however, that the date of purchase and the date of death of Madame Pallot roughly corresponded and Jeanne Gilbert was found guilty and subsequently executed.

Girard, Henri

Henri Girard and Louis Pernotte were like chalk and cheese. Girard was sophisticated, had expensive tastes, kept three mistresses and liked to spend lavishly on his friends. He had also been dishonourably discharged from the Hussars, had lived by a succession of insurance swindles and had been indicted for forming a crooked insurance company in 1909. Ominously, he was a keen amateur toxicologist who kept a laboratory in the precincts of one of his mistresses apartments. By contrast, Louis Pernotte was a rather lumpen, gullible, Paris insurance broker, settled into marriage and with two children.

Girard persuaded Pernotte to hand over the running of his finances to him and promptly arranged over 300,000 francs insurance on Pernotte's life through several companies. Girard then secured cultures of typhoid bacteria from scientific suppliers in Paris.

In August 1912, Pernotte and his family were planning to travel to Royan. Lunching with them, Girard secretly introduced typhoid germ culture into their drinking water. Later at Royan all the Pernotte family fell ill with symptoms of typhoid.

Returning to Paris to recuperate, Pernotte was visited by the solicitous Girard every day. Girard treated his admirer by injecting him in the thigh but soon afterwards Pernotte became paralysed. He died on 1 December 1912, doctors diagnosing cardiac embolism brought about by typhoid. Girard promptly told Pernotte's widow that her late husband owed him 200,000 francs.

In 1917, Girard set his sights on another potential victim, a certain Mimiche Duroux. He insured Duroux's life then accumulated a supply of the poisonous mushroom *Amanita phalloides*. Fortunately, the robust Duroux survived meals and aperitifs laced with the poison mushroom without realizing how close he was to becoming a murder victim. Girard gave up on ever being able to kill Duroux and looked elsewhere.

In April 1918 he decided he had found his next victim in Madame Monin, a war widow. He managed to get one of his mistresses, Jeanne Droubin to pretend to be a war widow herself. She visited the Phoenix Insurance Company where she took out a life policy on Madame Monin, making herself the beneficiary. This arranged, Monin was invited to Girard's apartment and served a poisonous aperitif. Later, in the Metro station she collapsed and died. But the companies who had arranged the policies were suspicious of the short time between the insuring and the death.

They looked closer into matters, and as a result, on 21 August 1918, Girard was arrested.

He was due to stand trial but killed himself before justice could take its course. His suicide too, was by poisoning. He swallowed germ culture and died in May 1921.

Groesbeek, Maria

After a brief, intense romance, 16-year-old Maria married Christiaan Burys in 1953. At first they lived with Christiaan's mother and his six brothers but this arrangement did not last long for Maria and her mother-in-law did not get on and the newly-weds left to set up on their own. A whirlwind start to the relationship lost its momentum as the years passed and Christiaan would accuse Maria of flirting, then become violent.

Seventeen years after they were married, Maria asked for a divorce having fallen in love with 20-year-old railway shunter Gerhard Groesbeek, a friend of her husband's. But Maria's pleas fell on deaf ears. In February 1969 Maria began purchasing 'Antexit' an arsenical ant poison and soon afterwards Christiaan fell ill. Suffering protracted vomiting, he was taken into hospital where on 28 March he died. Arsenic was detected in the body at the subsequent autopsy.

Maria married Gerhard Groesbeek on 11 June 1969 but their time together was short for soon afterwards both were arrested and charged with murder. Tried at Bloemfontein in November 1969, Maria admitted poisoning Christiaan with arsenic but denied intending to kill him and claiming that she only wished to make her stubborn husband sufficiently ill that he would grant a divorce. The jury, however, were not convinced and Maria was found guilty and hanged on Friday 13 November 1970. Gerhard Groesbeek, tried in May 1970, was acquitted.

Harris, Carlysle

On the coffin of Carlysle Harris, a plate was engraved on his mother's instructions: 'Carlysle Harris. Murdered May 8th, 1893'. But that sentiment arose from a mother's love rather than the sober judgement of society or the law, for Harris had been executed for first-degree murder. On 8 February 1890 Carlysle Harris secretly married Helen Potts. He was a 22-year-old medical student whose mother was active in religious and temperance circles while his bride was an 18-year-old student at a New York boarding-school. Shortly afterwards, Helen gave birth to a stillborn child.

The following year, in January, Helen began to suffer from insomnia and Carlysle acquired some capsules from a local druggist to help her sleep. They were compounded of four and a half grains of quinine and half a grain of morphine and Helen took three of the six capsules over the ensuing days with no adverse effects. On 1 February 1891, however, soon after taking the fourth capsule, the young woman died.

Dr Fowler, who was called in, noticed that Helen's eyes were tightly contracted and suspected some narcotic poison. The remaining two of the original six capsules had been kept by Carlysle and were correctly compounded but it began to look as if the fourth capsule which Helen had taken had been tampered with.

The *New York World* unearthed some sordid information about the young medical student. Secretary of the disreputable Neptune Club, Carlysle gambled and womanized. Helen's uncle, a doctor, added further seamy details stating that he himself had carried out an abortion on Helen, and that Carlysle had done likewise. Then the secret marriage was revealed, Helen's body was exhumed and an autopsy conducted. Morphine was detected but not quinine.

Helen's mother accused Carlysle of murdering her daughter, while Carlysle's mother for her part sprang to his defence and campaigned tirelessly on his behalf. On 30 March 1891, Harris was indicted by a Grand Jury and in January 1892 his trial opened in New York.

Francis Wellman, leading the prosecution, held that Harris had replaced the quinine in one of the capsules (the fourth one taken by Helen) with morphine. He had then administered what was now a lethal dose of morphine to his wife. Carlysle's motive was boredom, the excitement having gone from their clandestine relationship, Carlysle simply wanted to be rid of his wife. Evidence for this view came from the morphine found in the cadaver and from the observations of Dr Fowler who had examined Helen.

The defence lawyers, who included William Travers Jerome, argued that Helen may have suffered a kidney disease, a suggestion unsupported by autopsy reports. Harris himself did not testify. Found guilty of first-degree murder, Carlysle appealed unsuccessfully against the death sentence.

In Sing Sing Prison, on 8 May 1893, Harris was led to the electric chair vigorously protesting his innocence to the last.

Hilley, Marie

When eighteen-year-old Carol Hilley was hospitalized suffering from a mysterious wasting disease, her mother Marie was the model of a solicitous visitor. Emerging in 1979, the illness meant that much of Carol's time was spent in hospital undergoing tests. Despite the efforts of the medical staff, the affliction dragged on for five months. By this time, the teenager had endured great pain, could barely walk and had at one stage very nearly died.

Then quite casually, in conversation with a friend, Carol Hilley happened to mention that over the past months her mother's care and concern had extended to giving Carol injections. Yet Marie Hilley (born Frazier) possessed no medical qualifications and worked in fact as a secretary at the local foundry in Anneston, Alabama in the southern United States. As questions were asked about the strange injections Marie had been administering, suspicion began to spread to events in Marie's past.

She had apparently employed her syringe on her own mother Lucille who had died of cancer. The instrument had found further use on Marie's husband who had died in 1975 aged only 45 seemingly after a brief attack of infectious hepatitis. His life insurance made Marie $31,140 richer. Ominously, in July 1978, Marie took out life insurance for $25,000 on her daughter. As suspicion of poisoning strengthened, the sick teenager's urine and hair were sampled. Both were found to contain arsenic, the hair showing a hundred times more than the normal level.

Arrested on 17 September 1979, Marie was charged with no

more than passing worthless cheques. But she was also questioned about her daughter's enigmatic illness. Evidence began to roll in. When the bodies of Marie's husband and her mother were exhumed, both cadavers were found to contain arsenic. In Marie's jewellery box, a pill bottle containing the poison was discovered. Marie Hilley was charged with the attempted murder of her daughter. Admitting to police in a statement only that she had given Carol two injections without medical knowledge or approval, she was granted bail which she skipped in November 1979.

In her absence, she was indicted for the murder of her husband, but it was not until January 1983 that she was rearrested. Between her disappearance and her recapture events had taken further strange turns. In 1980 Marie married a boat builder and the couple settled in New Hampshire, where Marie found work as a secretary.

Announcing to her new husband that a relative had died in Houston, she explained that she had to go there to help sort out matters. While away, she set in motion a plan to convince her husband and others that she had died. Her obituary was published and an announcement was made that she had donated her body to medical research. Amazingly, Marie then reappeared saying she was her twin sister, Teri Martin and offered condolences to the 'bereaved' husband. She was arrested as Teri Martin in 1983.

Put on trial, Marie pleaded not guilty. The defence attempted to discredit Carol Hilley, implying that she was mentally unstable, used drugs and was sexually deviant. But that strategy was unsuccessful. Carol's brother testified in court, that in 1979 when his sister lay ill he had written to the coroner stating that he thought Marie had injected his father and his sister with arsenic.

Found guilty of the attempted murder of her daughter and guilty of the first-degree murder of her husband, Marie Hilley was sentenced to the maximum term of imprisonment allowed by law.

In February 1987, however, the prisoner was allowed out on a weekend furlough and absconded. Four days later and suffering exposure she was discovered. But Marie Hilley was to escape justice no more for shortly after she died in hospital.

Murderer of her first husband, would-be murderer of her daughter, refugee from justice, fabricator of her own 'death', impostor, and finally victim of her own flight from justice, Marie Hilley must rank as one of the strangest criminals of recent years.

Hinks, Reginald

James Pullen's sufferings began when the old man's daughter Constance Anne Pullen remarried. Constance was divorced with one child and lived with her 85-year-old father in the city of Bath. The senile old man was not without money and should he die, his daughter would inherit.

In 1933, Constance met Reginald Hinks, a Hoover salesman who had also been involved in petty thieving. After a brief courtship, they were married. Hinks moved in with his new wife. James Pullen was cared for by a male nurse. But Hinks soon got rid of this medical help and insisted that Pullen was kept on a spartan diet.

Hinks's designs on the old man's money became clearer. He got £900 from his father-in-law and bought his own house in Bath with it. But this was not enough and Hinks tried to get his hands on more of Pullen's money. The old man's solicitor was wary enough to protect Pullen's wealth with legal safeguards. Hinks's tactics changed.

He began taking the confused old man for long exhausting walks, hoping that the strain would prove too much and hasten Pullen's end. But this failed. Finally, Hinks thought he had the solution.

On 1 December 1933 Hinks telephoned the fire brigade. He informed the officers that Pullen had poisoned himself by putting his head in the gas oven. Hinks claimed to have pulled the old man out and in doing so may have bruised the back of Pullen's head.

But medical examination of Pullen's body did not verify Hinks's claim – far from it. The cause of death was ascertained as gas poisoning, but the bruise on Pullen's head had been caused before death.

Hinks was arrested and charged with murder. Standing trial at the Old Bailey, Hinks wore a black armband to signify mourning for his father-in-law. The prosecution case that Hinks had struck Pullen then gassed him trying to make it seem like suicide prevailed. Hinks died at the end of the hangman's rope on 4 May 1934.

Hirasawa, Sadamichi

Exchanging business cards is a deeply ingrained Japanese custom which led to the downfall of a mass murderer.

On 26 January 1948 the Shiinamachi branch of the Imperial Bank of Tokyo was about to close. A man entered wearing an official armband which indicated that he represented the Tokyo Metropolitan Disinfectant Corps. Wearing special clothing, rubber boots and carrying a medical bag, he handed over his business card which bore the name of Dr Jiro Yamaguchi. Saying that there had been an outbreak of dysentery in the region he claimed he had to give out some medicines to the staff.

The man then gave each of the staff a pill. Using a dropper bottle, he then placed a little liquid into several small cups. The staff drank the 'medicine' and fell to the floor, for the 'medicine' was cyanide. Of the sixteen staff only four were to recover later in hospital. While ten died immediately, two expired later. The bogus Disinfectant Corps representative then gathered more than 180,000 yen in cash and cheques.

But the police did have something to go on. A man calling himself Dr Yamaguchi had visited the Mitsubishi Bank a few days earlier leaving a business card. A similar procedure had taken place there without harm coming to any staff. It looked as though this had been a practice run using harmless 'medicine' for the mass murder which was to be perpetrated at the Imperial Bank of Tokyo.

A similar *modus operandi* had occurred some months previously at the Yasuda Bank. Someone presenting a card bearing the name 'Dr Shigeru Matsui' had given 'immunization' treatment to the staff, again without any harm coming to the bank employees. This also appeared like a practice exercise.

The name of Yamaguchi is very common in Japan, so police hopes of tracing the business cards bearing that name to someone who had placed an order for them were slim. If the same person had been involved in the two practice runs and the mass murder, however, it was not clear why he should have presented a card bearing the name 'Yamaguchi' on two occasions and a card carrying the name 'Matsui' on one occasion. Assuming that they were obviously false names, why not stick to one?

A possible explanation came when someone who was actually called Dr Shigeru Matsui called the police. He said he had read descriptions of the man calling himself 'Dr Yamaguchi' and thought he might have met the murderer some time in the past and exchanged business cards with him. If this was so then, when the murderer presented the business card at the Yasuda Bank he had intended that it should be a false one naming him as 'Dr Yamaguchi'. By error he had given the bank officials a card which had originally belonged to the real Dr Matsui.

If this was the case, then it was possible that Dr Matsui had among his collection of business cards, one bearing the real name of the murderer. The murderer would have had no cause to present other than his genuine business card in normal day-to-day dealings. Only in the bank visits doing practice runs were the false 'Dr Yamaguchi' cards necessary.

Sifting through the collection of business cards given to them by Dr Matsui, they were able to identify the suspected murderer as Sadamichi Hirasawa.

Hirasawa, an artist, fitted the descriptions of the killer given by survivors. His home was searched and clothing, rubber boots and a medical bag like those worn in the murderer's visit to the bank were found.

Hirasawa confessed to the crime, standing trial for murder in December 1948. His defence was to claim partial insanity. This had been caused he said by an anti-rabies injection administered in 1925. He also claimed that his original confession had been forced out of him and he withdrew it. Found guilty, he was sentenced to be hanged.

An appeal against hanging was made by defence lawyers. A Japanese law protects citizens from assisting their own demise. Hanging argued the lawyers, means that the victim's own body weight facilitates death thus violating the law. This appeal was successful. An appeal was made against the conviction but this was rejected by the Supreme Court in 1955.

In prison, Hirasawa painted pictures, although he had claimed that the same anti-rabies injection that allegedly made him partially insane had damaged his ability as an artist. He also wrote his autobiography.

Campaigners made a case for freeing Hirasawa, claiming that he had not committed the murders at all. The real murderer was a Japanese man who had served as an officer in the Imperial Army. He was a member of a secret biological warfare unit. He and other unit members were trained to get behind enemy lines and kill with toxins including cyanide. When the war ended, so the campaigners claimed, these assassination squad members were allowed by the occupying forces to return home on one condition. They were to hand over documents about the work of their unit, which included research into untraceable poisons. The prime suspects then for the murders in the Imperial Bank of Tokyo, were ex-members of these units. But the occupying forces were afraid that the police investigations would uncover these clandestine activities. Japanese and American governments colluded to keep the past quiet, and

Hirasawa was a scapegoat. This in essence was the campaigner's story.

But it did not lead to Hirasawa's release, for he spent forty years in prison, dying in his 90s in 1987.

Historical Sketch of Poison Use

The use in hunting of poisoned arrows, darts and spears by our primitive ancestors may be reflected in their use by groups still living today.

Bushmen of the Kalahari Desert in South Africa employed a particularly deadly poison derived from the entrails of a caterpillar. Pygmies in central Africa used a lethal poison extracted from the red ant.

Malayan natives shoot palm fibre blow darts projected by bamboo blow guns which can propel the little arrows as far as sixty metres. Tipped with dried gum from the upas tree, these darts can kill a man instantly.

In Java and Borneo, the sap of the upas tree (*Antiaris toxicaria*) might be mixed with snake or scorpion venom. The sap is collected in a vessel and cooked over an open fire. It is then rolled up, and tied in leaves until it dries into a hard stick, which is stored until needed. It is then scraped until the required amount is acquired. This is crushed and mixed with water. Dart tips dipped in the resulting paste are dried near a fire.

The Hairy Ainus of Northern Japan poisoned their whaling harpoons with aconite (q.v.). The root *Aconitum japanicum* was ground between stones and mixed with water to form a paste which was dried on to the harpoon.

Cholo Indians in western Colombia use a poison batrachotoxia which they call kokoi. It comes from jungle frogs and blocks the transmission of nerve impulses to muscles so causing death. One frog can yield enough poison for fifty lethal arrows. The Indians skewer the frog on a wooden spit, roasting it alive until it releases its poison. Arrows are touched onto the blisters on the creature's skin. Alternatively the kokoi is caught in a bowl as it drips from the frog and the arrows are dipped in that. South American Indians use the poison bufotenine from the skin of poisonous toads.

Poisonous plants and animals were important to ancient priests and magician healers both for their use on enemies and in connection with finding treatments for poisons such as snake bites.

Some time between 1900 BC and 1100 BC in Egypt, eight papyri were written describing Egyptian arts of medicine and poisons. One of these, the Ebers papyrus, an eighteen-metre long scroll, lists drugs and poisons. Probably the first written record of a poisonous concoction is contained on one of the papyri: 'Pronounce not the name of I.A.D. under penalty of the peach'. It is thought to refer to distilling cyanide from peach seeds.

Persian Queen Parysatis, wife of Artaxerxes 2nd (405–359 BC) was said to have poisoned her daughter-in-law Satira in a particularly cunning way. Sharing a meal of a game bird with Satira, the Queen carved the meat with a knife which had a blade coated on one side with venom. By being careful to eat meat carved only by the clean side of the knife Parysatis was able to share the meal unharmed while her victim died.

Mithridates the 6th, King of Pontus in Asia Minor (132–63 BC), experimented with poisons and antidotes. He also tried to develop a universal antidote which came to be known as 'Mithridates' or 'Mithridaticum' and contained numerous ingredients including viper flesh.

Strongly opposed to Roman infiltration of the Near East, he sought revenge on the military power. In 110 BC he displaced his mother in government and put to death 80,000 Italians in the region of Asia Minor. Roman armies were sent to deal with Mithridates who met his defeat some years later. Ironically the King killed himself by taking poison.

The Renaissance (1400 to 1700) was a heyday for poisoners and Italy seems to have been the centre of activity. In Venice a secret circle was developed within the government which arranged for the demise of anyone who displeased it. Professional poisoners carried out the secret sentence of the so-called 'Council of Ten'.

Baptista Parta in *Poison Formulas* published in 1589, included instructions for poisoning someone while they were sleeping. Opium, belladonna, hemlock and stramonium were mixed together then stored in a closed box for three days to ferment. The box was placed under the sleeping victim's nose and the lid removed to carry out the poisoning.

Cesare Borgia, son of Pope Alexander 6th by Vanozza de'Cattanel was rumoured to have poisoned people for the Pope. He was supposed to have a secret room where he mixed his poisons and only the Pope and Cesare's sister Lucretia were allowed to enter. Among Cesare's victims it is thought were the Duke of Grandier and Prince Djem, a Turkish royal.

Hoch, Johann

Johann Hoch, 'The Stockyards Bluebeard', worked in a Chicago packing house. In December 1904, he placed a matrimonial advertisement in a local newspaper – 'German, own home, wish acquaintance of widow without children; object matrimony'. Julia Walcker, a 46-year-old widow who owned a candy store at 12 Willow Street was among those who responded. By 12 December, within days of the advertisement appearing, the two were married.

Claiming to be temporarily short of money, Hoch persuaded Julia to withdraw all her savings, which amounted to $300 and to sell her shop for $175. A month after the wedding, Julia died after a short illness which a Doctor Reece who attended her diagnosed as kidney disease and inflammation of the bladder.

Four days later, Johann married Amelia Fischer his dead wife's sister whom he had met when she visited the dying Julia. Amelia withdrew her savings of $750 and signed the money over to her new husband. There was a scene when the newly-weds visited Mrs Sohn, another of Amelia's sisters, who saw Johann as a heartless money grabber, and soon after, Hoch disappeared. Police enquiries were made when the two sisters reported Johann missing and it came to light that Hoch had made a career of similar conduct using various aliases. After several national newspapers published Hoch's picture, police received a telephone call on 30 January 1905. Mrs Katherine Kuemmerle who kept a boarding house in 546 West 47th Street in New York said that a man who looked like Hoch was staying in her lodgings and had proposed marriage to her.

Within the hour, police arrested Hoch and found in his possession a fountain pen concealing white powder. After initially claiming that the device was simply 'my way of carrying toothpowder', Hoch later admitted that it was arsenic but maintained that he intended to use it to kill himself. Back in Chicago, Julia Walcker-Hoch's body was exhumed and an autopsy revealed the stomach and liver to be saturated with arsenic.

Police enquiries suggested that between 1881 and 1892, Hoch had married up to thirty-five women. About a half of them had made their savings and possessions over to him and had then suffered acute illnesses before dying suddenly. Found guilty of murder at Chicago on 19 May 1905 before an Illinois jury, Hoch was hanged on 23 February 1906. His final words were, 'Father forgive them – they know not what they do. I must die an innocent man. Goodbye'.

Hofrichter, Adolph

A wave of public sympathy greeted the news that 28-year-old Adolph Hofrichter an infantry officer in the Austrian Army was to be tried by closed court martial for the murder of another officer Captain Richard Mader.

Lieutenant Hofrichter protested his innocence, the evidence against him was circumstantial and there was concern that the case was not to be heard in an open civil court. The facts were plain enough. In December 1912 some twelve officers in the Austrian Army had received through the mail boxes of capsules. A letter sent with each parcel explained that the capsules were a nerve tonic. The only officer to bother trying the remedy was Captain Mader. He took one of the capsules and within seconds he was dead.

The capsules left in the box were examined and found to contain fatal doses of potassium cyanide. Enquiries established that eleven other officers had been sent similar poison capsules. If a common link between the twelve could be found, it might suggest the murderer's identity.

A common feature was that the officers concerned had all been promoted recently. Could the murderer be an officer who had failed to get promotion, who badly wanted it and who was wreaking revenge on the twelve successful officers?

A possible candidate was Hofrichter, based at Linz, who fitted the requirements of the theory. His quarters were searched and several pill boxes and capsules were found. There was no evidence, however, to show that Hofrichter had purchased any poison.

Nevertheless the lieutenant was arrested. Given these facts, the spread of public support was perhaps not surprising. But another side of Hofrichter's character began to be revealed. It emerged that he had been leading a double life. Posing as a doctor, he would advertise for a governess, drugging the young women who applied and then forcing himself on them.

This news punctured public sympathy. Hofrichter wrote a complete confession, the court martial found him guilty of murder and he was sentenced to death. But the sentence was not carried out. The Emperor of Austria instructed that the lieutenant serve a prison sentence on the grounds that he was 'morally abnormal', Hofrichter served twenty years.

Howard, Frances

Frances Howard, the daughter of the Earl of Suffolk, was one of several people implicated in the murder of Sir Thomas Overbury.

She was married to the Earl of Essex as a young girl. But the marriage was not yet consummated when in 1610 at the age of 15 she came to the court of King James VI of Scotland, James I of England. A stunning beauty, she soon caught the attention of Scotsman Robert Carr who was a favourite of the King and acted as his political advisor.

Carr's secretary, Thomas Overbury, was a most able man who was eleven years Carr's senior. They had been friends since Carr was a Royal page boy of 11 years old. Overbury, knighted in 1608, handled all the King's letters and even wrote love letters for Carr to Frances Howard when she arrived at court.

Carr and Howard soon became lovers but not long afterwards, the Earl of Essex, Frances's young husband returned from overseas. He took her to their country home, but Frances, distraught at parting from her lover, refused to consummate the marriage. She even consulted Mrs Turner, a local woman thought to be a witch, about casting spells to make the Earl of Essex impotent.

In 1613, Frances and her husband spent some of their time at Court and she resumed her role as Carr's lover. Carr was by now the Duke of Somerset and enormously influential, indeed, he was the first Scot ever to reach the English peerage.

The Earl of Northampton, Frances's manipulative great-uncle decided that Frances should divorce the Earl of Essex and marry Carr. King James consented, but Sir Thomas Overbury disagreed and argued fiercely with Carr. Eventually, the King felt it necessary to remove Overbury from the scene for a while and offered him a post abroad. When Overbury adamantly refused, the King resorted to having him locked in the Tower.

Carr persuaded Overbury not to resist and that the situation would soon be resolved. Frances, however, wanted Overbury out of the way permanently. Her great-uncle, the Earl of Northampton arranged for a confidant of Frances, Sir Gervase Elwys, to become Governor of the Tower. Northampton also managed to have Weston, a friend of the 'witch' Mrs Turner, made Overbury's jailer. Another friend of Mrs Turner, Dr Franklin, supplied sublimate of mercury and Weston himself was to see that the poison was administered.

Over a five-month period, Overbury's food, including game and tarts, was laced with sublimate of mercury. Sir Gervase suspected nothing at first and when he did discover what was happening, he chose not to intervene. After great suffering, Overbury died in September 1613.

Carr and Frances Howard married. King James appointed a new secretary whom Carr disliked. Carr made a constant nuisance of himself with the King, stretching the monarch's affection for him to the limit. George Villiers, a young Cambridge student, began to replace Carr in the King's affections. (He was later to be made Duke of Buckingham.)

A year and a half after the marriage of Carr and Howard, a chemist's assistant who had actually administered the fatal dose of poison to Overbury made a deathbed confession. When news of this reached the King, he had the pugnacious Sir Edward Coke, Chief Justice of Common Pleas, investigate.

As a result, the trial took place of Sir Gervase Elwys (the Tower Governor), Mrs Turner (the 'witch'), Weston (the jailer) and Dr Franklin (who supplied the poison). All were executed late in 1615.

Letters surfaced incriminating Frances Howard and Robert Carr and Sir Edward Coke had both of them arrested. In December 1615, Frances gave birth to a daughter but the baby was taken away from the mother in March 1616.

At her trial in May, held in Westminster Hall, Frances, Countess of Somerset, pleaded guilty and was condemned to death. Carr's trial reached a similar conclusion and both were consigned to the Tower. Before Carr's trial, however, the King had secretly promised him that the death sentence would not be carried out. Now painfully alienated from one another, the couple were incarcerated together for six years. They were then released from the Tower and allowed to retire in shame to their country home. Frances suffered a disease of the womb, became mentally unstable and died at the age of 39.

Hyoscine

Henbane (*Hyoscyamus niger*) comes from the same family of plants as the deadly nightshade, that is the solanaceae family and is found occasionally on waste ground in southern England. It yields an alkaloid hyosine.

Medically, hyoscine was used to discourage sickness, for instance seasickness. With morphine it has been administered to control acute mania. As a sedative, in the form of hydrobromide, it was administered by hypodermic needle. In the mid 1920s, it was sometimes used to induce a twilight sleep (along with morphine) during delivery. (Polson, C.J., Green, M.A., Lee, M.R., 1983). Hyoscine hydrobromide also has anti-aphrodisiac effects.

Hyoscine, like atropine (q.v.) is an anticholine. That is, it blocks the effect of acetylcholine which is a nerve-muscle transmitting substance. Hyoscine depresses the CNS whereas atropine has an excitor effect followed by a depressant effect on motor areas of the brain. A lethal dose is between a quarter to half a grain of hyoscine hydrobromide.

Inorganic and Organic Poisons

When poisons are considered according to their source, a useful way of broadly grouping them is as inorganic or organic.

Organic poisons include animal poisons (q.v.), plant poisons (q.v.), bacterial poisons (q.v.), and a series of synthetic organic compounds.

Among the latter are chloroform, an organic chemical with industrial applications which was once used as an anaesthetic. Seconal and succinylcholine chloride are synthetic drugs while Paraquat is a commercial contact herbicide. Also included among organic poisons would be cyanides as salts of hydrocyanic acid.

Regarding inorganic poisons, elements in the form of their salts have been used homicidally on many occasions, notably arsenic, lead, mercury, antimony and copper. Rarer use has been made of phosphorus and thallium.

Insulin

Insulin is a polypeptide formed by the B cells of the islets of Langerhans situated in the pancreas and secreted from there into the body. Secretion appears to be controlled by the amount of glucose in the blood supplying the pancreas. Increased blood glucose initiates the secretion of insulin which maintains blood glucose within normal levels.

Diabetes mellitus a condition in which blood sugar levels are too high is associated with the absence or decreased effect of insulin and insulin from an external source is used to treat diabetes where the body does not produce sufficient insulin itself. Insulin was first isolated by Nicolai Paulesen in Romania in 1920 and the results published in Paris. Banting and Best of Toronto isolated insulin in 1921 since when various sources have been used. Recently 'human insulin' has become available with the help of genetic engineering.

Diabetes mellitus gets its name from the fact that urine is passed plentifully and tastes sweet as Avicenna (980–1037) discovered. (An unrelated condition diabetes insipidus on the other hand is characterized by tasteless urine). Mehring and Minkowski in 1889 demonstrated that diabetes mellitus was caused by pancreas failure when they removed the pancreas of dogs and brought about the condition.

Insulin is injected subcutaneously to treat insulin-dependent diabetes (another form of diabetes mellitus being non-insulin dependent). Insulin enables muscles and other tissues to take up sugar from the blood. When insulin is insufficient, then blood glucose concentration increases and glucose is passed out in urine. Injections of insulin enable blood sugar to be utilized fully.

An overdose of insulin effects the brain. Glucose is an important source of energy for the brain so the blood glucose concentration needs to be sufficient. If insulin reduces this too much then hypoglycaemia (a deficiency of blood sugar) ensues. This can lead to permanent damage to the CNS, to convulsions, coma and death. Overdose can be treated by dextrose or ordinary sugar which helps restore blood sugar level.

Jegado, Hélène

French housemaid Hélène Jegado appears to have begun her career as a serial murderer when she was about thirty years old, although it is uncertain whether she committed any earlier undetected poisonings. Certainly from that age, she was associated with a series of killings and thefts.

In a household where she worked as a cook, seven of the inhabitants died in agony after showing symptoms of violent sickness. Hélène's attentions as a nurse did nothing to delay their death. Later, claiming to be deeply religious she entered a convent where during her stay several inmates became ill and died.

Moving to Rennes, she worked as a domestic servant for a M. Rabot but was dismissed after being caught stealing wine. On her departure, several members of the Rabot family became ill. Next, she worked in an inn where her employer's child died suddenly and in great pain. Later another domestic servant and the landlord's wife, died in a similar way. Eventually, Hélène was dismissed because she was caught stealing wine.

In 1850, she began working for Professor Théophile Bidard who taught in the University of Rennes. Not long after her appointment, another servant girl became ill. Hélène nursed her but her condition grew worse and she died leaving Hélène apparently grief-stricken. After a time, another servant girl was employed, (Rosalie Sarrazin) and she and Hélène became firm friends. When Rosalie was given the important task of keeping the household accounts because Hélène was illiterate and could not perform the duty, the relationship soured. Rosalie fell ill with vomiting and stomach pains and in July 1851, she died.

The doctor called to attend Rosalie suspected poisoning and reported the death to the authorities. A police magistrate visiting the Bidard home spoke to Hélène who immediately blurted out that she was innocent before anyone had accused her of anything. His suspicions heightened, the magistrate returned to his office and started enquiring into Hélène's background. What emerged were links between Hélène's employment and many suspicious illnesses some twenty-three of which ended in death.

Arrested on suspicion of poisoning Rosalie with arsenic, Hélène was eventually accused of three murders and tried at Rennes in December 1851. Proclaiming her innocence before the president of the court, Hélène was found guilty and was guillotined in 1852.

Jennings, Thomas

Thomas Jennings lived in a Berkshire cottage with his wife and four children. In order to help look after the children, Jennings' niece Maria Carter also lived with the family.

On the 23 December 1844, Mrs Jennings was not at home at dinner time when the rest of the family settled down to a basic dinner of bacon and potato. Everyone at the table had a pinch of salt with the meal except Jennings' infant son Eleazar. For seasoning for Eleazar's meal, Jennings left the table and returned with a pinch of white powder between his fingers which he sprinkled on the side of the child's plate.

Only half an hour after consuming the food, Eleazar became ill, suffering sickness, vomiting and stomach pains. His condition continued to deteriorate and on Christmas Day he died. An inquest, held on 27 December delivered a verdict of death from natural causes.

In the second week of January 1845, another of Jennings' children died and an inquest into the death held on 11 January also reached the conclusion that death was natural. But this time, Mr Lamb, a surgeon who had helped investigate cause of death, decided to check the medical findings. Taking an ounce phial of the liquid contents of the child's stomach, he sent these to Dr Alfred Swaine Taylor at Guy's Hospital. A pioneer toxicologist, Taylor was at that time lecturer on medical jurisprudence at Guy's.

Reporting his findings, Taylor (Taylor, A.S., 1845 in Ober, W.B., 1973) gives an interesting insight into tests used at the time to detect possible poisons. The poison he identified was in fact arsenic and one of the tests illustrates the sort of chemical analysis involved. Two drachms of deep red liquid found in the stomach were diluted with distilled water, acidulated with acetic acid, boiled for forty-five minutes and filtered. The resulting almost colourless liquid was mixed with ammonio-nitrate of silver, and produced a light yellow precipitate. This was just one of a series of tests which indicated the presence of arsenic.

Faced with these findings, the coroner ordered Eleazar's body to be disinterred, the exhumation being carried out on 24 January. The child's stomach and intestines were examined at Guy's the following day and it was estimated that five to six grains of arsenic were present in these organs.

Police arrested Thomas Jennings and charged him with the murder of Eleazar. Put on trial at Berkshire Lent Assizes, Jennings was found guilty and was subsequently executed.

King, Dr William

In 1858, Dr King's practice in Brighton, Ontario was thriving and his charm made him particularly popular with women patients. He was newly qualified having obtained his medical degree at Philadelphia in March 1858 and had been married for three years.

At the same time, it was rumoured that another side to King's character asserted itself where his wife Sarah was concerned. He was said to ill-treat her and to have told her that she was suffering from an incurable illness. In October 1858, Sarah became ill with severe abdominal pains, and Dr King's treatment appeared only to make matters worse. Becoming increasingly concerned Sarah's father asked for a second opinion, but when the second doctor called, Dr King got rid of him by saying his wife was pregnant.

After three weeks of agonizing illness, however Sarah died and her husband appeared to be consumed with grief. But Sarah's mother, while she had been attending Sarah during her final days, had discovered a love letter to Dr King from Melinda Vandervoort, a 20-year-old patient. Also, enquiries revealed that Dr King had bought arsenic only two days prior to his wife's demise. Once the coroner was informed, Sarah's body was exhumed, and an autopsy revealed that the stomach contained eleven grains of arsenic. A coroner's inquest was held, finding that Sarah King had died of arsenic poison administered by Dr King. King absconded but was soon arrested and stood trial in April 1859 at Cobourg Assizes. No fewer than twelve doctors gave expert testimony.

The defence argued that the arsenic discovered in Mrs King's stomach could have found its way there when the body was being handled for the autopsy. Dr King pleaded not guilty to no avail and was sentenced to death, meeting his end on the hangman's noose on 9 June 1859.

Lafarge, Marie

Born Marie-Fortunée Cappelle, Marie Lafarge had married an industrialist and may have thought that her future was set fair. But Charles Lafarge's business was bankrupt and the couple lived unhappily at Le Glandier with Charles's mother.

As if fate had to rub salt into the wound, a school-friend of Marie's had married a vicomte from one of the highest families in France.

Vicomtesse de Léautaud in contrast to Marie, lived in splendour in a château at Busagny. In May 1839, she discovered that a diamond necklace was missing and reported the matter to the police as theft. Marie Lafarge, then aged 23, had been a house guest at the time the jewellery had disappeared and the finger of suspicion began to point her way. The old school-friend withdrew the charge, however.

In December of the same year, Marie bought a quantity of arsenic. It appeared that her house was overrun with rats and she wanted to get rid of them.

Charles was in Paris and Marie made him some cakes and sent them to him. He fell ill and came home on 3 January 1840. After appearing to recover a little, he fell ill again and died on 14 January. Suspicion fell on Marie as it was rumoured that she had poisoned her husband. An autopsy revealed arsenic in Charles's stomach and Marie was arrested.

News of the arrest reached the Vicomtesse de Léautaud and the Léautauds resurrected the theft charge. Le Glandier was searched and the diamond necklace found. Marie claimed that there had been an agreement with the Vicomtesse that she, Marie should have the necklace but the Vicomtesse denied any such arrangement. Tried for robbery in July 1840, Marie was found guilty and given a two-year suspended sentence.

In September, Marie stood trial once more, this time accused of the murder of her husband. At Tulle, where the trial took place, the defence lawyers called in Professor Orfila, a leading toxicologist from Paris. Professor Orfila, however, concluded that Charles had died from criminally administered arsenic.

Found guilty, Marie was sentenced to hard labour for life. King

Louis-Philippe commuted the sentence to life imprisonment, and Marie served ten years at Montpellier, where she wrote her memoirs. Marie Lafarge died a year after her release.

Lamson, Dr George

What appeared to be a family holiday turned out to be the first attempt on the life of Percy John by his brother-in-law Dr George Lamson.

Lamson was in financial difficulties. Born in 1850 in England, he had qualified as a doctor and served in the Russian-Turkish War as a surgeon. On returning to England, he married in 1876 making himself financially much better off, for his wife had, with her brothers, inherited shares in the estate of their parents.

By this time, however, Lamson had developed an addiction to morphine and this coupled with his liberal spending meant that his wife's money was soon depleted. In 1879 one of Lamson's brothers-in-law, Herbert, died and his wife came into a further share of the inheritance. Having free use of his wife's money, Lamson now bought a medical practice in Bournemouth on the south coast. But the venture failed and in 1881, Lamson visited America possibly looking for ways to make money. On his return he was still in financial straits, and began writing false cheques.

It was at this point that Lamson's attention turned to his second brother-in-law, Percy. It is possible that the death of Lamson's first brother-in-law, Herbert, may have been his first murder. If this was so, then it was an obvious step to use the same means to increase his wife's wealth and hence his own. If Lamson had no part in the earlier death, then it may be that the inheritance from it gave him the notion of similarly benefiting from the demise of Percy. In fact, Percy was already unwell, suffering from a curvature of the spine. Only eighteen years old he lived in Blenheim House, a private school in Wimbledon. Lamson shared a holiday with Percy in the summer of 1881 on the Isle of Wight and it was there that the first attempt on the boy's life was made. Lamson obtained some aconite and administered it to Percy but the poison failed to prove lethal. It did make Percy very ill, but he recovered.

Lamson visited America once more and on returning to England, he had another plan to get rid of Percy. His pressing need for money at this time is indicated by the fact that he had to pawn his surgical instruments.

Having obtained some more aconite, Lamson wrote to Percy at the school saying that he was to travel to France but would visit him briefly on the evening of 3 December 1881 at 7 p.m. Accordingly, Lamson and Percy joined the school principal over refreshments and Lamson offered round some ready-cut pieces of Dundee cake, ensuring that Percy ate a poisoned section. Lamson also produced some capsules. With much show, he filled one of these with sugar and administered it to Percy as a medicine.

Taking his leave at about 7.20 p.m., Lamson explained that he had to catch the Paris train. Ten minutes after his departure, Percy became ill and later that night he died in great pain. Despite the showmanship with the capsule which was presumably to confuse matters if ever Lamson was accused, the doctor was a prime suspect. He stood to gain financially from the death and doctors at the school suspected poisoning. On top of this, staff at Allen & Hanbury's where Lamson had purchased the aconite, read of the death of Percy in the newspapers and informed police of Lamson's purchase. Lamson was sought, in the immortal phrase, to 'help police with their enquiries'.

In sheer bravado or conceit, Lamson returned from France and reported to Scotland Yard to try to resolve matters. Arrested and charged with murder, he stood trial on 9 March 1882 at the Old Bailey. Before Mr Justice Hawkins, the prosecution led by Solicitor-General Herchel presented the overwhelming evidence against Lamson. For the defence Montague Williams called in toxicologists to point out that (at that time) aconite could not be detected chemically and to try to cast further doubt on the evidence surrounding the alleged poisoning.

Lamson was found guilty and sentenced to be hanged. As he awaited execution in Wandsworth Prison, his morphia addiction was not fed and he was affected by withdrawal symptoms being semi-conscious much of the time. After confessing his guilt regarding Percy's murder to the chaplain, but denying any involvement in the death of Herbert, Lamson was carried swooning to the scaffold where the sentence was carried out on 28 April 1882.

Lead

Lead is found in nature mainly as galena, a lead sulphide ore, which is heated to yield metallic lead. Among the properties of the metal are its heaviness and its easy fusibility. Its forms are inorganic lead salts and organic lead compounds such as tetraethyl. Lead acetate, which used to be called sugar of lead is an inorganic salt of lead and acetic acid. The usefulness of lead was recognized in antiquity and emphasized in the Bible where both Moses and Jeremiah speak of it. Ancients used lead in jewellery, for dishes and as fishing net weights. (The modern day use of lead fishing weights has poisoned swans and other birds.)

If the use of lead has a long history, so does lead poisoning.

Nicander in the first century BC wrote a book on poisons in which he refers to lead oxide and the symptoms of intoxication it induces. Dioscorides, the Greek physician under Nero, and Pliny the Elder also noted the effects of lead. Romans made great use of it and may have even used it to sweeten food. Wine was prepared in pots with a lead lining and the substance also found its way into the water system because Roman aqueducts were lined with it. When the Roman Empire fell, in AD 4000 its use declined until around AD 1000 when Germany began to mine lead ore.

In Europe, it was the practice to add lead salts to wine to sweeten it and consequently lead colic became widespread. Today lead is used in solder, glazed earthenware, leaded glass, pewter, hair dye, paper pigments, battery casings and engine oil.

Lead may be absorbed by the gastro-intestinal tract if swallowed or by the respiratory tracts if inhaled or through the skin. About 15% to 20% of the metal taken by mouth is kept in the body, the rest being excreted in faeces. Carried through the body in red cells, lead is deposited in the bones, teeth, kidneys and liver. It binds to the sulphydril groups of proteins in the body and acts with carboxyl and phosphory groups too, damaging cell metabolism.

Lead poisoning is associated with effects on the gastro-intestinal tract, the nervous system and kidneys. Symptoms may include headache, tetchiness, tiredness and jaundice in which skin and whites of the eyes may become yellow. A 'lead line' on the gums is a well-known sign as are dental cavities. Severe poisoning leads to blindness, emaciation, kidney damage, convulsions and paralysis and death.

Legal Aspects

All countries have wrestled with the control of poisoning as a crime and England serves as an example of the strategies used.

In England the crime of poisoning is specifically enshrined in the Offences Against the Person Act 1861. Section 23 of the Act deals with endangering life or causing grievous bodily harm by poisoning. Even the intention to annoy is included (Section 24). While no distinction is made between a drug and a poison, in the case of drugs, the dose and its mode of presentation is central to the definition. For instance the issue of whether or not the drug takes the form of a reputable pharmaceutical preparation may be crucial. Also the intention of the user is of great importance. In Scotland, the situation is somewhat different, poisoning being a crime under common law.

Having defined the crime, the measure of whether a set of circumstances warrants being classed as that crime is related to the proof needed. For legal proof of murder by poison, three components are necessary. It has to be shown that:

(1) the deceased died from poisoning
(2) the accused administered the fatal dose
(3) the accused intended to kill the deceased in doing so

Of equal importance to defining the crime, however, is the law's role in restricting the purchase and sale of poisons. This may be illustrated by a series of laws enacted in Britain in the nineteenth and twentieth centuries.

The Arsenic Act 1851 was the corner-stone of control of the sale of poisons to members of the public. Before this act, no legal restrictions existed on the sale of arsenic or other poisons. Arsenic was the first poison to come under control because as the preamble to the act frankly stated, 'unrestricted sale of arsenic facilitates the commission of crime'.

The act decreed that anyone selling arsenic must record the sale in a book, following a set pattern. This had to be performed immediately and before delivery. Arsenic sold had to be distinctively coloured – to help its detection if it was used criminally. The purchaser (or a witness to the sale) had to be known to the seller. Summary conviction and a fine to a maximum of £20 was the penalty for not conforming. Exemptions were made for dispensed medicines and for sales by wholesalers to retailers.

The Pharmacy Act 1852 gave the Pharmaceutical Society of Great Britain the powers to hold examinations and issue certificates. Before the act, anyone could use the title 'pharmaceutical chemist', but the act restricted the title to members of the Society. Anyone could still, however, call themselves a 'chemist' or a 'druggist' quite freely.

In 1868 a further Pharmacy Act went on the statute books. Its aim was to 'regulate the sale of poisons' and to amend the 1852 act.

Section one of the Pharmacy Act 1868 made it unlawful for all and sundry to 'sell or keep open shop for retailing, dispensing or compounding poisons'. A poisons list of fifteen substances was introduced and to avoid the problems arising from the slippery nature of the term, a poison was simply defined as a substance on the list. With approval from the Privy Council, the Pharmaceutical Society could extend the list. Under a schedule of the act, retail sale of poisons in the schedule had to conform to the 'poison book' and 'known to seller' requirements. Substances containing poisons could be sold retail only by a 'pharmaceutical chemist' or a 'chemist and druggist'. The latter were defined legally. (Later, the Pharmacy Act 1953 combined the two qualifications into one Register of Pharmaceutical Chemists.) Fixed penalties recoverable in civil courts could be imposed for not conforming to the act.

The question of whether a corporate body could be liable for keeping open shop for the sale of poisons arose in 1880. An appeal case was heard by the House of Lords between The Pharmaceutical Society and The London and Provincial Supply Association Ltd. The Lords found in favour of the corporate body, so company chemists did not come under the control of the Pharmaceutical Society until the Poisons and Pharmacy Act 1908. This required corporate bodies to make special arrangements for aspects of their business to do with keeping, retailing and dispensing poisons. They were to be 'under the control and management of a superintendent who is a duly registered pharmaceutical chemist or chemist and druggist'. The act also allowed poisonous substances to be sold by dealers in agricultural and horticultural products.

A series of Dangerous Drugs Acts and regulations from 1920 to 1932 channelled the control of dangerous drugs through prescriptions. Such drugs were only to be dispensed by someone lawfully keeping 'open shop for the retailing of poisons'. The Dangerous Drugs and Poisons (Amendment) Act 1923 introduced the provision of signed orders from a doctor.

The Pharmacy and Poisons Act 1933 provided for the forming of a Poisons Board. They were to advise the Secretary of State what substances should be on the Poisons List. Part 1 of the list comprised substances which could be retailed only at a pharmacy. Part 2 poisons could be sold both at a pharmacy and by traders approved by the local authority. A statutory committee was set up under the act which had powers over pharmacists committing misconduct and over corporate bodies guilty of offences under the Pharmacy Act. It became a duty of the Pharmaceutical Society to enforce the act. Also action was to be taken in court of summary jurisdiction rather than civil courts.

The 1933 Act was later replaced by the Medicines Act 1968 and The Poisons Act 1972. The Medicines Act 1968 controls the sale of poisons with medical uses and regulates the standards of pharmaceutical practice. The Poisons Act 1972 was concerned with non-medical poisons, their storage, and their sale and supply to members of the public and health professionals. It covers the registration of those who sell poisons. It is concerned with categorizing poisons according to how they must be supplied or sold, and Poison Rules (and their modification) both of which topics are dealt with by the Poisons Board. The lists of substances considered poisons under the Pharmacy and Poisons Act 1933 would continue. The 1972 Act restricts the sale of certain 'Part 2' poisons to general sale by pharmacists or to sale by listed sellers only to those in the horticulture, agriculture or forestry business. This restricts the sale of poisonous herbicides and pesticides to the public.

Throughout such a brief historical sketch, trends begin to emerge. Many criminal cases of poisoning in the past involved using substances that were available in rodenticides but the modern rat poison is now mainly made up of biological substances. It may not now contain strychnine.

Another thread that is apparent is the development of the medical and related professions into an overall system of National Health. This has enabled potentially poisonous substances to be channelled to members of these professions whereas in the past some would have been sold openly cover the counter.

Lehmann, Christa

Born Christa Ambros, Christa Lehmann's childhood was far from happy. Her mother was incarcerated in Alzey mental hospital and her cabinet-maker father married again but neglected his daughter. Later Christa worked at the Hoechst chemical factory where she met Karl Lehmann whom she married in 1944.

The couple moved in with Karl's parents on Paulusstrasse in Worms and Karl set himself up as a tilesetter. Christa argued with Karl's mother and after her mother-in-law's death, Christa was at loggerheads with her father-in-law, Valentine. While Christa had several affairs, Karl drank heavily and eventually died on seventeenth September 1952 suffering violent convulsions. Cause of death was put down to stomach ulcers. With the death of Karl, Christa was able to be as free as she wished with her lovers and she and Valentine continued to argue. On 14 October 1953, however, Valentine fell from his bicycle and died in the street of what appeared to be a heart attack.

In 1954 an incident occurred which was to reveal Christa's more sinister aspects. At a house on Grosse Fischerweide lived Eva Ruh (a 75-year-old widow), her son Walter, her daughter Annie Hamann who was a war widow, and Annie's 19-year-old daughter Uschi. On the afternoon of Monday 15 February Annie returned home from an errand and found a cream-filled chocolate truffle on a plate in the kitchen cupboard. Eva had left this for Uschi who was visiting relatives, but Annie took it. Noticing a bitter taste she spat the confection out, complained to her mother that she suddenly could not see and staggered to the bedroom where after suffering painful cramps and convulsions she died. By the time a doctor was called the family's white Spitz dog had licked up the chocolate that had been spat on the floor and had also died.

Autopsy revealed an accumulation of blood in the brain and lungs indicative of poisoning and samples of organs were sent for examination to Professor Kurt Wagner, Director of the Institute of Forensic Medicine in Mainz. Police led by Chief Inspector Dahmen established that Annie Hamann was a friend of Christa Lehmann. On the day before Annie's death, that is on Sunday 14 February, Christa had visited the Hamann household and offered round a bag of truffles to those present; Annie, Walter, Eva and a neighbour. Christa also ate one of the truffles herself. Eva saved hers saying she would eat it later but kept it in the cupboard planning to give it to Uschi. It was this truffle which Annie discovered on Monday 15 February and which she had eaten prior to her death.

When police interviewed Christa, she admitted buying chocolates from a Wortmann department store in the company of Annie. Inspector Dahmen checked with the confectionery section of the store who had sold 133 out of a batch of 140 truffles. Police sent the remaining seven truffles to the Institute of Forensic Medicine in Mainz for analysis while radio broadcasts warned the public not to eat the confections. At the University clinic in Mainz, Wagner was searching for evidence of convulsant poisons and eventually on a hunch tested for E605 an organic phosphorus compound and got positive results.

Annie Hamann was buried on Friday 19 February and Christa Lehmann was arrested after the funeral. Imprisoned on a murder

charge, she denied poisoning Annie while intending to kill old Eva
Ruh. On Tuesday morning 23 February, however, Christa asked for
her father and a clergyman to visit her cell and confessed. Taken to
an examining magistrate, she repeated her confession claiming at
first that she had only intended to make Eva poorly but later
admitting that she wanted to get rid of the old woman because Eva
had accused her of corrupting Annie. Christa also confessed to
killing her father-in-law by pouring a vial of E605 into Valentine's
breakfast yoghurt. Twenty minutes later he had died in the street.
On Wednesday morning Christa confessed killing her husband by
mixing E605 in his breakfast milk.

Karl Franz and Valentine Lehmann's bodies were exhumed on 12
March when parts of the bodies were sent to Mainz for analysis,
E605 was found. At her trial which began on 20 September 1954
Christa Lehmann was sentenced to life imprisonment.

Lipski, Israel

On 28 June 1887, a relative ascended the stairs at 16 Batty Street, a
lodging-house in the East End of London to visit Miriam Angel
who rented a room there. Finding the girl lying in her bed with a
bubbling yellow mucous around her mouth, the visitor quickly
realized Miriam was dead. A doctor called to the scene suspected
corrosive poisoning suicide and the room was searched to try and
find a container that would help identify the particular substance.

Under the bed a man was discovered, semi-conscious and with
yellow corrosive stains round his mouth. Police enquiries revealed
the man to be Israel Lipski, a 22-year-old Jewish immigrant, who
occupied the attic room above Miriam's chamber. Nitric acid was
identified as the poison which had caused Miriam's death and
made the stains round Israel's mouth. Factors including the
position of Miriam's body indicated that a sexual assault had
taken place, possibly necrophilia.

Lipski recovered, was arrested, charged with murder and tried in
July 1887 before Mr Justice Fitzjames Stephen. Prosecution lawyers
suggested Lipski had seen Miriam in her room through a window on
the stairs leading to his attic. Filled with lust, he had sexually
assaulted her, murdered her then attempted suicide. For the
defence, it was argued that two workmen had attacked and poisoned
Miriam and had then turned on Israel forcing him to drink the acid
too. Found guilty and sentenced to death, Lipski confessed to the
murder the day before his execution at Newgate Prison.

Major, Ethel

In Lincolnshire, in 1934 a dog's body was exhumed on the suspicion that it contained strychnine. Someone signing themselves 'Fairplay' had sent an anonymous letter to the police saying that the hound had died after eating some food scraps put out by Ethel Major the 43-year-old daughter of a gamekeeper.

The importance of this strange exhumation lay in the fact that, some days earlier, on 24 May 1934, Ethel's husband Arthur, a lorry driver had also died after two days of excruciating pain.

The same anonymous letter had explicitly linked the two events, the death of Arthur Major and the demise of the dog. Part of the letter reads: 'Have you ever heard of a wife poisoning her husband? Look further into the death of Mr Major of Kirkby-on-Bain. Why did he complain of his food tasting nasty and throw it to a neighbour's dog, which has since died? ...'

Before this startling development, the certificate of the cause of death had put Arthur's death down to status epilepticus. Despite his occupation as a lorry driver, Ethel claimed that her husband had suffered from epilepsy for years. She had told this to the doctor who had made out the certificate.

Now the death of Arthur Major took on a more sinister aspect. The funeral was stopped. Dr Roche Lynch carried out an autopsy in his laboratory at St Mary's Hospital, London, establishing that Arthur's death was caused by strychnine poisoning. Some 1.27 grains of strychnine were found in the man's organs. The terrier's remains contained 0.12 grains.

Evidence began to point towards Ethel Major. Her father in his capacity as a gamekeeper, kept a small amount of strychnine which meant that Ethel had access to the poison. Also, when interviewed by police Ethel made the classic mistake of mentioning information which they had not revealed to her. Stating that she was unaware that Arthur had 'died of strychnine poisoning', Ethel overlooked the fact that no mention had been made of strychnine.

Events which led to the killing made a sorry tale. In 1915, when Ethel was 24, she had given birth to an illegitimate daughter, Auriel. Not wanting the world to know, Ethel's parents brought the child up as their own. Three years later, Ethel married Arthur Major and kept the secret from him. The couple lived with Ethel's parents and in 1919 had their first child.

Then in 1929, after 11 years of marriage, Arthur and Ethel moved to Kirkby-on-Bain and into their own residence at 2 Council House. Soon, gossip reached Arthur about the origins of his wife's supposed sister, Auriel. He demanded to know the name of the child's father and was enraged when Ethel refused to tell him. Cracks began to appear in their relationship, and Ethel was developing a reputation for being extravagant, spending too much on herself and not enough on her children.

In 1934, Ethel discovered that her husband was getting letters from another woman, Rose Kettleborough. Complaining far and wide about her husband's infidelity, Ethel even wrote to the Chief Constable. For his part, Arthur publicly announced that he would meet none of his wife's debts. His death on 24 May 1934 was the tragic outcome.

Ethel was tried at Lincoln Assizes in November 1934 before Mr Justice Charles with Norman Birkett as defence counsel. No defence witnesses were called and Ethel herself did not give evidence.

In his summing up, the judge mentioned a theory of Dr Roche Lynch that the dead man had received two doses of strychnine. The implication was that one dose was in the corned beef and another dose was given some other way, perhaps in a glass of water. Drawing attention to the inconsistency of the theory, Mr Justice Charles observed: 'Strychnine is exceedingly bitter in taste, and if the second dose was in the glass of water that Major drank, then that small bulk of water had to contain a quantity of strychnine which, according to the medical evidence, would require two and a half pints of water to dissolve it.'

Finding the defendant guilty after retiring for an hour, the jury recommended mercy. Nevertheless, Ethel Major was hanged on 19 December 1934 at Hull Prison.

Marek, Martha

Emil Marek, an Austrian engineering student, was felling a tree when the axe slipped. So deep was the wound that his leg was practically severed and a surgeon had to amputate the limb below the knee.

But Emil was insured against accident in the sum of £10,000. In fact the policy had been taken out only a short time prior to the accident. But things began to go wrong with the insurance claim.

The surgeon who operated on Emil's leg, noted that there was not one wound, but three. The story that the wound was accidental looked suspect and the surgeon concluded that the injury was intentional. When the police were informed, a charge of fraud was brought against Emil and his wife Martha. At this point Martha gave a hospital orderly a bribe to say that he had witnessed the suspicious surgeon meddling with Emil's injuries. It was this bribe which earned the couple four months in prison. Ironically, they were cleared of fraud.

As Martha languished in her cell, she might have considered that she had squandered an opportunity to turn the inauspicious start she had had in life into something positive. Poverty characterized Martha's early life. Born Martha Lowenstein, she was an orphan and was adopted by a poor family in Vienna.

In 1919, however, it looked as though her luck might change. Martha, aged 15, was working in a dress shop. There she was noticed by a rich store owner who made her his ward, sent her to finishing schools in England and France, and left her a considerable amount of money.

Martha married Emil Marek in 1924 and had soon spent the inherited wealth. Facing poverty, they hatched the plan to acquire insurance money through staging the accident with the axe. Once this had failed, the pair left prison to face lean times.

In 1932 Emil died of tuberculosis. Less than four weeks after Emil's death, the couple's baby daughter breathed her last. Martha became a companion for an elderly relative, Susanne Lowenstein, who died soon after. Martha came into the old woman's property. But Martha could not hold on to money and soon she had to rent out rooms to make ends meet.

One of her boarders, a young woman, died suddenly and suspicion arose that Martha had poisoned her. An autopsy revealed that the woman's body contained thallium. As a result three more bodies were exhumed and examined: the husband Emil, the baby daughter, and the old woman Susanne Lowenstein. All contained thallium.

It was established that Martha had purchased the substance at a chemists. On 6 December 1938, Martha Marek paid for her crimes. She was decapitated.

Marymont, Marcus

In April 1958, Mary Marymont, a 43-year-old service wife discovered an unposted letter in her husband's handwriting to his lover Cynthia Taylor. It dealt the death blow to their marriage and led ultimately to the death of Mary herself. The letter helped slot recent events into perspective. Marcus Marymont, Mary's husband, was a 37-year-old Master Sergeant with the United States Air Force based at Sculthorpe, Norfolk, England. The couple had three children, but the previous Christmas, Marcus did not stay with his family. Now it emerged that he had spent that time with Cynthia Taylor, a 23-year-old married woman separated from her husband and living in Maidenhead.

Although Mary Marymont had been unaware of it until she came across the letter, Marcus and Cynthia had been seeing each other for some time. Having met at a club in July 1956, they became lovers in December of that year. The discovery of the letter understandably made Mary irritable and unhappy and the marriage which had lost its lustre for Marcus Marymont and led to his affair with Cynthia, also collapsed from Mary's point of view.

Soon after this Mary also became physically ill, suffering vomiting, diarrhoea and stomach pains. On 9 June, critically ill, she was admitted to the base hospital where she soon afterwards died.

Events accumulated which raised strong suspicions about Mary's death and pointed to poisoning by her husband. When the doctor told Marcus that Mary was dying, the Master Sergeant seemed only disposed to talking about the difficulties of his marriage. Also Marcus first consented to an autopsy on his wife's body then changed his mind. Nevertheless, a post-mortem examination was carried out and organs and other samples were sent to Scotland Yard's laboratories for analysis. Arsenic was found in the liver and there was evidence that the deceased had taken arsenic or been given it in the twenty-four hours before she died. An examination of arsenic in the hair showed that arsenic had also been present in the body several weeks before death occurred.

Two cleaners at the airbase reported seeing Marymont looking round the chemical laboratory one evening expressing concern to them that the arsenic supplies were not under lock and key. Bernard Sampson, a chemist in Maidenhead where Cynthia Taylor lived, stated that Marymont had enquired about buying arsenic at his shop. Told that he would need documentation to buy the poison, Marymont left.

In December 1958, Marcus Marymont stood trial before a US general court martial at Denham in Buckinghamshire. The prosecution case was that Marcus had poisoned his wife to be free to consort with Mrs Taylor. The defence emphasized the circumstantial nature of the evidence and Marymont's good war service record.

Marymont was found guilty on two counts: the murder of his wife with arsenic and misconduct with Mrs Taylor. Sentenced to life imprisonment, he was transferred to Fort Leavenworth Prison, Kansas.

Maybrick, Florence

Florence Chandler's chance meeting with James Maybrick in the tea-room of a transatlantic liner could have leapt from the pages of romantic fiction. In fact, the liaison was a link in a chain of events that led to Florence becoming the first American woman to stand trial for murder in Britain.

It was April 1880 and Florence was just seventeen years old. She had been born in Alabama, a child of the third marriage of her mother, Baroness Caroline Holbrook von Roques. Both the baroness and Florence's brother accompanied her on the voyage from New York to Liverpool from where the party planned to travel on to Paris.

James Maybrick was a wealthy English cotton trader, twenty-three years Florence's senior. Despite the age difference the couple discovered common interests – among them horse racing – and Florence was clearly attracted to the older man. Soon they were engaged and in July 1880, they married in London.

For the first three years of marriage, the couple divided their time between Virginia, which was a centre of the cotton trade, and Liverpool. Then in March 1884, James leased Battlecrease House in a suburb of Liverpool.

It was already known by James's associates that he took arsenic powdered with his food in daily doses in the belief that it acted as a strengthening tonic. Not long after moving into Battlecrease House, James discovered that he had malaria, which be believed he had contracted in the swampy atmosphere of Virginia. Dr Arthur Hooper prescribed an arsenic based treatment. But James, even after recovering, continued to take the substance supposedly as a preventive measure.

The couple had a son in 1883 and their second child, a daughter was born in June 1886. Not long after, Florence made a discovery that broke the sexual bond with her husband. She found out that James had a long-standing mistress in Liverpool who had borne him five children. Two had been born after James and Florence had married, though all died in infancy.

About this time, James regularly visited Edwin Garnett Heaton, a chemist, for a tonic containing arsenic liquor. As 1888 came to an end, the hostility between the married couple led to James destroying his will which had solely benefited his wife.

James complained of headaches and pains in his stomach and limbs. He obtained arsenic from a new supplier, Valentine Blake, a clothier who was using it for his business in an imitation cotton material. In March 1889 Blake handed over 150 grains of arsenic in three paper packets. Some of the powder was white, the remainder was black being mixed with charcoal. In 1889, when James visited London, Florence became close to another cotton broker, 28-year-old Alfred Brierley a friend of James who had first visited Battlecrease House for dinner the previous December.

On 21 March 1889, Alfred and Florence secretly checked into a London hotel where they spent three days together. Discovering about the liaison, James remonstrated with his wife and beat her.

On 13 April, Florence visited Wokes', a local chemist, where she had an account and bought a dozen fly papers containing an arsenic base. Back at home, she soaked the fly papers in a basin of water in her bedroom where Nanny Alice Yapp, one of the servants saw them. She had heard a housemaid talking about having seen them and mentioning in a joking fashion the murderers Flannagan and Higgins.

James wrote a new will leaving most of his estate in trust to the children and providing Florence with only an allowance. In the last week of April, Florence bought arsenic cat poison from Richard Aspinall, a local chemist but refused to sign the register recording the sale as was legally required.

On the morning of 27 April, James fell ill, vomiting and complaining of numbness in the legs. He told the housemaid Mary Cadwallader, that he had taken an overdose of a medicine containing strychnine. Dr Humphreys, a local doctor, diagnosed indigestion although Florence had informed him that her husband had been taking a 'white powder'.

By Tuesday 30 April, James was recovered sufficiently to go to his office. That afternoon, Florence bought two dozen fly papers from Hansons, another chemist shop. On 1 May, she bought a

second packet of cat poison from Aspinall's. James's health
fluctuated. Five days later Dr Humphreys prescribed Fowler's
Solution, a medicine containing arsenic and carbonate of potash.

By 8 May, James was very ill and a nurse was called. Florence
sent for James's brothers, Michael and Edwin. Alice Yapp
observed Florence at James's medicine table transferring liquid
from one bottle to another. Later the same day, Mrs Briggs, a
friend of Florence's visited the house and Alice Yapp told her that
she believed Florence was poisoning 'the master'.

Florence gave Alice Yapp a letter to post which was addressed
to Brierley. But Nurse Yapp found a pretext to open the letter and
noticed that Florence had written that James was 'sick unto death'.
She passed the letter to Edwin Maybrick who showed it to his
brother Michael. He in turn informed Dr Humphreys that Nurse
Yapp suspected Florence of poisoning James.

On Thursday 9 May, Mary Cadwallader discovered fly papers
left soaking in a tray in the pantry and destroyed them. Dr
Humphreys tested samples of Maybrick's faeces and urine for
arsenic but the results were negative.

On Saturday 11 May, with Maybrick's condition deteriorating,
Dr Humphreys tested a bottle of Valentine's Meat Juice which was
at James's bedside and this time traces of arsenic were detected.
James Maybrick breathed his last at 8.40 that evening.

Next day, Florence was effectively held captive in her own
house while her husband's brothers Michael and Edwin went
through the place with a fine tooth-comb. Discovering a packet in
Florence's room labelled 'Arsenic: Poison for Cats', they called
in the police. Over the following days, police discovered 117
medicines from twenty-nine different chemists all compounded
for 'J. Maybrick'. Sufficient arsenic was discovered to have
poisoned fatally some 150 people.

Noticing inflammation in Maybrick's stomach and intestines,
doctors decided the cause of death as being some unspecified
irritant poison. Mrs Maybrick was detained on suspicion of causing
James's death and taken to Walton Jail.

Maybrick's body was exhumed and examined in detail. Traces
of arsenic, strychnine, morphine and hyoscine were found in the
body. The total amount of arsenic amounted to one tenth of a
grain. The average fatal dose being around two grains. At the
coroner's inquest, the jury returned a verdict on 6 June 1889 of
murder by Florence Maybrick.

Her trial opened at St George's Hall, Liverpool, on 31 July 1889
and Florence pleaded not guilty of the charge. Mr Justice Stephen

presided, the prosecution was led by John Addison QC and Sir Charles Tussell defended. Much was made of Florence's liaison with Alfred Brierley, but no specific mention was made of James Maybrick's long running relationship with his mistress. Florence's letter stating that her husband was 'sick unto death' was seized upon by the prosecution as indicating her intention that James would die.

It has been pointed out (Christie, T.L., 1968) that 'sick unto death' was an expression used in the United States to refer to a serious illness but not necessarily one expected to actually end in death.

Evidence concerning the exact cause of James's death was not conclusive. Prosecution witness Dr William Stevenson of Guy's Hospital maintained that Maybrick had died of a poisonous dose of arsenic. On the other hand, Dr Charles Tidy of London University maintained that Maybrick's symptoms were not sufficiently conclusive to point to arsenic poisoning.

The defence held that James had died of natural causes and that the poisons found in his body were no more than the self-administered doses of a hypochondriac. Florence, it was admitted, had bought arsenic based fly papers but only to use in making cosmetic preparations.

Trial Judge Mr Justice Stephen gave a long, circuitous and prejudicial summing up. Although an expert of criminal law, his faculties were failing and four years after the trial he was to die in a lunatic asylum.

A guilty verdict was returned by the jury and Florence was sentenced to death. The sentence was commuted to penal servitude for life by the Home Secretary. His grounds were that the evidence did not 'wholly exclude' a reasonable doubt regarding whether James Maybrick's death was caused by the administering of arsenic.

Queen Victoria said of the case that she regretted that such a wicked woman should escape because of a legal quibble. But efforts were made on Florence's behalf both in America and England. American presidents and English politicians as well as English lawyers took an interest in the case. After fifteen years in prison, Florence was released in 1904, the year her own account of events was published.

She lived to the age of 79, dying in the United States in 1941. But the case had aroused great controversy (*Solicitors Journal* 133, 34, 1069) and pressure to reform the law grew. Florence had been unable to give sworn evidence on her own behalf. Nor had she

137

been permitted to appeal against the guilty verdict. The Civil
Evidence Act 1898 and the Court of Criminal Appeal Act 1907
filled in these gaps in legal proceedings.

Mercuric Chloride

Mercury, a metallic element, is usually found combined with
sulphur in the form of cinnabar (red mercuric sulphide) or in its
metallic form as quicksilver. Mined in countries where volcanoes
have been active, mercury is extracted in Italy, Spain, Mexico and
elsewhere. While cinnabar and quicksilver are two naturally
occurring forms, many other compounds of mercury exist,
mercuric chloride being an inorganic salt.

Named after the Roman God, Mercury has been mined as
quicksilver or cinnabar for thousands of years. It was known in
Egypt certainly before 1550 BC. The distillation apparatus used to
extract quicksilver is described by the Greek physician Dioscorides
and by the naturalist Pliny the Elder.

Mercury and its salts were used medically by the ancients in
China and India. In the west, however, possible therapeutic uses
were not explored until the sixteenth century. Then, Paracelsus,
the travelling doctor, drew attention to the use of mercury as a
treatment for syphilis. Attitudes went to the opposite extreme
after this and the substance came to be regarded as a cure-all, even
though its poisonous qualities were also appreciated.

Mercury and chalk ('grey powder') or mercurous chloride
(calomel) has been used as a laxative particularly for children.
Mercuric oxide was an antiseptic and cinnabar was a treatment for
syphilis. Mercury has even been used as teething powder! Its use in
fur processing and hat manufacture in the past led to the
expression 'mad as a hatter' because of the effect it had on the
mental state of workers. Barometers, thermometers, mirrors, tilt
security switches and dental amalgams are among other uses of
mercury.

Mercuric chloride has itself had several uses in the past. As an
antibacterial agent, it acted on bacteria because the mercuric ion
in its structure forms insoluble complexes with proteins and
precipitates them so killing the bacteria. It also had a fashion as an
agent of abortion where it was causing fatalities reported as late as
1934. In 1951 it was introduced as an anti-cancer agent in the
bowel. But in 1979 a patient died following irrigation of the
abdominal cavity and it is believed mercuric chloride is no longer

used for this purpose.

Taken by mouth, about two grammes of mercuric chloride can be lethal while taken intravenously only ninety-seven milligrams could kill. In cases of homicide the chosen method of administration has been by mouth, where its corrosive action causes the mouth and throat to become pale and very painful. (Its metallic taste needs to be disguised). The victim salivates freely, may vomit after about fifteen minutes and experiences abdominal pain, diarrhoea and cramp in the limbs. Mercuric chloride is excreted by the kidneys where it causes damage, by the salivary glands where it causes irritation and excessive salivation and by the large bowel where it may cause ulceration. After twenty-four hours ulcers may form on the gums and teeth may loosen. If the dose is sufficiently large it causes shock and death.

Treatments for mercuric chloride poisoning are Dimercaprol (British Anti-Lewisite).

Merrifield, Louisa

Strains of 'Abide With Me' rose from the Salvation Army band playing outside the bungalow in Blackpool, Lancashire, England. Inside, the police were searching for phosphorus poison.

Louisa Merrifield, who had requested the melody, was staying in the bungalow with her 71-year-old husband Alfred. The 46-year-old woman had been married twice before and with her third husband Alfred had held a succession of domestic jobs. She had also served a prison sentence for fraud involving ration books which after the Second World War were an aid to the equitable distribution of food.

They had moved into the bungalow on 12 March 1953 as companions and housekeepers to the owner elderly Mrs Sarah Ann Ricketts. On 9 April, Louisa summoned a doctor. She asked him to ensure that Mrs Ricketts was in a fit condition to write a new will. On the 14th of that same month, the old woman died. When an autopsy showed that death had been caused by phosphorus poisoning, the police searched the bungalow but found no poison. The Merrifields stood trial for murder in July 1953.

Prosecuting counsel argued that Mrs Ricketts had died after being given rat poison containing phosphorus.

Witnesses testified that Louisa Merrifield had somewhat

anticipated Mrs Ricketts' death by telling people while the old woman was still alive that her employer had died and left her the bungalow. When police asked Louisa who it was who had died, she intimated that Mrs Ricketts was not yet dead but soon would be.

Louisa was found guilty and hanged at Strangeways Prison, Manchester on 18 September 1953. But the jury could not reach a verdict on Alfred who was eventually released and inherited a half share in Mrs Ricketts' bungalow. He died in 1962 aged 80.

Methylphenobarbitone

Methylphenobarbitone, a barbiturate, is a white crystalline powder. While tasteless and odourless, it is practically insoluble in water. Taken in tablet form, it is an anticonvulsant used in the treatment of epilepsy and has been used to treat chronic alcoholism.

In toxic doses, methylphenobarbitone causes respiratory depression and the heartbeat becomes weak. The body loses heat, and coma ensues. Death is caused by paralysis of the respiratory centre of the brainstem.

The treatment for methylphenobarbitone poisoning includes artificial respiration and oxygen to maintain respiration and washing out the stomach with warm water.

Monahan, Annie

Jennie McNamee was 17-years-old when she died of tuberculosis on the morning of 7 March 1913. Of Irish stock, she was orphaned along with four brothers and the younger children were given homes with the mother's sisters. Jennie stayed with her aunt Annie Monahan at 43 Bassett Street, New Haven, Connecticut. At 15, Jennie took a job as a filing clerk and soon afterwards took out an insurance policy of $500 which would benefit her aunt if Jennie died. Annie helped the young girl complete the form on which they declared that there was no history of tuberculosis in the family.

By approaching several companies, Annie acquired insurance cover totalling $2,000 on Jennie's life of which $1,593 would directly benefit Annie herself. But when the aunt approached yet another insurance company and falsely claimed on the form that she had not taken out insurance elsewhere, the lie was discovered. Insurance companies involved investigated further and established that Jennie's father, mother and sister had all died of tuberculosis. Refusing any further insurance, the companies also tried to cancel the existing policies.

When Jennie died in 1913, the insurers looked into matters even more fully and unearthed some odd facts. One doctor who had attended the sick girl once or twice was surprised at her death for he had not thought when he visited that she was seriously ill. Another physician, Dr Isaac Porter was suspicious of the death but had finally diagnosed the cause as neuritis and heart disease, saying nothing about tuberculosis. Also, while Jennie was ill, her younger brother Frank was sent to get some arsenical rat poison.

Police investigating Annie's past unearthed further disquieting facts. Her first husband Joseph Pallman had died of 'dropsy and pneumonia' on 20 November 1906 and a small ($400) life insurance policy had benefited Annie. On 3 June 1908, Annie married Joseph Monahan, a labourer and mechanic who subsequently died on 14 November 1909 of 'gastritis'. Having just left the house after a visit to Joseph the doctor was called back. Joseph was dead, which surprised the doctor as only minutes before he had noticed no dangerous indications. Annie explained that immediately after the doctor had closed the door, Joseph had taken a swig of whisky which 'finished him'. Life insurance was again quite small at $500 but the doctor was concerned and suspected arsenic poisoning. When he came to the decision that Joseph's body should undergo an autopsy, however, the doctor discovered that the corpse had been embalmed and that the fluid used contained arsenic, as was traditional at that time. Insurance companies considered requesting an exhumation of Monahan and Pallman but were dissuaded because of the arsenical embalming fluid.

Only a month after Joseph Monahan's death, Annie married his brother John. By the time Jennie died, embalming fluid containing arsenic was forbidden in case it concealed poisoning, so in late June 1913, her body was exhumed from St Lawrence Cemetery. Dr M. Scarborough the city medical examiner conducted the autopsy and viscera were sent to Yale for chemical analysis. Sufficient arsenic being discovered in the body to kill three men, the coroner issued a warrant and next morning Mrs Monahan was taken to the county jail and held without bail. She was, however, released with no further legal proceedings except the coroner's findings.

Annie returned to her third husband John, a 34-year-old

mechanic at a hardware factory in New Haven. At his wife's instigation, John had taken out insurance on his life of $400. From Bassett Street, the couple moved to 137 James Street where John became ill in October 1916 suffering inflammation of the alimentary tract, weakness in the legs and kidney problems. Fortunately the doctor originally called in sought advice from a colleague who knew of Annie's earlier jail sentence in connection with suspected arsenic poisoning. Their suspicions aroused, the doctors sought a third opinion, then a fourth.

All this took from October 1916 until the Spring of 1917 when John was transferred to New Haven Hospital where physicians kept all the patients' bodily excretions for analysis. On 12 June, John died and the next day Annie was arrested, charged with poisoning him with arsenic and imprisoned. Prosecution evidence at the trial which opened in January 1919 before Judge Webb, highlighted the circumstantial evidence. Annie had purchased arsenic as rat poison during John's illness; a phial of medicine which doctors found in Annie's home had been dosed with arsenic, autopsy indicated death by corrosive poison and the symptoms of John's illness described by doctors were those expected in arsenic poisoning. Found guilty by the jury on 13 February 1919, Annie was sentenced to life imprisonment.

Moreau, Pierre-Désiré

As Madame Moreau suffering persistent vomiting lay dying, she said that she suspected that she was being poisoned by her husband, Pierre. Pierre Moreau was a 32-year-old pharmacist who ran a herbalist store in Paris. He had been married before but the first Madame Moreau had died three years after taking Pierre as her husband. In her brief final illness it had been Pierre who had treated her for the severe vomiting which afflicted her. But whereas Pierre's first wife had been far from financially well off, the second Madame Moreau had money. On marrying her, Pierre had received half her dowry and only on her death would he come into all her property.

The body of the second Madame Moreau was exhumed and found to contain excessive amounts of copper. The body of Pierre's first wife was also exhumed and also found to contain copper.

Pierre Moreau stood trial for murder. The motive of financial gain was clear. A book on pharmacy owned by Moreau was exhibited at the trial, marked at a passage on copper sulphate. A large crowd witnessed the end of Pierre Moreau in Paris on 14 October 1874 when Madame Guillotine had the final word.

Morphine

Morphine or morphia is an alkaloid derived from opium (q.v.). Until 1803 crude opium was used in medicine. Then Friedrich Sertürner isolated its main active ingredient testing the various components on animals and later on humans. Noting that, among other effects the principal ingredient caused cerebral depression, Sertürner called it morphine after Morpheus the Roman god of sleep and dreams.

Morphine was initially administered by doctors as a pain-killer. But it became perhaps too popular and doctors tended to use it rather liberally. Some patients became dependent on the drug.

In 1848, the invention of the syringe offered a safe way for doctors to prescribe morphine, or so it was thought. The belief was that, if morphine was not swallowed but was injected directly into the body, dependence would be avoided. What was not known was that the drug is even more potent when injected. Problems of addiction which resulted were further extended because morphine was freely available to the public. In the twentieth century morphine came to be used medically where opium had been used previously, mainly to ease pain.

Medically morphine is used among other things as an easer of pain and to control coughs or diarrhoea. It induces euphoria in the dying and eases anxiety in such conditions as shock or heart failure.

Morphine is absorbed well from the alimentary tract, except the mouth. It is not absorbed through unbroken skin. If it is important to speed up absorption morphine may be injected under the skin. The substance is detoxicated in the liver and excreted in urine.

Essentially, morphine is a cerebral depressant. It dampens down certain aspects of the CNS giving rise to an inability to concentrate, general lethargy and sleep. It depresses respiration and the cough reflex. At the same time the drug stimulates other aspects of the CNS, causing vomiting and causes the pupils of the eyes to contract. The central respiratory depression leading to respiratory depression can cause coma and death.

Euphoria is experienced and physical and psychological

addiction may develop. Withdrawal symptoms from morphine include muscle spasms noticeable particularly in the limbs and which gave rise to the expression 'kicking the habit'. Morphine also stimulates smooth muscle paradoxically causing constipation because the intestine contracts.

Drugs to try to prevent respiratory failure are used in treating morphine poisoning.

Motives for Poison Murder

While the motives for killing by poison cover the same spectrum as motives for killing by many other means, they offer an interesting side light on the cases.

Particularly noticeable is the number of cases where the motive was to dispose of a spouse. Sometimes this is to escape tyranny and perhaps to have the freedom to enjoy a general sexual freedom as in the case of Major Herbert Armstrong who soon after the death of his wife took a philandering holiday. In other cases, there is a lover waiting in the wings when the murderer is free of the existing marriage bonds.

It may have been part of Charlotte Bryant's motive for killing her husband to be able to spend more time with her gypsy lover, even though he already had a traveller wife. Edith Carew, Maria Groesbeek and Kitty Ogilvy all murdered their respective husbands so as to be with lovers. Florence Maybrick may have killed her husband for the same reason although it was clear that her lover would not stand by her. In addition, she was also unhappy with her hypochondriac spouse. Similarly, Dr Philip Cross, Dr William King and Marcus Marymont all killed their wives with a view to seeing more of a mistress. Dr Edward Pritchard (who also killed his mother-in-law) dispatched his wife for the same reason, as did Dr Crippen who then tried to flee with his lover dressed as a boy.

Among other husband killers are Susan Barber, Marie de Brinvilliers (who also murdered other relatives and was partly motivated by greed), Marie Lafarge, Ethel Major and Eva Rablen. Wife poisoners include Edward Black, Brian Burdett and Dr Robert Buchanan who actually killed his second wife so he could gain financially and remarry his first wife. Carlysle Harris tired of his young clandestine wife and murdered her, and Dr Carl Coppolino killed his wife with succinylcholine chloride.

Mason (Mason, J.K., 1983) suggests that the incidence of

poison murder to dispose of a spouse has declined as legislation and public attitudes have made divorce and separation easy. Poison murder as a last resort is in this respect unnecessary. Other reasons for the general decline in poison murders are legal restrictions on the sale and purchase of poisons and the development of organized medical professions to whom potentially poisonous drugs are channelled. Improved forensic tests to detect poisons at the scene of crime or as part of autopsy procedure have also played an important part. But Mason's hypothesis seems sound where murder has been a way of escape from an unbearable relationship. Not all spouse murders, however, hinged on this sort of escape.

Monetary gain played a part in some spouse murders, notably in the murders by Eugène Chantrelle and by Dr Robert Clements and the killings by Daisy de Melker who murdered two husbands and a son. Johann Hoch who married several times, killed each spouse for monetary gain. Martha Marek who killed her husband, also dispatched a daughter and another relative, inspired at least when she killed Susanne Lowenstein by financial gain. Pierre Moreau also killed his wife with the prospect of money before him. Mary Cotton is said to have committed some fourteen murders, some in order to profit monetarily, others to clear the way for another marriage.

Greed was a motive for murders other than spouse murders, notably in the case of Frederick Seddon, the insurance agent who was hanged for the murder of his lodger. It has even been said that Seddon's blatant lust for money that came across in the witness box was what sealed his fate rather than the trial evidence. Lawyer Albert Patrick administered chloroform and mercury to his employer to benefit financially from the death. Dr William Palmer murdered a racing companion so as to acquire his friend's gambling winnings. The bogus Count de Lacy (O'Brien) killed his brother-in-law from greed. Louisa Merrifield, Louisa Taylor and Dorothea Waddingham were similarly motivated. Nurse Amy Archer-Gilligan killed five of her patients to make money while Dr Pierre Bougrat injected a patient with a fatal dose of cyanide to rob him. Having come across a problem when trying to claim on a will he had forged, Richard Brinkley tried to poison an acquaintance who had unknowingly signed as a witness to the will (thinking he was signing for a seaside trip). He only succeeded in killing the acquaintance's landlord and landlady who drank the poison stout intended for their lodger.

Dr de la Pommerais dosed his mother-in-law and his mistress

with digitalis and Captain Donellan dispatched his brother-in-law. Both murderers were out to benefit financially. Dr Edme Castaing poisoned a friend and partner in crime so as to gain from the friend's will and insurance dealer Henri Girard stood to gain from insurance on a fellow broker and on a widow both of whom he murdered. Money was the motivator when Reginald Hinks gassed his father-in-law with carbon monoxide, when Dr George Lamson poisoned his brother-in-law, and when Comte Hippolyte De Bocarme murdered his brother-in-law with nicotine (although in the latter instance the financial gain was small).

While profit from theft was part of the motive for Hélène Jegado to get rid of fellow housemaids with arsenic, jealousy was also a strong factor. Jealousy was also the major emotion which led Adolph Hofrichter to poison fellow soldiers promoted above him.

Complicated relationships were behind several murders. Frances Howard, the Countess of Somerset, plotted the murder of King James's secretary because he was against her marrying her courtier lover. Using strychnine, Jean Vaquier ended the life of his lover's husband so he could take over the husband's role. John Tawell administered prussic acid to a mistress because he was worried that another woman whom he hoped to marry would find out about her. Cordelia Botkin became the lover of a married man who later left his wife. Trying to ensure that the wife did not pose a further threat, Cordelia sent poisoned chocolates through the post to kill her.

Perhaps one of the oddest justifications for poison murder and complex relationships was that of Arthur Deveureux who killed his wife and son so he could better care for the remaining son, his favourite. Another is the murder by Mary Blandy of her father because he objected to her choice of fiancé.

Clear sexual or sadistic motives arise but are comparatively rare. Dr Etienne Deschamps chloroformed a girl of twelve with whom he had regularly been having sexual intercourse and she died. He claimed that the death was accidental but a jury decided that he had murdered the child to prevent her talking about Etienne's sexual practices with her. George Chapman appears to have been motivated primarily by sadism as does Graham Young. While claiming to be motivated by a desire to end suffering by mercy killing, Arnfinn Nesset seems to have been driven by sadistic impulses into killing the patients at a nursing-home he was managing. While poisoning was only one mode of murder alleged in the Werner Boost case, the motivation was thought to be sexual sadism.

Nagyrev Murders

In 1929, a medical student, called to examine the body of an apparent suicide washed up by the River Tisza near Nagyrev in Hungary, discovered that the cadaver contained a large amount of arsenic in the stomach. The police were informed just at a time when they were suspicious of two deaths which had recently occurred in the district. Josef Nadarasz and Michael Szabo had died mysteriously and their bodies were now exhumed revealing that both corpses contained arsenic.

Police enquiries indicated that a local midwife, Susanne Fazekas had been supplying poison over a period of twenty years to women who wanted to get rid of husbands or brothers. Nine women claimed to have obtained poison from Susanne, but before police could arrest her, the midwife committed suicide. In her cottage piles of fly papers were found from which it appeared Susanne extracted the arsenic to sell to her clients.

Exhumations of fifty 'suspect' bodies were conducted in Nagyrev Cemetery and police were posted there night and day as women tried to remove incriminating evidence or attempted to deface the tombstones so the deceased could not be identified. Arsenic was detected in forty-four bodies and in most of these, the poison was present in large quantities. In one case it was reported that a bottle of arsenic solution was found in the coffin itself.

Arrests of women aged from twenty to seventy years old followed and fifty-three were sent for trial in three batches. In most instances, the motive was to be rid of an old husband to take on a new or to benefit financially from the death. Held at Szolnok, the first batch of trials beginning on 13 December 1929, involved thirty prisoners all of whom were imprisoned for life except one who was sentenced to death. A typical case was that of Holyba who claimed that a friend had advised her to approach Susanne Fazekas the midwife for 'medicine' to dispatch Holyba's husband. His death had been achieved by lacing his coffee with poison.

A second batch of prisoners began trial on 17 January 1930 and included among them was a certain Maria Szendi, who admitted to conniving in the deaths of her son and husband. Having bought arsenic from Susanne Fazekas, she killed her 23-year-old son

Hardor by poisoning his supper apparently because she disliked him drinking and playing cards. Next, in collaboration with Susanne, Maria set about poisoning her husband with arsenic first dosing his brandy, then mixing the substance with his soup and finally poisoning his food. Maria was condemned to death.

On 7 February 1930, the trials of the third and final batch of prisoners got under way. Maria Varga, aged 41, was charged with poisoning her husband (who had been blinded in the war), her lover Michael Ambrus, and his grandfather. Although she claimed that the fatal dose was administered in each case by Susanne Fazekas, Maria was found guilty of the murder of her husband and sentenced to hard labour for life although she was acquitted on the other charges. Another defendant, Maria Kardos was found guilty of the murder of her second husband and her eldest son Sandor and sentenced to death.

As well as the deaths by poisoning and the sentences of death passed on some of the prisoners, five of the women who were originally arrested committed suicide before the trials took place.

Nesset, Arnfinn

Arnfinn Nesset was born illegitimate and reared in an isolated country community in Norway. In 1977 he became manager of the Orkdal Valley Nursing Home for old people. He was not a happy man, feeling rejected and suffering acute feelings of inferiority. Over the following three years after his appointment, an unusually high number of old people in the home died, thirty in all.

Then routine police enquiries revealed an odd circumstance. In Nesset's office large quantities of curacit were found which the manager claimed was to put down his dog. But the amounts were a great deal more than would be necessary and rather more to the point, Nesset had no dog.

Arrested in March 1981, Nesset confessed to killing twenty-seven of the old people in his care but subsequently withdrew the admission. At his trial for murder at Trondheim in October 1982 at which Nesset pleaded not guilty the defence case was that Nesset had been carrying out euthanasia on his patients. The use of curacit for this would have been quite inappropriate, however, because of the painful death it incurs. Nesset may have enjoyed a feeling of power over the old people and this may have led to him taking their life as though he knew best.

Gain may have been another motive for the killings. It was

shown that he embezzled small amounts of money from his patients but it appeared he intended this to be used for charitable purposes and missionary work. Nesset himself is supposed to have given various 'reasons' for the killings: mercy killing; pleasure; a morbid desire to kill; schizophrenia and self-assertion.

The jury found Nesset guilty on twenty-one charges of murder and he was sentenced to twenty-one years imprisonment, the maximum term allowed under Norwegian law.

Nicotine

Nicotine is an alkaloid derived from the tobacco plant (*Nicotiana tabacum*). The oily liquid which is pale yellow to clear in colour is named after Nicot who introduced tobacco to France.

Nicotine is used in the form of a vapour or spray as a horticultural insecticide. It is readily absorbed through the gastro-intestinal tract if swallowed. If it passes through the skin surface or is injected subcutaneously, its absorption is slower. It is in part destroyed by the body and in part excreted in urine and sweat.

A fatal dose for an adult is between 40 and 60 mg. Acute poisoning and death may take place within minutes (Goodman & Gilman, 1980).

Nicotine at first stimulates then paralyses all autonomic ganglia, that is, it effects clusters of nerve cells in that aspect of the nervous system which regulates the involuntary action of some internal organs. It also effects the CNS; small doses encouraging respiration, but large doses causing convulsions and arresting the muscles of respiration. Heart failure and death result.

Symptoms of nicotine poisoning emerge clearly from its action and include vomiting, convulsions, paralysis and eventually death.

In treating nicotine poisoning, activated charcoal may be used to absorb the nicotine. Artificial respiration perhaps supplemented by intravenous stimulants to counteract respiratory depression may be employed.

Nitric Acid

Nitric acid is a fuming liquid which is either colourless or nearly so. In the past, it has been used to get rid of warts because of its strong corrosive action. Very dilute nitric acid has been used in mixtures with vegetable bitters and also as an astringent for certain forms of diarrhoea. Weaker solutions applied to the skin surface have been employed to ease itching in pruritic skin conditions.

Almost immediately the acid is swallowed intense pain occurs and vomiting. Often having the appearance of coffee grounds, the vomit contains blood from which water has been lost, bits of mucus and remnants of food. Substances gather in the mouth: pieces of tissue and foaming mucus which is white or bloodstained and later becomes yellow or brown.

A powerful oxidizing agent, nitric acid reacts with organic matter, that is protein, to form trinitrophenol. Nitrogen monoxide is given off and organic matter is turned yellow, hence the discolouration of tissues and sometimes clothes. As gas is liberated, the abdomen becomes distended and the sufferer eructates (belches) to release some of the gas. Collapse follows and suffocation may be caused by the irritant fumes. A lethal dose is about 30 ml. although patients have recovered after 60 ml.

A treatment of nitric acid poisoning comprises about four tablespoons of magnesium (or calcium) hydroxide to neutralize the acid, followed by demulcents such as white of egg.

O'Brien, Patrick

When Irishman Patrick O'Brien resolved to murder his brother-in-law, Captain Buturlin, it was the culmination of a thoroughly deceitful phase of O'Brien's life. He had previously dropped out of a Russian school then married a woman who was already married but who agreed to divorce her first husband. Having spent the woman's money, O'Brien divorced her just at the time she was divorcing her first husband.

Having left Ireland for Vilna in 1905, he claimed lineal descent from ancient Irish kings and posed as Count de Lacy a wealthy Polish nobleman. A favourite at the residence of the rich General Buturlin, O'Brien became attracted by the daughter's generous dowry and married her.

Moving to Petrograd with his new wife, 'Count de Lacy' became well liked at the Tzarist court. Eager to replenish the money he was rapidly depleting, he hit on the plan of killing his brother-in-law, Captain Buturlin. By the Captain's death, de Lacy's wife would inherit more wealth which would then fall into his own hands. When the Captain visited Petrograd, de Lacy approached Dr Panchenko, who worked at the laboratory of Plague Cultures, and bribed from him some cholera endotoxin. Panchenko's mistress Madame Muravieva hovered in the background.

At a meal with the Captain, de Lacy fed him with bread and butter which had been spread with the deadly micro-organism. What de Lacy had not calculated was that the young officer had taken the precaution of being inoculated against cholera which was rampant at that time in Petrograd. Consequently he was quite unaffected by the poison sandwiches. (Also such a method of administering poisonous micro-organisms is not very effective.)

Next, de Lacy suggested that he, his wife and the Captain should all receive cholera inoculations – in the Captain's case a 'booster' inoculation. Dr Panchenko was to administer these but de Lacy arranged with the doctor that he and his wife would receive a harmless injection while the Captain should be given diphtheria bacteria. Panchenko obtained the bacteria from the Zabolotny Institute of Experimental Medicine in Kronstadt and administered to the Captain one, possibly two phials each of thirty to forty cubic centimetres. As a result, after suffering nose bleeds, vomiting and sharp pains, Captain Buturlin died in agony.

Old General Buturlin arrived from Vilna before the funeral and demanded an autopsy which only indicated the cause of death as blood poisoning. But Madame Muravieva, Panchenko's mistress, confided to another of her lovers, Petropavlovski, that she was suspicious about de Lacy's visits to the doctor. Petropavlovski in turn informed the police.

Panchenko was charged with the murder of Captain Buturlin although the evidence was circumstantial and hearsay. Panic stricken, he told the whole story and as a result de Lacy was arrested on a murder charge. Standing trial in Petrograd in January 1911, Panchenko entered a guilty plea and received a fifteen-year prison sentence while de Lacy pleaded not guilty but was convicted and sentenced to a life of penal servitude.

Occupations of Poisoners

Members of the medical and related professions figure largely in the ranks of poisoners. Doctors, nurses, managers of nursing homes, dentists, chemists and their assistants, medical students – all these occupations have produced poisoners.

Doctors can put themselves into a position to murder and possibly make detection difficult. (Simpson, K., 1978) The doctor has access to potentially poisonous drugs as well as a knowledge of the symptoms of poisoning and how such symptoms might pass as disease or illness. Dr Henry Clark and Augusta Fulham used this knowledge to try to pass off their victim's death from arsenic poisoning as heat stroke.

Both doctors and nurses are society's interpreters of symptoms and preside over periods of deterioration and death. Particularly in such periods, drugs used to ease pain can be abused to kill. Nurse Dorothea Waddingham killed patients with overdoses of morphine which was kept to relieve pain, and even claimed to have done so on doctors' instructions.

Assessing cause of death and completing the death certificate is part of a doctor's duties and this too can be abused. So when Dr Philip Cross killed his wife with arsenic, he got a young inexperienced doctor to concur with his own diagnosis of typhoid.

The victim of poison murder by doctors is often the wife. To this end Dr Carl Coppolino, an anaesthetologist, used an injection of succinylcholine chloride. Dr William King employed arsenic, and medical student, Carlysle Harris used morphine. Dr Robert Buchanan even murdered his second spouse using morphine in order to remarry his first wife. Dentist and germ researcher Dr Arthur Waite turned to arsenic while pharmacist Pierre Moreau employed copper.

It is difficult to estimate how many 'medical' poisonings might have escaped detection. But certainly some doctors have been brought to justice by blatant mistakes. Crippen foolishly lied about his wife's disappearance, allowed his mistress to flaunt the deceased's jewellery and, disguising his lover as a boy, tried to flee with her to America. Thomas Cream drew attention to himself by publishing letters and circulars and complaining to Sergeant McIntyre of Scotland Yard about the poisoning of prostitutes by strychnine for which he, Cream, was responsible. Attempts by George Lamson to distract attention from the murder of his brother-in-law with poison cake were pure pantomime and attracted more suspicion than they averted.

If wives have often been victims of poisoning by doctors, so have mistresses. Prussic acid mixed in to a bottle of stout was used by chemist and businessman John Tawell to get rid of his mistress. In order to gain financially, Dr de la Pommerais poisoned not only his mistress but his brother-in-law too.

Morphine is commonly used in medical murders. Dr Edme Castaing poisoned his partner in crime and chemist's assistant Arthur Devereux killed his wife, their twin children and himself using morphine. Suspicion fell on Dr Robert Clements when it was discovered that he had prescribed morphine for a patient but had not administered it. Also Carlysle Harris the medical student and Nurse Dorothea Waddingham employed the drug.

Antimony was used by Dr William Palmer to murder a fellow horse-racing enthusiast so he could acquire his companion's winnings and by Dr Pritchard to get rid of his wife and mother-in-law (Pritchard also used aconite).

Ex-nurse Mary Cotton committed a series of arsenic poisonings either to clear the way for marriage or to make money from the death while Amy Archer-Gilligan killed patients in her nursing home with arsenical rat poison. Among the strangest cases in the catalogue of medical poison murders are those of dentist Dr Etienne Deschamps and Dr Pierre Bougrat. Etienne killed a 12-year-old girl with chloroform having previously on several occasions had sex with her while convincing her gullible father he was using the child as a spirit medium. Bougrat injected a patient with cyanide in order to rob him then tried hiding the body in a surgery cupboard where the smell of decomposition became so strong it aroused suspicion.

Arthur Ford, the general manager of the office of a wholesale and manufacturing chemist stole cantharides from the stores and administered it to girls in the office hoping to sexually excite one of them but succeeding in killing two of the girls.

Members of the nobility occasionally figure in poison cases, the most famous examples being Frances Howard, the Countess of Somerset convicted of poisoning King James I's secretary; and Comte Hippolyte De Bocarme who despatched his brother-in-law with nicotine. O'Brien posed as the Count de Lacy and murdered with diphtheria bacteria.

The legal profession are represented by the case of Major Armstrong in England and by Albert Patrick in the United States.

Members of the armed forces who have poisoned include Marcus Marymont of the US Air Force and Adolph Hofrichter of the Austrian Army. John Donellan who switched his brother-in-law's medicine for cherry laurel water had been a captain.

Where poisoners were employed as sales people, or specifically as insurance agents, the motive for killing is sometimes financial. Henri Girard murdered a fellow insurance broker and a widow to make money from their deaths. A similar motive drove Hoover salesman Reginald Hinks to gas his father-in-law; and insurance agent Frederick Seddon to poison his lodger with arsenic. Insurance salesman Edward Black, however, seems to have been mainly motivated by a desire to be rid of his wife.

Domestic servants have resorted to poison murder, notably housemaid Hélène Jegado who killed other housemaids from motives of jealousy and theft. Also Anna Schönleben took domestic posts in various parts of Germany, murdering her employers. Housekeeper Louisa Merrifield ended her employer's life with phosphorus, Catherine Wilson used colchicum seeds and chauffeur William Waite dispatched his wife with arsenic.

Graham Young may have benefited from his role as general factotum in a photographic instruments factory. While Young was poisoning his workmates with thallium, their symptoms were put down to possible chemical contamination or a 'bug' in the factory.

Mary Bateman's practice as a fortune teller enabled her to work her way into a victim's confidence, overawe them with her supposed powers and find out a great deal about their personal circumstances. All this made it easier for her to plan and carry out her poisonings, the murder of Mrs Perigo and the attempted murder of Mr Perigo being an example of this.

Murderers in the hospitality business include pub landlord George Chapman and hotel worker Jean Vaquier.

Other occupations represented in a poisoners' catalogue include a teacher of French (Eugène Chantrelle), packing-house worker (Johann Hoch), artist (Sadamichi Hirasawa), secretary (Marie Hilley) and a milliner (Louisa Taylor).

Ogilvy, Kitty

In a run-down four-roomed house in Eastmiln, Forfar, Scotland in February 1765, a strange cluster of people were drawn together in a situation which was to end in murder.

Among these were a newly married couple Thomas and Kitty Ogilvy. Thomas was middle-aged and far from wealthy. His new bride, born Katherine Nairn was nineteen years old and the daughter of a knight. While unequal in age and social status, they appeared to be in love.

Anne Clarke, Thomas Ogilvy's cousin also lived in the house. She was the lover of Thomas's youngest brother Alexander who was away studying medicine. Alexander was a spendthrift and womanizer and his family were becoming impatient with his reckless ways. He had sent Anne Clarke into the household to help pave the way for a better relationship with his family.

Thomas Ogilvy's mother and his younger brother Patrick (a lieutenant) completed the family circle living in the house. (There were also three servants.)

Kitty Ogilvy and Patrick developed a deep attraction for each other although there is no evidence of a sexual relationship between them. Nevertheless they were indiscreet in their displays of affection. Anne Clarke and Mrs Ogilvy (Thomas's mother) did not like Kitty anyway and Anne Clarke lost no time in spreading rumours that Kitty and Patrick were lovers. Mrs Ogilvy colluded in the suspicion.

In March 1765 Thomas had a heated argument with Patrick over Kitty and the atmosphere in the house must have been fraught with undercurrents of suspicion and resentment.

Kitty wrote Patrick a letter and in it reminded him that she had asked him to perform a service for her. Soon afterwards, Patrick visited Brechin and bought laudanum and arsenic which were delivered to Kitty by Andrew Stewart, a brother-in-law. Kitty talked freely to Andrew Stewart about her unhappiness and the deterioration of her relationship with her husband. Stewart was not slow to read between the lines and that same evening told Mrs Ogilvy (Thomas's mother) that he thought Kitty was planning to poison Thomas with arsenic. Surprisingly, they did nothing.

Next day Thomas Ogilvy fell ill and the tea which Kitty solicitously gave him only made him worse. Thomas voiced his belief that his wife was murdering him but he was failing fast and on 6 June 1765, he breathed his last. At this point the profligate younger brother Alexander made an appearance and ordered the funeral to be stopped because Thomas had been murdered. Kitty and Patrick were arrested and charged with murder (and also incest).

The trial took place in Edinburgh and both were found guilty. Patrick was executed in September 1765 but Kitty's death sentence was postponed until March the following year because she was pregnant. This would allow time for the baby innocent of any crime to be born and taken away from the mother before she met her end.

Incarcerated at Tolbooth Jail, Kitty disguised herself as a midwife and escaped. Changing into an officer's uniform she fled by coach to Berwick and from there made it to London. There she chartered a boat to Calais where she arrived safely and was never heard of again.

Opium

Opium, a Greek word for juice, is an extract of the poppy *Papaver somniferum*, Somnus being the Roman god of sleep. The milky juice is tapped from the unripe head of the plant and dries into a brownish elastic substance. This is scraped off and collected as raw opium. It contains many alkaloids, principally morphine (about 10%) but also codeine, narcotine and others.

One of a collection of medical papyri, the Ebers papyrus of 1550 BC mentions poppy opium which the ancient Egyptians mixed with pepper and fragrant spices in wine. The plant in fact originated in Turkey.

In AD 900 Arabs introduced opium to various countries including India where Bengal was to later become the world's greatest producer. In the 1830s, with the British Empire reigning supreme, the East India Company turned its eyes to China as a vast potential market for opium. Chinese government resistance set against British persistence escalated into the Opium War

(1839–42). Britain prevailed and by 1940, some 20% of China's population ate or smoked opium as a soporific.

At the same time that the addictive power of opium was being abused, its medical uses continued. One compound of opium has particularly interesting connections. Dover's Powder was used in less severe cases of fever to encourage sleep and sweating. This medicine was first formulated by Dr Thomas Dover who took up general practice after an earlier career as a licensed pirate.

Captain Dover rescued Alexander Selkirk from his lonely island. (Selkirk served Daniel Defoe as the model for Robinson Crusoe). Dover's Powder cleverly combined opium with *ipecacuanha*, the dried root of a South American plant which is an emetic in strong enough doses. This meant that any accidental overdose of the opium component would be ejected from the system by the emetic.

The principal active ingredient of opium is morphine (q.v.) and the two substances are essentially similar in terms of absorption, distribution, excretion, toxicity action and symptoms. These topics are therefore covered under the entry for morphine.

Palmer, Dr William

Palmer's trial in 1856 focusing on the death of his racing companion John Cook, has been extensively written about and debated. Palmer's early life, however, is full of interest and intrigue also. Born in Rugeley, Staffordshire, in 1824, Palmer attended school up to the age of 17 when he left to work in Liverpool. There, working for a drug firm, he stole money from his employer's mail and was obliged to leave. For the next five years he was apprenticed to a medical doctor, Edward Tylecote of Hayward in Cheshire. After this he worked briefly in the Stafford Infirmary where it appears he committed his first murder. An acquaintance of Palmer, a man called Abbey, died after drinking brandy in Palmer's company and it seems Palmer may have laced the drink with strychnine.

When Palmer reached the age of 22, he studied at St Bartholemew's Hospital, London where he qualified as a doctor. Returning to the place of his birth he set up a practice. For some years Palmer had experienced money difficulties, despite inheriting £9,000 when he was twenty-one years old, and was often in debt. Betting heavily on horse racing did nothing to help his financial state.

One of Palmer's creditors, Blandon was a guest at the doctor's house when he became gravely ill. Dr Bamford, an elderly local doctor was called in but Blandon was clearly dying. Mrs Blandon had scarcely arrived at Palmer's house when her husband died. Suspecting Palmer had a hand in the death, friends advised Mrs Blandon to inform the police but she declined.

Another creditor called Bly died with Palmer owing him £800. When Bly's widow requested the money, Palmer told her that it was her husband who owed him the £800. One of Palmer's uncles died within days of a drinking contest with him.

Palmer married Annie, the illegitimate daughter of an army officer and benefited from the substantial dowry that went with her. He may have murdered four of his children, all of whom died suffering convulsions in infancy. Certainly, his mother-in-law died two weeks after staying with him, her estate passing to Palmer's wife and consequently to him.

In 1853, he insured his wife's life for £13,000 and in September that year Annie died of what was diagnosed as cholera. Next, Palmer insured the life of his brother Walter for £82,000 and Walter later died after a drinking session. The insurance company were suspicious by this time and refused to pay. Making further enquiries, they found a hotel employee who claimed to have witnessed Palmer adding some substance to Walter's drink.

At this stage, Palmer planned the murder of his companion, John Cook, which was to bring him to trial. Palmer accompanied Cook to the races at Shrewsbury on Tuesday 13 November 1855. Palmer lost money there but Cook, backing his own horse, won handsomely. The pair celebrated with a dinner and drinks at the local Raven Hotel. On Wednesday, they returned to the hotel for more drinks and in the evening were joined there by two more racing enthusiasts. Cook complained of something in his brandy that burnt his throat and that night was very ill. On Thursday, Cook had recovered somewhat and Palmer borrowed some of his friend's money to bet at the races, losing all of it.

Palmer and Cook returned to Rugeley and Cook stayed at the Talbot Arms opposite Palmer's house on Thursday evening. Next morning after Palmer rejoined him, Cook drank some coffee and became ill again. For the rest of Friday and on Saturday and Sunday, Cook lay ill in bed. On Monday 19 November, Palmer travelled to London to collect his friend's racing winnings. By the time he returned Cook seemed to be recovering a little and had dressed. Dr Palmer continued to give him doses of 'medicine', and that evening administered some pills which had a dramatic effect on the patient. Cook became so racked by convulsions that his head and heels touched. Within minutes he was dead.

Cook's stepfather was not convinced that all was well and poisoning was strongly suspected. An autopsy was carried out and Professor Alfred Swaine Taylor, the toxicologist at Guy's Hospital analysed the organs and concluded that death had been caused by the administration of antimony.

At the Coroner's Court in Rugeley, the inquest verdict was one of wilful murder against Palmer who was subsequently arrested on Friday 15 December 1855. The accused was committed to Stafford Gaol and House of Correction and citizens of Rugeley reacted so strongly against Palmer that he was transferred to London to stand trial.

Transferred to Newgate Gaol, Palmer was tried at the Old Bailey in May 1856 before Lord Chief Justice Campbell. Defence counsel led by Mr Serjeant Shee made an eight hour plea for

Palmer's innocence. But the prosecution under Attorney-General Sir Alexander Compton were able to marshal an enormous amount of circumstantial evidence and a guilty verdict was returned sentencing Palmer to death.

Public hanging being still customary, the 32-year-old Rugeley poisoner was dispatched outside Stafford Prison on 14 June 1856 before a crowd of some 30,000 after having shaken hands with the hangman.

Paraquat

Paraquat is a commercially produced contact herbicide which is extensively used in agriculture and horticulture. Gramoxone is a concentrated solution of Paraquat and Weedol is a granular preparation of Paraquat. When using Paraquat for legitimate purposes, care has to be taken to protect the eyes and skin.

The fatal dose of Gramoxone is about two teaspoonfuls taken in a single dose. Death is almost always delayed. Death in the first few days is due to liver and kidney damage. After one to three weeks respiratory damage is the usual cause. A mouthful of Paraquat could prove fatal, eventually.

Paraquat causes fibrosis of the lungs which makes breathing increasingly difficult. It burns the throat and attacks vital organs.

Pavulon

Pavulon is a muscle relaxing drug in some respects similar to succinylcholine and curare. Used as an anaesthetic it quickly paralyses the muscles and its effects also disappear quickly from the system. When the muscles controlling breathing are paralysed, artificial respiration is necessary to preserve life.

Pearson, Sarah and Black, Mrs

Sarah Pearson and Mrs Black were charged at Armagh in Ireland in June 1905 with the murder of 74-year-old Alice Pearson. The old woman's son had married Sarah, making Alice Sarah's mother-in-law. Alice's daughter had married a Mr Black, so Mrs Black was in fact Alice's daughter.

Sarah had been arrested in Montreal, Canada, where she

confessed to the murder and implicated also her husband (Alice's son) and her sister-in-law (Alice's daughter). Sarah stated that she had bought 'three pennies worth' of strychnine in Armagh and had mixed it with mashed potato and eggs given to the old woman. Old Alice had complained of the sour taste of the meal but had eaten most of it. The motive was monetary gain, for Alice had £40 and her life was insured.

Previously, Sarah Pearson and Mrs Black had tried to kill Alice with metallic mercury. They seem also to have prepared neighbours for Alice's death, encouraging their superstitious beliefs. One male witness at the trial said that Sarah had been to his house saying she had seen 'Old Alice's Ghost'. She added that her husband had dreamed that his mother Alice was going to die.

At the autopsy, 296 grains of pure metallic mercury were found in the body but, as the mercury had not acted as a poison in its metallic state, this was not the cause of death. The fatal dose was of strychnine and one seventh of a grain was found in the stomach, liver and kidneys.

Pearson and Black were both found guilty by the jury and executed in 1905.

Perez, Leonora and Narcisco, Filipina

During July and August 1975, thirty-five patients at the Ann Arbor veterans' hospital in Michigan suffered cardio-pulmonary arrest, an episode of brief muscle paralysis. Perez and Narcisco, two of the nurses were often around to give the necessary artificial respiration in order to save life. Largely due to their quick action only five patients died.

Because the hospital was on federal property, the FBI called in a forensic pathologist, Michael Baden to investigate the deaths. Four bodies were exhumed and autopsied showing nothing suspicious. When tissues were sent to the FBI crime laboratory, however, Pavulon was found. Enquiries revealed that either Perez or Narcisco had been on duty when each crisis occurred and they were put on trial and found guilty of poisoning six patients.

But there had been strong interest in the trial in the Philippines where some of the defence costs had been raised. In particular Imelda Marcos, wife of the Philippines President had taken an interest in the trial and a government observer had been sent from her country. Imelda Marcos claimed that the US had an unfair immigration policy and that Perez and Narcisco were victims of false charges aimed at deterring Filipino nurses from coming to the United States. A few months after the trial, the judge announced that on examining the record he had realized that mistakes had crept in to the procedure. He set aside the conviction and ordered a new trial which did not take place.

Dr Baden reports that he was told Imelda Marcos was threatening to be difficult about American bases in the Philippines and US national security took precedence over the Pavulon victims (Baden, M. and Hennessee, J.A., 1991).

Petiot, Dr Marcel

Petiot, was born in 1897 in Auxerre, France and his early life was punctuated by theft and involvement with drugs. Conscripted into the army in 1917, he stole drugs intended for war casualties and sold them on the black market. He qualified as a doctor in 1921, opening a practice in Villeneuve, and there he married and his wife bore a son. In 1928, he was elected mayor but after being convicted of stealing from a municipal store and imprisoned, his mayoral duties ended in 1930. In 1939, at the outbreak of the Second World War, Petiot was convicted of illicit drug dealing, and claimed to be an addict himself.

September 1941, saw the completion of some rather unusual building alterations on his house at 21 rue Leseruer close by the Etoile. A small triangular room was built with cement walls and no windows, only a little trap-door in one side. Outside, a wall was heightened so neighbours were unable to see into the courtyard at one end of which was a cellar containing lime.

Earlier in his life several people around Petiot had died or disappeared including a pregnant housekeeper and a patient, Madame Debauve. But only gossip had made of these anything more than coincidence.

In 1941, however, Petiot appears to have methodically embarked on a career of murder. He employed a small group of men to keep their ears to the ground and inform him of anyone who wished to escape German occupation and flee abroad. Then Petiot, posing as a member of the French Resistance, arranged for the victim to visit his surgery at night bringing money and possessions with them. Under the pretext of vaccinating them against some disease supposed to be prevalent in the country to which they were to escape, Petiot would give them a lethal injection. He would then take them to the triangular room where he asked them to wait. As the victims died in great suffering, he would watch them (using a periscope) through the little trap-door. A succession of people, hoping to flee to freedom were murdered in this way, Petiot's motive apparently being huge financial gain and the sadistic pleasure of watching them die.

Then in 1943, the Gestapo, suspicious of Petiot, coerced a Jew into visiting him and requesting help to escape. The Jew was never seen again and assuming Petiot to be genuinely helping escapees, the Gestapo arrested him in May 1943. He was released in December 1943, perhaps after convincing the Gestapo of the real fate of his visitors. His murders continued.

On 11 March 1944, one of Petiot's neighbours, complained to the police about the disgusting smoke issuing from the doctor's house. When the police called, they found a note on the door requesting enquiries to be redirected to 66 rue Caumartin where Petiot had an apartment and a consulting-room. The police telephoned Petiot who said he would come straight over and then they summoned the fire brigade.

When the firemen arrived and broke into the house, they traced the source of the smoke to a stove in the cellar. There they also discovered the remains of twenty-seven bodies. The police went in and then Petiot himself arrived.

A police sergeant told Petiot he would have to be put under arrest. But incredibly, Petiot convinced the sergeant that the bodies were of Nazi supporters and collaborators killed by the French Resistance. Petiot was allowed to go free. But this was a close enough shave for the doctor who returned to the rue Caumartin to collect his wife, 17-year-old son and some belongings and fled. After leaving Paris, the family headed for Auxerre where Petiot's brother had a shop. Police investigators traced Petiot to Auxerre but then the trail went cold.

Paris was liberated by the Allies in August 1944. By this time Petiot had gone into hiding staying with George Redoute, a house-painter in the rue Faubourg St Denis and saying his wife had been killed in an air raid and his house obliterated. He joined the Free French Army on 27 September.

In October, as an officer in the French Resistance, Petiot wrote to a newspaper saying that, while he had been in prison the Gestapo had deposited corpses in his house and framed him. His handwriting, checked against Resistance officers enrolled in Paris identified the author as Captain Henri Valery serving at Reuilly. 'Valery' was arrested on 2 November in Paris.

Questioned at the Quai des Orfèvres, France's Scotland Yard,

Petiot claimed that the twenty-seven bodies in his cellar were nearly all German soldiers and repeated his story that he had been working for the Resistance.

On 18 March 1946, Petiot's trial began at Seine Assize Court. Pierre Duval prosecuted while René Floriot defended. Relatives of the victims were called, and genuine Resistance workers who demolished Petiot's claim to have worked for the movement over the years. The jury retired on 4 April 1946 and after two and a half hours returned with a verdict of guilty on twenty-four of the twenty-seven murders. Petiot's appeal was turned down and on 26 May 1946, he was guillotined.

Phosphorus

A white, waxy non-metallic element, phosphorus turns yellow on exposure to light. At normal temperatures it combusts slowly taking on a luminous quality. Its name reflects this luminosity. The Greek word 'phos' means 'light' and 'phorus' means 'bringing'. From this is derived the Latin phosphorus or 'morning star'.

Red and yellow (white) phosphorus are well known, the former, used in safety matches being almost harmless. Yellow phosphorus is dangerous, however, a fatal dose being as low as 50 mg. Matchgirls in Victorian England suffered phosphorus necrosis, that is gangrene of the jaw-bone because of the phosphorus fumes involved in their trade. 'Phossy Jaw' was the slang expression for the condition in which pieces of the jaw were known to crumble off. Phosphorus has been used in rat poisons and in chemical processes.

Yellow phosphorus has an unpleasant taste and a sulphurous odour but has been administered as a poison in spirits and coffee which sufficiently disguise it. The substance is slightly soluble in water and more soluble in alcohol or organic liquids such as olive oil.

When swallowed, phosphorus is absorbed by the gastro-intestinal tract and distributed to the internal organs where it does particular damage to the liver.

The initial action of phosphorus is irritant. Later it breaks up cells in the liver and other internal organs. It is essentially a protoplasmic poison.

In acute poisoning, symptoms include a garlic smell to the breath, vomit and faeces which may glow in the dark, burning pains in the stomach, convulsions and coma. After a day or two, symptoms may appear to subside before the delayed effects of phosphorus poisoning assert themselves. These are jaundice, collapse, coma and death.

Copper sulphate has been used as a treatment for phosphorus poisoning.

Pioneer Toxicologists

Many great and infamous names form the links by which systematic knowledge developed about poisons and antidotes.

Nicander of Colophon (second century BC) was physician to Attalus, King of Pergamum, Greece. A botanist and a keen researcher, Nicander was supplied with condemned criminals by the King on which to perform experiments with poisons and antidotes.

Among the poisonous plants, minerals and animals he listed were wolf's-bane and hemlock. One of his more successful antidotes, primarily an emetic was a mixture of warm water, linseed tea and warm oil.

Latin naturalist Pliny the Elder referred to poisonous plants and animals in his text *'Historia Naturalis'*. He also discovered several antidotes against serpent and other poisons. These remedies were known as *'theriaca'*.

Pedanius Dioscorides, the Greek physician who served the Emperor Nero from AD 54–68 was the author of a classic work on medicines. In five books, he describes some 900 drugs – most of them already known to the Greeks or Egyptians. A sixth book *De Veninis* concerns poisons and antidotes.

Galen, born in Pergamon in AD 129 worked in Alexandria the centre of Greek medicine and was a physician to athletes. His 'Nut Theriac', a remedy against poisons and bites included among its ingredients figs, salt, nut and the plant *Ruta graveolens*.

An interesting similarity is found in a medicine recommended by the tenth-century Arab physician Rhazes. His antidote for snakebite was a poultice of dried nut, salt, leaves of *Ruta graveolens* and white figs.

Avicenna (AD 980–1077) the great Persian physician, wrote a Canon of Medicine which included animal, plant and mineral poisons and their antidotes.

In the twelfth century, Maimonides, personal physician to the Sultan of Egypt, researched antidotes and treatments for poisoning including snakebites. For snakebites, he recommended that the part of the body above the wound was tied off quickly to prevent the poison spreading. Just above the wound an incision was then made and someone sucked out the poison. The patient was then forced to vomit then the antidote was given. Finally, a medicine was applied to the wound to draw out the poison.

Paracelsus was the name assumed by Philip Theophrastus Bombast von Hohenheim (1493–1541). In mines and smelting works in Switzerland where he worked in his youth, he gained knowledge of chemistry and metallurgy. After studying Art (possibly in Vienna) he studied medicine in Italy. Disenchanted by what universities could offer, he began a remarkable career of travelling and learning in Europe and elsewhere that continued for most of his life.

As an itinerant doctor, Paracelsus developed a somewhat mystically flavoured personal system of medicine. His wanderings were punctuated by a year (1527–8) in which he taught in Basel but he was obliged to leave after dramatically burning the medical classics of the time. He made much use of poisons in his treatments, a practice he defended in his, *The Reply to Certain Calumniations of his Enemies*. Despite his talents, Paracelsus died in Salzburg in poverty.

Landmarks in toxicology are the two books of poisons by Jacques Grévin the French founder of modern biotoxicology. The *Deux livres des venins* were published in 1568.

It is Mathieu Joseph Bonaventura Orfila (1787–1853), however, who is considered the founder of modern toxicology. Born in Minorca, he studied at several Spanish universities before pursuing advanced studies in Paris. After adopting French nationality he became a professor of legal medicine and professor of chemistry. Following initial experiments with arsenic, he spent several years carrying out experiments which meant the death of 4,000 dogs and in 1814 produced his volume on general toxicology, *Traité des Poisons*. This became a corner-stone of experimental and forensic toxicology.

François Magendie (1783–1855) was physician at the Salpétrière and later at the Hôtel-Dieu. He made valuable contributions to physiology particularly in relation to the central nervous system.

A pioneer pharmacologist, he published papers on arrow poisons from the Upas tiente plant and the Upas antiar plant (with a student R. Delille). Used by the natives of Java and Borneo, the poison was a vegetable extract of Upas tiente belonging to the Strychnos genus. Experiments were conducted where, for example, quills of wood covered with the poison were stabbed into the thigh muscle of various animals: horses, dogs or rabbits, leading in each case to convulsions, disturbed respiration, tetanus and death. Through such methods Magendie laid the foundations of experiments to determine the site of action of poisons on the body.

Robert Christison (1797–1882) was born in Edinburgh and studied medicine there. In Paris he studied chemistry and was influenced by the toxicologist Orfila with whom he came briefly into contact. At 24, he gained the chair of medical jurisprudence in Edinburgh and ten years later moved to the professorship of materia medica and therapeutics. His *Treatise on Poisons* first published in 1829 became a standard text. His work on poisons included studies of arsenic, opium, hemlock and lead.

Louis Lewin (1850–1929), born in Prussia, studied in Berlin and Munich before specializing in pharmacology and toxicology and earning a professorship in 1894. His many works include textbooks on toxicology and a volume on arrow poisons.

Through the painstaking work of these pioneers the study of poisons and antidotes emerged from the darkness of superstition and into the light of scientific knowledge.

Plant Poisons (Phytotoxins)

Poisonous plants, or extracts from such plants which are used as poisons, have been much favoured by poisoners. Aconite was used by Dr George Lamson to poison his brother-in-law. Crippen despatched his wife with hyoscine so he could be with his mistress. Cherry laurel water was the poison chosen by Captain John Donellan to lace his brother-in-law's medicine and so gain financially from the death.

Opium was employed by Eugène Chantrelle to get rid of his wife while morphine has been used by many poisoners particularly doctors and paramedics. Among these are Dr Robert Buchanan who killed his wife to gain financially and so he could return to his first wife. Arthur Deveureux, a chemist's assistant, called on morphine to kill his wife and younger children so that his eldest son could supposedly have a better start in life. Dr Edme Castaing poisoned his 'friend' and partner in crime with morphine while Dr Robert Clements used it to rid himself of his wife. Carlysle Harris, a medical student added morphine to capsules of medicine given to his wife to help her insomnia. Dorothea Waddingham, the manager of a nursing home, killed patients for monetary gain with morphine injections.

Comte Hippolyte De Bocarme despatched his brother-in-law with nicotine and the Bulgarian Secret Police assassinated Georgi Markov, the defector using a pellet containing ricin shot from an umbrella gun. Digitalis was employed by Dr Edmond de la Pommerais when he killed his mother-in-law and his mistress.

Strychnine was used by Dr Thomas Cream to kill prostitutes, by Daisy De Melker on two husbands and a son, by Ethel Major on her lorry-driver husband, by Eva Rablen on her spouse, and by Jean Pierre Vaquier on the husband of his lover. Colchicum seeds were used by housekeeper Catherine Wilson. In addition to all these substances, which have been used in well documented criminal cases, numerous other plant poisons exist.

Perhaps the best known of these is hemlock, famed as the Athenian state poison taken by Socrates in the fifth century BC. The species consumed by the famous philosopher was called cicuta. Plato's description of his friend's death gives a clear picture of the effects of hemlock. The body gradually becomes cold and paralysis creeps from the feet upwards until the muscles controlling breathing are affected. Eventually the poison reaches the brain and death ensues.

Cicuta was given its present name hemlock by the Anglo-Saxons in the tenth century and Linnaeus provided its scientific name *Conium maculatum* in 1737. It is the seeds and leaves of hemlock which contain the highest concentration of the poison conium which has five components the most lethal being coniine. The crucial effect of coniine in hemlock poisoning was revealed by the Scottish chemist and toxicologist Robert Christison (1797–1882) who established that the action on the body of hemlock and its alkaloid coniine are identical.

Another poison surrounded by myth is abrin which comes from rosary peas (*Abrus precatorius*). These peas grow on vines in pods and are used in jewellery beads, being bright orange at one end and black at the other. When the wearer perspires, however, the abrin can be absorbed through the skin. If one bean is chewed and swallowed it is almost certain to prove fatal.

Symptoms may be delayed as long as several days when the victim loses his appetite, suffers stomach pains and delirium before finally collapsing.

Oleandrin is a poison contained in the oleander tree (*Nerium oleander*). Just one leaf of this tree can be fatal to man if chewed, causing nausea, sleepiness, irregular heart beat, unconsciousness and paralysis of the muscles controlling breathing. *Thevetin* is contained in the Yellow Oleander Tree (*Thevetia perunriana*) and acts in a similar way to digitalis poison. (Tichy, W., 1977; Thompson, C.J.S., 1931)

Large fungi (as distinct from the minute fungi classified as bacteria) are loosely called 'poisonous mushrooms'. Many contain muscarine, a poisonous alkaloid, others phallin, another toxin. Among the best known of these is the death cap (*Amanita phalloides*) which displays a yellowish-green cap, white gills and a cup at the base of its stem. Three of these mushrooms constitutes a fatal dose and in the United States, this plant is responsible for nine out of every ten deaths from mushroom poisoning. Another well-known poisonous mushroom is the Fly Agaric (*Amanita muscaria*) which has a red cap with white patches and is lethal to flies when soaked in milk (hence its name).

After consuming such mushrooms there may be no effect for up to twelve hours when vomiting, diarrhoea and stomach pains occur. In severe cases this is followed a day or two later by jaundice, circulatory problems, kidney failure and internal bleeding. Liver failure and death may follow.

Poison Definitions

Poison appears to be an easy term to define, for everyone holds common-sense notions of poison and can readily think of several examples; arsenic, cyanide, strychnine being among the first to come to mind. But once one tries to sharpen the definition and be a little more precise about what a poison is in a general sense, the concept proves extremely slippery. (Farrell, M., 1990[a])

Some substances which can be beneficial in small doses can be lethal in larger ones. Morphine is a case in point. An easer of pain and a body relaxant in small amounts, in larger doses it can kill. Indeed this principle was used by Carlysle Harris to kill his unwanted secret wife. She had been taking capsules compounded of five parts quinine and one part morphine to help insomnia and Harris replaced the quinine component with further morphine making the capsule dose fatal.

To further confuse the issue, some poisons were erroneously thought to have a tonic effect in small doses although today the claim is known to be bogus. Arsenic is no longer recommended therapeutically except that an organic form is used to treat sleeping sickness. In the nineteenth century and even into the twentieth, however, it was taken as a pick-me-up.

Substances like powdered glass are incontrovertibly harmful if swallowed but are not classed as poisons because they depend on mechanical action for their effect on the body. Boiling liquids would exert a damaging influence but may not be in themselves poisonous, so something that depends for its harmful effect on temperature comes outside the remit of a poison. Nor can a substance be rightly called a poison if its damaging influence hinges on a bodily peculiarity. Illness may bring about susceptibility to a substance which would prove harmless to the same person in robust health. Allergies may produce dramatic reactions to substances harmless to others.

Drawing on these problems it is, however, possible to go some way to clarifying the notion of poison. Firstly, a poison must be able to kill, or seriously damage the functioning of organs or tissues. Also, despite the observations about morphine being potentially beneficial in tiny doses and lethal in larger ones, we are still dealing with very small dosages even when considering lethal amounts. A teaspoonful of arsenic for instance is several times the lethal dose while ricin is deadly in minute quantities. The substance must not depend on mechanical action or temperature for its effect nor on a bodily peculiarity particular to a person.

Whereas most people immediately think of a poison as a substance taken by mouth, poisons can be injected under the skin or into the bloodstream. They can also be absorbed through the skin (Renaissance poisoners were said to dust the gloves of victims with arsenic powder). Gaseous poisons or poisons in fine powder form can be inhaled, passing from the lungs to the bloodstream.

Good definitions encapsulate most if not all these points.

Blakiston (1979) defines poison as: 'A substance that in relatively small doses, has an action, when it is ingested by, injected into, inhaled or absorbed by, or applied to a living organism, that either destroys life or impairs seriously the functions of one or more organs or tissues.'

Dorland (Dorland, W.A., 1985) gives the following definition. '... any substance which when injected, inhaled or absorbed, or when applied to, injected into, or developed within the body, in relatively small amounts, by its chemical action may cause damage to structure or disturbance of function.'

Words relating to poison or describing certain types of poison also help to indicate the breadth and complexity of the term. 'Venom', the poisonous fluid produced by certain snakes, spiders and insects, derives from the Latin word *venenum*, meaning poison. 'Virus', the poison associated with a contagious disease, has a similar derivation. Toxin, while often thought to be another word for poison, refers in fact to poisons having a natural origin. Included among such poisons are plant poisons such as ricin or aconite, animal poisons like snake or insect venom and bacterial poisons such as typhoid. Taken together this group are sometimes known as biotoxins. To further complicate the picture, the term 'toxin' is sometimes reserved for poisons secreted by a microbe and causing a particular disease.

Legal minds wisely got round the problems of definition by accepting as a poison as a substance regarded as poisonous for the purposes of the law; as indicated by lists and schedules under Poison Acts. These can be amended as necessary.

Pritchard, Dr Edward

When, in August 1865, Dr Edward Pritchard was led to the scaffold, a crowd of 100,000 jostled for a view of what was to turn out to be the last public hanging in Scotland. A pitiful and self-deluded though evil life ended that day.

Son of a Royal Navy captain, Pritchard was gazetted in 1846 as a naval assistant surgeon. Four years later, he married an attractive Scottish girl, Mary Taylor and resigned his commission to pursue a private practice in Hunmanby in Yorkshire.

While as time passed Mary was occupied raising a family of five children, Edward was raising local ill-feeling by philandering with a succession of women. Attracting further unpopularity by his incessant lying and bragging. Pritchard decided to leave Hunmanby after eight years there. He first spent a year travelling abroad as a gentleman's doctor then moved to his wife's home country.

Living at 11 Berkley Terrace in Glasgow, Pritchard began his new practice in 1860. But three years later his house was damaged by fire while he was away from home for the night and a young servant girl perished in the flames. Although death was put down to misadventure, Pritchard had to press for his claim against a suspicious insurance company.

In 1864, Mary's mother, Mrs Taylor, a formidable 70-year-old who lived in Edinburgh gave the couple money to buy a house in Sauchiehall Street, Glasgow. There he seduced a 15-year-old servant girl, Mary M'Cleod saying he would marry her if his wife died. M'Cleod became pregnant but Pritchard carried out an abortion.

In November 1864 Mary Pritchard became ill and went to stay

with her family in Edinburgh. Recovering, she returned to Glasgow where she fell ill again, and was confined to her sick bed. Pritchard diagnosed the symptoms as stomach irritation but knew the real cause, for in December 1864 and January, February and March 1865 he made purchases of Fleming's Tincture of Aconite. By February 1865, Mary was so ill with violent sickness that her mother moved into Sauchiehall Street to nurse her.

Old Mrs Taylor had barely arrived in the house, when, having eaten some tapioca pudding, she too became ill. It was later established that the food contained antimony. In the early hours of 25 February, Mrs Taylor died. Dr Patterson who was called thought that the old woman had been affected by a narcotic. Pritchard told him that the old woman may have overdosed herself with an opium mixture which she used to ease neuralgia. But unconvinced, Patterson refused to sign the death certificate. Pritchard himself finally signed the certificate putting the death down to apoplexy.

The following month, on 18 March, Mary Pritchard died too and Pritchard certified cause of death as gastric fever. An anonymous letter sent to the Procurator Fiscal, however, pointed the finger of suspicion at Pritchard. Consequently, as he returned to Glasgow from Edinburgh where he had attended his wife's funeral, Pritchard was arrested. Autopsies carried out on the exhumed bodies of the old Mrs Taylor and Mary Pritchard indicated the presence of both antimony and aconite, the antimony being present in organs but not in the stomach indicating sustained chronic poisoning. In July 1865, Dr Pritchard appeared in the dock at the High Court of Justiciary, Edinburgh before the Right Honourable John Inglis. Defence lawyers, who included Mr Rutherford Clerk, suggested Mary M'Cleod had administered the poisons. But the prosecution team which included the Solicitor General Mr Gifford carried the jury with them and they returned a guilty verdict. Awaiting execution, Pritchard confessed to both murders.

Prussic Acid (Hydrocyanic Acid)

Prussic acid is also known as hydrocyanic acid. As its less familiar name suggests, its salts are the deadly cyanides. Prussic acid itself was once used in medicine in dilute form because it numbs the sensory nerves and therefore eased the discomfort of irritable skin diseases. It was also used to control vomiting or coughing.

Prussic acid when swallowed is very quickly distributed through the body, so symptoms appear after only a few minutes or even seconds. A fatal dose is about 50 mg. Large doses cause unconsciousness in seconds and death in about five minutes. Prussic acid is not difficult to administer as a poison owing to its sweet smell and pleasant taste.

Its action, symptoms and antidote are the same as for cyanide (q.v.) and essentially its effect is to block the action of cytochrome oxidase enzymes at the cellular level. This prevents the cells taking up oxygen. All tissues, especially the heart may be affected and the CNS is very vulnerable. Symptoms of prussic acid poisoning are that breathing becomes slow and heart beat grows slow and irregular. Face and lips become blue and sometimes there are convulsions. Unconsciousness follows then breathing and heart-beat cease. Nitrates such as sodium nitrate injections are used as an antidote because they convert cyanide in the blood into cyanmethaemoglobin which is harmless.

Rablen, Eva

Dance figured largely in the life of Eva Rablen. Her husband Carroll, deaf owing to a First World War injury, accompanied her but did not dance himself. He seemed content to watch while his attractive wife had a good time.

On 26 April 1929 the couple went to the weekly dance at Tuttletown, California. Carroll staying in his car, Eva danced the evening away inside.

Eva came out around midnight with a cup of coffee for her husband, then slipped back into the dance hall. Within seconds Carroll was crying out. His father and some others, hearing this rushed to the car where they found Carroll contorted with agony. He said the coffee had tasted bitter. Soon after he died.

Carroll's father was inclined to think Eva had poisoned his son for insurance money. But an autopsy in which the dead man's stomach contents were analysed revealed no poison.

When police first searched the dance hall, they drew a blank too. But the second search revealed a bottle labelled 'Strychnine'. On it was the address of a local druggist. Checking with the store, it was established that a bottle of strychnine had been sold on 26 April to Eva Rablen, and she was arrested.

But there was still the puzzle about the stomach contents analysis. A second analysis cleared this up. Traces of strychnine were found. As if to clinch matters, traces of the poison were also detected in the coffee cup.

The case attracted much public interest and was held outdoors to accommodate observers. Eva began by pleading not guilty but changed her plea to guilty as the evidence against her accumulated. She was sentenced to life imprisonment. Even in her trial the dance theme was ironically continued. It was held in an open-air dance pavilion.

Richeson, Revd Clarence

On the evening of 14 October 1911, a group of girls in Warrenton Street YWCA, Boston, were ready to go out to a concert. Having waited in the hallway for some time for Avis Linnell a 19-year-old singing student who was to go with them, they went to her room to hurry her along. Avis's door was locked, however, and groans were heard from inside. Breaking the door lock and entering Avis's room, the girls found her naked in a bath of hot water and writhing in agony.

A doctor was called who managed to get Avis into bed but ten minutes later she was dead. An autopsy revealed two major findings: that death was caused by potassium cyanide poisoning, and that Avis Linnell was pregnant. At this point, Avis's brother-in-law informed the police that he believed Avis had been killed by a clergyman with whom she had been having an affair. The minister in question was 35-year-old Reverend Clarence Richeson of Immanuel Baptist Church in Cambridge. He had recently become engaged to a wealthy socialite, Violet Edmands, the daughter of Moses Edmands of Chestnut Hill who was head of the Baptist Missionary Society of America.

Reverend Richeson was routinely interviewed by police and admitted to having been engaged to Avis but claimed they had split up months before. But events were given a new twist when on 19 October an attorney appeared before the chief of Boston detectives explaining that he was retained by William Hahn the owner of an apothecary shop in Newton. Revd Richeson and William Hahn were old school friends and on 10 October, four days before the death of Avis Linnell, Richeson had bought fifteen grains of potassium cyanide from the shop which he claimed was to kill a dog. Hahn had thought no more about the purchase until he had heard of the death of Avis.

Acting on this information, police officers went to Edmands' mansion to arrest Revd Richeson, but found the house in darkness and were unable to rouse the occupants. Eventually, they woke the chauffeur from his sleeping quarters above the garage and confirmed that the family were at home. An officer was then sent to the police station to try to wake the family by telephoning but this too was unsuccessful. The police waited at the house until next morning when they arrested Richeson and took him to the Charles Street jail. The Edmands family stood by the accused minister but had no choice but to begin returning the wedding gifts for the ceremony which had been planned for 31 October.

Police inquiries established that, contrary to what Richeson had claimed, he and Avis had met at the Sea Grill, a restaurant in Dartmouth Street on the afternoon of the day Avis died. Suspicions grew that Revd Richeson had given Avis a cyanide capsule and told her that it was a drug to induce abortion. The fact that Avis had been found in a hot bath presumably to also encourage abortion supported this theory. Indicted by the grand jury, Richeson was returned to jail on 31 October, the very day he was due to marry.

He had, until the death of Avis Linnell, almost escaped an inauspicious early life. Born on a poor mountain farm in Rose Hill, Virginia, he had later moved to Carrollton, Missouri as a farmer's help. His next step was employment as an elevator attendant in a St Louis hardware store, then promotion to clerical duties. In 1900 he became a street car conductor and was a leader and talented orator in the St Louis car strike. At 24 years old, while working as a bread salesman, he joined the Third Baptist Church of St Louis and two years later enrolled in the William Jewell College in Liberty, Missouri. But throughout he had a succession of women friends and several scandals arose. When faced with problems and when under severe stress, Richeson tended to have fits which may have been epilepsy. While at William Jewell College, he became minister of Budd Park Baptist Church but was expelled from college in 1908 for cheating in the examinations. Admitted to another school, he eventually graduated at Hyannis where he had his fateful affair with Avis Linnell.

As he languished in his cell at Charles Street jail, Richeson became increasingly depressed. Then on 20 December 1911 at 4 a.m., cell guards heard screams emerging from his cell and rushing there found Richeson on his back covered in blood. He had emasculated himself with the jagged top of a marmalade can which he had sharpened on the cell floor.

Richeson was rushed to hospital where, two weeks later, he wrote a confession of the murder which was delivered to newspaper reporters on 3 January 1912 and published everywhere. On 9 January, the minister was carried to the courthouse on a chair and pleaded guilty before Judge George Sanderson who sentenced him to die in the electric chair. On January 26, his church held a meeting which expelled him and on 20 May at seven minutes past midnight. Clarence Richeson was executed.

Ricin

Ricin comes from the seeds of the castor-oil plant, the castor bean (*Ricinus communis*). It is a toxalbumin, that is a form of toxin protein molecule. Research into the effects of the poison has been mainly conducted in Czechoslovakia and Hungary.

Ricin is a by-product of castor-oil production. During the extraction process, when castor oil is expressed from the seeds, steaming is carried out to remove the small amount of ricin which the oil contains. Ricin remains in the seed cake which eventually may be used as a fertilizer as it is useless for feeding cattle. As little as one hundredth of a milligram of ricin injected into the bloodstream can prove fatal. One estimate gives a dose as small as two millionths of the body weight as fatal, making ricin, weight for weight twice as poisonous as cobra venom (Knight, B., 1979).

Ricin leads to internal bleeding and kidney failure. It irritates all tissues with which it comes into contact. Symptoms of ricin poisoning include fading vision, abdominal pain, a burning sensation in the mouth and throat, and nausea. Vomiting and bloody diarrhoea ensue. Eventually as the blood becomes increasingly effected death occurs, sometimes preceded by convulsions.

Similar irritant proteins are crotin in crotin seeds and abrin from the jequirty beans which are used for necklaces.

Robinson, Henrietta

In May 1853, Mrs Henrietta Robinson paid several visits to the grocers across the street from where she lived in Troy, New York, which were to lead her to stand in the dock.

She was an eccentric, volatile woman whose relationships with people tended to blow hot and cold. It was during one of the frosty periods in her relationship with the grocer that she paid her three visits. The grocer was an Irishman, Timothy Lanagan who lived with his wife and his sister-in-law Catherine Lubee.

Henrietta's first call was at 6 a.m. when she bought beer and soda crackers. At 8 a.m. Mrs Robinson's gardener entered the shop asking for a loan of two dollars for Mrs Robinson soon followed by Henrietta Robinson herself complaining that she was being made to wait.

At 1 p.m. Mrs Robinson called a third time and the Lanagans invited her to lunch. She treated the family to beer to which she added a white powder which she said was sugar. Mr Lanagan and Catherine Lubee drank the doctored beer and two hours later suffered violent vomiting and diarrhoea. Next day both died in great suffering. Arsenic was found in the corpses. Mrs Robinson being the prime suspect, had her house searched and more arsenic was discovered under a carpet.

Arrested and charged with murder, Henrietta Robinson tried to fake insanity in court. But the jury found her guilty and she was sentenced to death. The death penalty was commuted to life imprisonment and Mrs Robinson was incarcerated in Sing Sing. Later moved to Matteawan State Asylum in 1874 she died there in 1905, aged 78.

Schönleben, Anna

Serial poison murderer Anna Schönleben, exercised a gift for gaining people's confidence which allowed her to remain undetected when many others might have fallen under deep suspicion. The daughter of an innkeeper at Nuremberg, Germany, she had, by the age of 20, married an alcoholic notary whose health was failing. After his death, Anna tried her hand at a variety of occupations: confectioner, doll-maker, housekeeper and cook to a touring circus. Eventually, she settled into a series of domestic jobs in different parts of the country.

Her parallel career in crime seems to have started at Rosendorf in Bavaria where she became housekeeper to a Judge Glaser. Anna's plan was to win the Judge's affection and marry him but a stumbling-block existed in the form of Glaser's wife, although the couple were separated. Accordingly, Anna acted as an intermediary to reconcile the Judge and Frau Glaser who reunited. The next step being to get rid of Frau Glaser, to achieve this Anna laced the woman's tea with arsenic gradually increasing the dose so that after three days sickness, Frau Glaser died. But the plan that the Judge would then be disposed to marry his housekeeper was in the realms of fantasy and never materialized.

Anna left for better prospects, working for 38-year-old Judge Grohmann at Sanspariel. A similar plan, to achieve marriage with a successful man, again began to develop but soon after employing his new housekeeper, Judge Grohmann became engaged – to a woman other than Anna. Soon the judge became ill with vomiting and diarrhoea and Anna became his attentive nurse. Unsurprisingly his condition grew worse, for the reason for his illness and further deterioration was that Anna was poisoning him with arsenic. Such were Anna's powers of deception that when Judge Grohmann died her services as a nurse were sought by Frau Gebhardt the wife of a local magistrate.

A chronic invalid, Frau Gebhardt had noticed how caring Anna had been in nursing the judge and was keen to secure her services. Soon the familiar pattern re-emerged with Frau Gebhardt becoming ill with sickness and diarrhoea while Anna took care of her. This time it was Magistrate Gebhardt who was taken in and once Anna had poisoned his wife to death, he was quick to retain her in his household agreeing with popular sentiment that she was a 'pious, worthy creature' (Thompson, C.J.S., 1931).

But over the following three months several of the domestic servants fell ill with attacks of vomiting and abdominal pains after drinking coffee or other beverages prepared by Anna. Even Herr Gebhardt had to admit to some suspicions and decided to dismiss her while at the same time, in case he was completely misjudging the situation, giving Anna a good reference.

The day of Anna's departure came and a carriage which had been hired to take her to Bayreuth arrived at the door. That same morning, Anna had served coffee to the maids and dosed it with arsenic. She had also mixed arsenic with salt in the kitchen salt box and for good measure had mixed 30 grains of the poison in the salt barrel. As she was about to enter the carriage, Anna gave Herr Gebhardt's infant child a biscuit which she had earlier soaked in arsenic-laced milk. With this she climbed into the carriage and waved goodbye. Half an hour later the whole household were ill with the usual symptoms of arsenic poisoning.

Magistrate Gebhardt immediately called in the police who discovered the poisoned salt box and salt barrel. Suspicion now at last fell on Anna and the body of Frau Glaser, the wife of her earlier employer Judge Glaser was exhumed. Its state of good preservation indicated arsenic poisoning. The exhumed body of Judge Grohmann, her employer at Sanspariel showed similar signs of preservation while Frau Gebhardt's body had arsenic in the intestines.

While these discoveries were implicating Anna Schönleben increasingly deeply, she had found work in Nuremberg. On 18 October 1809 police traced her there and, arresting her, found arsenic in one of her pockets.

At her trial she denied all charges but in July 1811 the court found her guilty. After her sentence was announced, Anna confessed her guilt to the judge, stating that she took pleasure in watching the sufferings of her victims and that it was probably for the best that she was to die because she could not imagine herself resisting the urge to poison again. (Thompson, C.J.S., 1937).

Her sentence of death was duly carried out, and Anna Schönleben was publicly decapitated with a sword after which her body was exposed on the wheel.

Seconal

Seconal (Seconal sodium) is another name for the barbiturate quinalbarbitone sodium. It is a white, odourless but bitter tasting powder.

Barbiturates themselves are comparatively modern, emerging from the search for an ideal hypnotic drug in the late nineteenth century. Barbituric acid, supposedly named after a woman called Barbara by its discoverer, yielded several effective derivatives. One of these, barbitone began to be used in clinical practice in 1903.

Seconal is used as a sedative taken by mouth in capsules of methyl cellulose, although before the 1950s, gelatine capsules were used.

Absorbed by the gastro-intestinal tract, seconal is excreted in urine after the body has absorbed most of it (and in the normal course of events destroyed it).

Like other barbiturates, seconal depresses the CNS. Acting on the higher centres first, it then works down the CNS mainly effecting the cerebral cortex and the thalamic region of the brain. Overdoses of seconal block autonomic nerves, that is those which regulate the function of certain internal organs. Also an overdose acts directly to depress the vascular smooth muscle.

Symptoms of seconal poisoning are failure of the circulatory system leading to kidney failure. This is accompanied by the passing of only very small quantities of urine or none at all. The respiratory system also fails and coma and death follow. Respiratory failure is almost invariably the cause of death where a fatal overdose is taken. This is due to central depression of respiratory centres in the brainstem.

Seddon, Frederick

In early September 1911, Eliza Barrow, a 49-year-old unmarried woman lay gravely ill in the bedroom of her top-floor lodgings in North London. By day, among the smell of sickness and diarrhoea flies buzzed around in the late summer heat. By night, throughout her illness, Miss Barrow insisted that 8-year-old Ernie Grant, the orphaned son of a woman friend continued to sleep in her sick bed.

She had fallen ill on 1 September. Dr Henry Sworn, a local doctor prescribed various remedies including Valentine's Meat

Juice to be drunk each night.

The house, 63 Tollington Park, Islington, was owned by Frederick Seddon, a successful insurance agent who with his wife Margaret and their five children occupied the ground and first floors of the spacious residence.

Mrs Margaret Seddon did her best to nurse the sick woman and Frederick Seddon once persuaded her to take her medicine when she had neglected doing so.

On 13 September, Frederick went to the theatre accompanied by his sister and niece who were visiting them. At 11.30 p.m. Ernie Grant came downstairs for Mrs Seddon who found Mrs Barrow in agony on the floor of her sickroom. Frederick and Margaret Seddon got Ernie into another room, then Margaret sat at the bedside while her husband sat on the landing. But at 6.30 a.m. on Thursday 14 September, Eliza Barrow died.

That same morning, Frederick Seddon obtained a death certificate from Dr Sworn giving the cause of death as epidemic diarrhoea. The doctor did not think it necessary to see the body.

Although Miss Barrow was entitled to burial in a family vault, Seddon arranged for her to be buried in a common grave and claimed a commission from the funeral director for putting business his way. None of Eliza Barrow's relatives were informed so none were present when she was buried on Saturday 16 September.

Before moving into the lodgings at Tollington Park on 25 July 1910, Eliza Barrow had been staying in the same locality with her cousin Frank Vonderahe and his wife but had left after a quarrel. It was only when Frank Vonderahe called at Tollington Park to see his cousin that he learned of her death. When Vonderahe questioned Seddon about Eliza's assets Seddon assured the cousin that all Eliza's property had been made over to Seddon himself in exchange for an annuity. It was obvious that now the annuity no longer had to be paid. But as Vonderahe knew, Eliza's assets despite her appearance were quite considerable.

He reported the matter to the police and Miss Barrow's body was exhumed. Sir William Willcox, a Home Office forensic pathologist discovered two and a half grains of arsenic in the cadaver. Both Frederick and later Margaret Seddon were arrested on a charge of murder.

Seddon asked police if they had found arsenic in Eliza Barrow's body and told his solicitor that the deceased may have drunk liquid in which fly papers had been soaked. (In fact on 26 August, Seddon's daughter had bought fly papers and some had been hung in Miss Barrow's room).

The Seddons' trial before Mr Justice Bucknill, opened on 4 March 1912 and much was to be made of Seddon's financial agreements with Miss Barrow.

Seddon was an agent of the London and Manchester Industrial Assurance Company where for eleven years he had been district superintendent in North London. Miss Barrow and Ernie Grant had taken lodgings at Tollington Park in July 1910. It emerged at the trial that Miss Barrow held stocks, leasehold interests, cash and other assets which she gradually signed over to Seddon between October 1910 and June 1911 for a fairly generous annuity of £3 a week.

Prosecuting, the Attorney-General Sir Rufus Isaacs QC, who specialized in commercial cases, painstakingly worked through the transactions.

Defending Frederick Seddon (and effectively his wife also) was the illustrious Sir Edward Marshall Hall. The defence was that Miss Barrow had died of chronic arsenic poisoning, not acute poisoning as the prosecution alleged.

Sir William Willcox, the Home Office Pathologist testified that he had carried out the Marsh Test and concluded that about five grains of arsenic had been given to Miss Barrow a short time before she died.

Marshall Hall seized on the fact that this was the first time evidence based on the Marsh Test had been given in a British court. Arsenic was present in the deceased's hair and William Willcox had to admit that this suggested arsenic had been introduced to the system a year before death. Overnight Willcox conducted a further experiment, however, indicating that fluid found in Miss Barrow's coffin may have introduced arsenic into her hair.

Frederick Seddon's obsession with money and lack of fellow feeling came through his evidence on the detailed transactions by which he came to acquire Miss Barrow's assets. What also emerged was the unattractiveness of Miss Barrow. Perhaps not surprisingly Seddon at his trial said she was not someone 'you could be in love with'. But subsequent writers have described her unflatteringly, for instance, as 'an even less lovable character than Seddon' (Lustgarten, E. 1951). But whatever her shortcomings may have been these were not the issue of the trial.

The jury retired on the tenth day of the trial, taking an hour to find Frederick Seddon guilty and his wife not guilty. The trial judge was a mason like Seddon himself and before sentence of death was made, Seddon made a Masonic sign and declared his innocence before the Great Architect of the Universe. Mr Justice

Bucknill passed sentence but was clearly moved as he often was when having to pass the ultimate sentence.

On 2 April 1912, Seddon's appeal was turned down. At Pentonville Prison on 18 April he was hanged.

Strychnine

Strychnine is an extremely bitter-tasting vegetable alkaloid obtained from plants of the genus *Strychnos*. In tiny doses, strychnine is a nerve stimulant. It has been used medically as a tonic or as a 'bitter' to improve appetite. Used as a 'vermin' killer for animals it is a cruel method of dispatch.

Strychnine is quickly absorbed from the intestine and rapidly distributed in the body. But is only slowly excreted, partly unchanged in urine. Some of the substance is destroyed by the liver. About 100 mg of strychnine taken by mouth represents the fatal dose, the minimum lethal dose being about 36 mg.

Strychnine stimulates the CNS, particularly the spinal cord. It inhibits the nerves of the spinal cord from counteracting over stimulation. Consequently overdoses cause twitching then convulsions. The cortex is affected and senses are heightened. Following stimulation of the CNS, there is a phase of CNS depression.

After strychnine poisoning, convulsions seize the sufferer so that the body is arched backwards with arms and legs extended. Face muscles contract to produce a characteristic sardonic grin. At the same time as this painful wave of convulsion is taking place the senses are sharpened. The contraction of the diaphragm and related muscles prevent breathing while convulsions last. Typically, convulsions persist for a minute or two with ten or fifteen minutes between them. Death occurs usually after the second to fifth seizure. Asphyxiation is brought about by the effect of the poison on the respiratory muscles. A massive overdose of strychnine can kill suddenly without convulsions. In attempting to treat strychnine poisoning, intravenous injections of a quick-acting barbiturate and muscle relaxants are administered.

Succinylcholine Chloride

Succinylcholine chloride is a synthetic drug used to relax muscles. It is also known under the trade name of Scoline. An off-white crystalline powder, it has little odour, a salty taste, and is soluble in water.

Succinylcholine chloride is widely used in anaesthetics. It is particularly useful for brief operations such as when a tube needs to be inserted down the trachea to aid breathing. The drug is administered intravenously for medical use.

Succinylcholine chloride is a neuro-muscular blocking agent which paralyses the muscles for a brief period when given in a small dose. It acts by depolarization, as it were stopping the nerve 'communicating' with the muscle and vice versa. (All bodily processes are chemical or electrical and the polarity refers to the positive or negative electrical charges involved in a process.)

An overdose of the drug can cause irregularities in heart action; slow beats, extra contracting as opposed to 'resting' phases of heart action, and even heart failure. All this appears to be caused because of the stimulation of the vagal nerve which supplies branches to the heart and other organs. In treating succinylcholine poisoning, blood transfusion may help replace cholinesterase (the nerve-transmitting agent) rendered inactive by the drug.

Tawell, John

Between 6 p.m. and 7 p.m. on 1 January 1845 a woman neighbour of Sarah Hadler who lived in Salt Hill, near Slough heard muffled screams and saw a man coming out of Sarah's cottage. She tried to talk to the man but he rushed by. Looking into the cottage, the neighbour saw Sarah on the floor convulsed in agony. Minutes later Sarah died.

Police were alerted and a telegram was sent from Slough to Paddington describing the man's appearance and saying he was a murder suspect. Police spotted the man and followed him to his lodgings. Next day they questioned him and he claimed not to have been out of London the previous day. He was arrested.

The man was a Quaker, John Tawell, whose past had been quite remarkable. As a young man of 20 he had been transported to Australia after being found guilty of forgery. After serving his time, Tawell opened up a chemist business and through this and other business dealings became rich and successful.

Returning to England, he bought a house in Berkhamsted and married. His wife died after a few years and Tawell planned to marry again.

At the same time he kept a mistress, Sarah Hadler for whom he provided lodgings first in Paddington and later in Salt Hill. She bore Tawell two children.

The autopsy on Sarah's body indicated that she had died of prussic acid poisoning. (It may have been administered by a drink of stout). A Bishopsgate chemist reported to police that he had sold prussic acid to a man on the morning on the 1 January, and identified Tawell as the customer.

At Tawell's trial, Fitzroy Kelly, the defence lawyer drew attention to the fact that a basket of apples had been in the room when Sarah died. Sarah, it was argued, had died from the cyanide in the apple pips. The prosecution, however, were able to close this line of defence by pointing out that cyanide is only released from crushed, distilled apple pips.

On 14 March, Tawell was found guilty. He soon after confessed to the murder saying that he was worried his new wife would find out about his mistress.

Tawell, the first murderer to be arrested through the use of a telegram, was hanged at the end of March 1845.

Taylor, Louisa

From August to October 1882, Dr Smith, a local physician in Plumstead, made several visits to an ailing old woman, Mrs Tregillis. She lived with her 85-year-old husband William and a 37-year-old lodger, Louisa Taylor, who had been widowed a short time previously. Occupying only two small rooms of a larger house, the three inhabitants had to use both rooms at night, Louisa sleeping in one with the old woman while the old man rested in the other. Throughout the old Mrs Tregillis's illness, Dr Smith noticed Louisa nursed her with great care.

Mrs Tregillis showed symptoms of shivering and vomiting, while her teeth and gums became discoloured and Dr Smith diagnosed ague. He asked Louisa to bring him a sample of the old woman's vomit but Mrs Taylor did not comply. Nevertheless, Dr Smith had no cause to see Louisa as other than a kind and considerate lodger.

He began to wonder if he was right when on 6 October police charged Louisa with stealing from Mr Tregillis. What had been happening during the previous months was strange to say the least.

Louisa had formed an attachment to Edward Martin a watercress seller. Yet as Mrs Tregillis lay suffering Louisa had shocked William Tregillis by suggesting that she and the old man elope. Louisa later told William that he was a beneficiary under her will and gave him a copy showing him other documents suggesting she was worth some £500. Yet, soon after William had drawn £10 of pension back pay, Louisa told the old man that his wife wanted to keep it safe under her pillow. Word reached William from neighbours that Louisa had got her hands on the money and this was when he reported the matter to police.

Dr Smith began to review the symptoms in a new light (just as Dr Thomas Hincks was to review the symptoms of Mrs Armstrong in the Herbert Armstrong case in 1921). He remembered that Louisa had been seeing him for a supposed skin condition and had obtained quantities of sugar of lead (lead acetate) from him. Mrs Tregillis's symptoms now began to take shape as those of lead poisoning. Consequently on 9 October 1882, Dr Smith requested that a police surgeon examine Mrs Tregillis and his fears were confirmed.

A legal enquiry was held in Mrs Tregillis's sickroom as was

customary at the time. Local magistrates gathered there and
Louisa was brought in custody. Mrs Tregillis was clearly dying but
was able to give evidence that she had witnessed Louisa adding
white powder to her (Mrs Tregillis's) medicine. On 23 October,
1882, the old woman died.

At the coroner's inquest, Mr Tregillis stated that he believed
Louisa intended to acquire his pension and then put him in a
lunatic asylum (he had previously been admitted to one). Louisa
stood trial at the Old Bailey in December 1882 before Mr Justice
Stephen and was found guilty. On 2 January 1883, Louisa Taylor
was executed.

Thallium

Thallium is a soft, white metallic element. Its name derives from
the fact that the element produces a green line in the light
spectrum, *thallos* being Greek for 'green shoot'. Among its forms
are thallium sulphate, and oxide and bromide salts of thallium.
Thallium salts were discovered in 1861 by Crookes and Lany, two
chemists working independently.

Thallium salts were used therapeutically for a time to help in the
treatment of ringworm of the scalp because they caused hair loss
and therefore cleared the scalp for treatment. More recently
thallium salts have found uses in the manufacture of dye, paint and
window glass. Ant bait and rodenticides such as rat poison may
also contain thallium. Oxide and bromide salts of thallium are
used in making optical lenses.

Thallous salts are absorbed readily from mucous membranes of
the mouth and gastro-intestinal tract as well as from the skin. The
metal accumulates in the muscles, kidneys and spleen and to a
lesser degree in the skin and hair. Thallium is excreted in the urine
up to two months after it has been taken.

Thallium is one of the most toxic of metals. Odourless, tasteless
and colourless, it can be easily added to food or drink for
homicidal poisoning.

The minimum lethal dose for an adult is about 800 mg of
thallium sulphate which is 12 mg per kg of body weight for a
person weighing 70 kg.

The action of this toxic substance is not fully known. It appears
to compete with the body's potassium at enzyme active centres and
elsewhere.

At certain stages, symptoms of thallium poisoning can resemble

poisoning by arsenic, lead, mercury or carbon monoxide. Acute
symptoms include waves of severe abdominal pains, vomiting and
diarrhoea and haemorrhage. Proteins are passed in the urine and
only very small amounts of urine are excreted. Bodily extremities
become very painful so that even the pressure of a bed sheet is
intolerable. Delirium, convulsions and coma follow. Circulatory
collapse and respiratory failure may occur twenty to forty hours
after symptoms first appear.

Chronic symptoms show effects mainly on the nervous system.
The nerves serving the hands and feet become inflamed. Loss of
the power to control movement, facial paralysis or squinting
occurs. Pupils become widely dilated. Eruptions appear on the
skin and the palms of the hands and the soles of the feet assume a
horny quality. Hair loss is noticeable about twenty days after the
initial dose. Slight loss of appetite, vomiting and stomach pains
develop.

Thallium is probably the only homicidal poison to have been
detected in a victim after cremation.

Toffana

It is said that Toffana began her career in poisoning as a girl in
Palermo, Sicily. After moving to Naples in 1659 when Alexander
VII was Pope, she became known for selling solutions of skin
cosmetics to women. Phials containing the solution usually bore
the representation of a saint, often Nicholas of Bari who was
associated with a healing spring.

Arsenic was the main constituent of the solution and rumours
spread that Toffana was involved in many poisonings, either
administering them herself or advising her clients on their use.
Certainly she moved house often, it was said to avoid detection.

But Toffana reached the age of 70 before the judicial authorities
sought to bring her to trial for the crimes. Taking refuge in a
convent, Toffana was forcefully removed by the authorities and
imprisoned much to the annoyance of the clergy who felt that
church privilege was being eroded. Put on the rack, the old woman
confessed and was then strangled and her body thrown into the
courtyard of the convent in which she had hidden.

Vaquier, Jean-Pierre

A French guest registered at the Blue Anchor Hotel, Byfleet, Surrey on 14 February 1924. He was 45-year-old Jean-Pierre Vaquier who said he was waiting for payment for an invention while he stayed there.

But Mrs Jones, the wife of the landlord, knew Vaquier's real motive was to be close to her. Mabel Jones and her lover had met only the previous month. He had been working at a hotel in Biarritz where she had been staying on holiday. Their attraction for one another was not hampered by the fact that neither spoke the other's language.

When in February, Mabel returned home, Vaquier came over to England too and stayed in London. Mrs Jones visited him in the capital and soon after the Frenchman moved into the Blue Anchor.

He returned to London on 1 March but only long enough to buy some poison at a chemist. The purchase of twenty grammes of perchloride of mercury and 0.12 of a gramme of strychnine were recorded in the poison book. Vaquier, who said the poisons were for wireless experiments, signed the book in the name of 'Wanker'.

Back at the Blue Anchor on the morning of 29 March, Mr Jones came down into the bar parlour. Having drunk heavily at a party the night before he had a hangover. He took a bottle of Bromo-salts and poured some into a glass of water, but, taking a drink, commented on the bitter taste. His wife took the bottle of salts to the kitchen where she placed them in a drawer.

Mr Jones fell ill and the doctor was called, but, while the doctor was attending to the sick man, Vaquier ran into the kitchen and removed the Bromo-salt bottle.

Mr Jones died a painful death, and an autopsy established strychnine poisoning as the cause. The Bromo salts container was discovered in the kitchen but it had been emptied and rinsed. Traces of strychnine were still detectable in the bottle, however.

Vaquier's versions of who might be implicated were, to say the least, fanciful. At first he blamed the postman. Vaquier himself however, was identified by a London chemist as the Mr Wanker

189

who had bought strychnine from his store. At his trial for murder at Guildford Assizes in July 1924, Vaquier tried to implicate Mabel Jones's solicitor. It was the lawyer, he claimed, who had requested Vaquier to buy strychnine and sign for it under an assumed name. But in the end the responsibility for the crime came to rest inevitably at Vaquier's door. Found guilty, the Frenchman was hanged on 12 August 1924 at Wandsworth Prison, London.

Waddingham, Dorothea Nancy

When Dorothea Waddingham's husband died, she set up a nursing home for old people and the long-term disabled in Nottingham, despite having no nursing qualifications. Her helper was 39-year-old Ronald Sullivan.

The year 1935 was a fateful one for 'Nurse' Waddingham, Sullivan and more particularly for two patients Mrs Baguley aged 89 and her 50-year-old invalid daughter Ada.

The two patients were admitted in January, and needed a great deal of care. Ada Baguley, the daughter, told her solicitor that she wanted to leave property to Nurse Waddingham. In exchange Waddingham would agree to take care of both the old Mrs Baguley and Ada as long as they lived. On 6 May, Ada made a will citing Waddingham and Sullivan as beneficiaries. Six days later the old Mrs Baguley died. In September Ada also died, apparently from cerebral haemorrhage.

Then a strange letter was received by the nursing home physician. It was supposedly written by Ada Baguley and made two requests: that her body be cremated and that her relatives should not be informed of the death. Sullivan had witnessed the letter.

An autopsy was carried out on Ada revealing traces of morphine. Next, the body of the old Mrs Baguley was exhumed and morphine detected.

Waddingham and Sullivan were jointly charged with Ada Baguley's murder, but Sullivan was released for lack of direct evidence against him.

The trial took place at Nottingham Assizes in February 1936. Waddingham testified that she had given morphine on the instructions of the doctor, Dr Manfield. He, however, said that he had given no such instructions.

Waddingham was found guilty with a strong recommendation to mercy. On 16 April 1936, however, she was hanged at Winson Green Prison, Birmingham.

Wainewright, Thomas Griffiths

De Quincey, Hazlitt and Lamb were among the literary acquaintances of Thomas Wainewright, who turned to writing and painting after a spell in the army. His grandfather who had reared him was an editor of *The Monthly Review*.

Wainewright dressed elegantly and spent lavishly. In 1821 he married Eliza Frances Ward but marriage did little to change his habits and he seemed to be constantly in debt. Even £2,000 which he obtained from his stock by forging the signatures of his trustees did little to help.

In 1829, Wainewright's grandfather died of a fit and most of his estate passed to Wainewright. Most went to settling debts. It was suspected that Wainewright had poisoned the old man with strychnine.

Next, Mrs Abercromby, Wainewright's mother-in-law moved in with him and Eliza. Madeleine and Helen, two daughters by Mrs Abercromby's second marriage came too.

In 1830, Mrs Abercromby died. Again it was rumoured that Wainewright had poisoned her. He then insured Helen, his 20-year-old sister-in-law through several policies for £18,000, using Madeleine as the apparent beneficiary. In reality Madeleine assigned the interest in two of the policies to Wainewright.

In December 1830, Helen, aged only 20, died and Wainewright asked Madeleine to collect the insurance money. But the insurance company was reluctant to pay, being suspicious of the death. Wainewright sued for the insurance money. But after a case that continued over five years, the decision favoured the company.

Wainewright had gone to France in 1831. There, having met a young woman and insured her father's life for £3,000, he poisoned the man. When he returned to England in 1837, he was recognized. Sent for trial only on a charge of forgery, he was sentenced to transportation for life to Van Dieman's Land (Tasmania). There he died aged 58.

Waite, Dr Arthur

At his trial for the double murder of his in-laws, American dentist Dr Arthur Waite entered a plea of not guilty but in his evidence to the court he admitted poisoning both Mr and Mrs Peck for their money. At appeal, Waite pleaded insanity, claiming to have a dual personality, half of which was an Egyptian acquaintance of Queen

Cleopatra. Doctors were called to concur with a diagnosis of insanity but the jury were unimpressed and returned a guilty verdict.

Waite's early career was one of deceit and theft, but he eventually qualified as a dental surgeon at Glasgow University. After working in South Africa for six years, he returned to the United States. In 1915, he married Clara Peck whom he had known since childhood, but who was seemingly unaware of Arthur's dishonest side and noticed more his immense charm and sociability. Clara's parents were wealthy inhabitants of Rapid Falls in Michigan, but the newly-weds settled in Riverside Drive, New York. There he ran his dental surgery and conducted research on germ culture at Cornell Medical School.

Over Christmas, 1915, four months after he had married Clara, Arthur invited his mother-in-law to stay with them. Implanting her food with diphtheria and influenza germs, Waite soon got rid of her. When Mrs Peck died on 30 January 1916, supposedly of a kidney disease, Waite had the body cremated.

Naturally upset by his wife's death, Mr Peck went to stay with his daughter and son-in-law in February. Arthur Waite tried various strategies to hasten John Peck's end. Treating the millionaire's food with diphtheria and influenza bacteria was unsuccessful so Waite tried giving Mr Peck a nasal spray implanted with tuberculosis bacteria. Believing that chlorine increased susceptibility to germs, Waite released tubes of chlorine in Mr Peck's bedroom. When soaking the old man's bed sheets to try to induce pneumonia failed, Waite resorted to arsenic, administering some eighteen grains to kill his victim. Death again appeared to be from kidney disease. In his will John Peck left his children over $1,000,000.

Peck's cadaver was embalmed and transported back to Michigan where Mr Peck's son Percy, suspicious of Waite, had the body examined. Arsenic was detected.

On 23 March 1916, Waite was found unconscious by police having taken a drug overdose. He later recovered. Suspected of murder, Waite paid the embalmer of Mr Peck's body to state that arsenic was present in the embalming fluid, but this did not prevent the police from arresting him for suspected double murder.

After his trial, Arthur Waite was taken to Sing Sing Prison where on 24 May 1917 he died in the electric chair.

Wilson, Catherine

In April 1862, Catherine Wilson was charged at Marylebone Police Court with administering oil of vitriol to a certain Mrs Connell of Marylebone in an attempt to kill her. Mrs Connell was separated from her husband and had sought Catherine's help to bring about a reconciliation. She had invited Catherine to tea in February 1862 to discuss this but Mrs Connell had suddenly become ill. Catherine Wilson had rushed round to a local chemist and brought back a 'black draught' which she urged Mrs Connell to swallow. The draught burnt Mrs Connell's mouth and made her sick and, once she had recovered, she reported the incident to the police. By this time Catherine Wilson was nowhere to be found and it was some weeks before she was arrested and charged. After a trial at the Central Criminal Court, however, Catherine was acquitted by the jury.

But the police were not idle while Catherine stood awaiting trial and unearthed a series of deaths which seemed to occur wherever she had lived. From 1853 to 1854, Catherine was housekeeper to Captain Peter Maiver of Boston, Lincolnshire. A sufferer from gout, the captain used colchicum (q.v.) as a treatment. In October 1854, he died suddenly, leaving his estate to his housekeeper.

The following year found Catherine living with a Mr Dixon in a house in Alfred Street, Bedford Square, London, which was owned by Mrs Soames. At the end of 1855, Dixon died suddenly leaving his money to Mrs Soames. Around Christmas, however, Mrs Soames also fell ill, feeling weak and vomiting violently. Cathering nursed her, but Soames's condition deteriorated and within a few days she died. An autopsy put cause of death down to natural causes.

In 1859, Catherine lived with Mrs Jackson who died suddenly showing symptoms similar to those of Dixon and Soames. After her death, Mrs Jackson's money disappeared unaccountably. A year later Catherine played hostess to Mrs Atkinson, a milliner of Kirkby Lonsdale, who was visiting London. After staying with Catherine for four days, the visitor died and her money disappeared. Her husband who was summoned by telegram to London questioned Catherine about the money and was told that Mrs Atkinson had been robbed on the way to London and had arrived at Catherine's house penniless.

As a result of police enquiries, once Catherine had been acquitted of attempting to kill Mrs Connell, she was re-arrested and charged with the murder of Mrs Soames of Bedford Square, London.

At the trial, Dr Taylor, called for the prosecution, stated that Mrs Soames's symptoms indicated colchicum poisoning. Also, the doctor who had attended Mr Dixon now recognized the symptoms of his patient as indicating the same cause. It appeared that the colchicum seeds may have been infused in wine, brandy or tea before the beverages were administered. The jury found Catherine Wilson guilty and she was duly executed, showing not a flicker of emotion, before a crowd of twenty thousand spectators.

Young, Graham

The managing director of Hadlands, a Herefordshire photographic instruments firm, attended the funeral of one of his employees in June 1971. The dead man was 60-year-old Bob Egle who had been a storeman at the firm. Egle had suddenly become ill at work that June. Peripheral neuritis was diagnosed but treatment proved ineffective and Bob Egle died in hospital.

With the director was one other employee, 23-year-old Graham Young. The director noticed that Young used medical terms fluently.

What he did not know was the past history of the man beside him. Young as a boy of 13 had confessed to murdering his stepmother with poison and attempting to poison his father, his sister and a school-friend. The boy was sent to Broadmoor, an institution for the criminally insane. He was released nine years later and managed to get a job at Hadlands without his past being known. But none of this had come to light as Young and his boss paid their last respects to the dead storeman.

Back at Hadlands, employees had been falling ill for some time, and attributed this to some mysterious 'bug'. In October Fred Biggs became a victim of the 'bug'. But he became worse over a three week period and died. Young was unusually interested in Biggs' sickness.

The 'bug' continued to make workers ill. Two employees complained of stomach pains and numbness in the legs. Their hair started to fall out. They also complained that their tea was bitter to the taste. One of Young's duties was that of tea boy.

Naturally, in the course of manufacturing photographic instruments, Hadlands used chemicals. It seemed that these might be causing the trouble. A medical team was called in to investigate.

The doctor heading the team was aware that rumours were circulating and that staff had questions and concerns. To try to deal with these matters, he called the employees to a meeting. Young continued to draw attention to himself, asking many questions including directly asking the doctor if he thought the symptoms complained of were consistent with thallium poisoning.

The medic simply thought Young was a show off. Thallium after all was not even used in the factory. But management had their suspicions by now and contacted the police. To their horror, when Young's records were checked, his past incarceration for murder by poisoning was revealed. When Young was arrested, thallium was found stored in his pocket.

Police got hold of Young's diary. In it were the names of six people marked out as victims. Two of these were Bob Egle and Fred Biggs. Egle had been cremated but his ashes were analysed. Some nine milligrams of thallium were identified.

In 1972, Young stood trial at St Albans. He pleaded not guilty. The diary entries he claimed were background notes for an intended novel. Found guilty, he was sentenced to life imprisonment. Young died in prison in 1990.

Bibliography

Arthur, H., *All the Sinners* (John Long, 1931)

Atholl, J., *The Reluctant Hangman* (John Long, 1956)

Atlay, J.B., *Famous Trials* (Grant Richards, 1899)

Baden, M. & Hennessee, J.A., *Unnatural Death – Confessions of a Forensic Pathologist* (Sphere Books, 1991)

Barker, D., *Palmer: The Rugeley Poisoner* (Duckworth, 1935)

—— *Lord Darling's Famous Cases* (Hutchinson, 1936)

Beal, E. (ed.), *The Trial of Adelaide Bartlett for Murder* (Stevens and Haynes, 1886)

Bedford, S., *The Best We Can Do* (Penguin, 1958)

Bennett, B., *Murder is My Business* (Howard Timmins, 1951)

—— *Genius for the Defence* (Howard Timmins, 1967)

—— *The Noose Tightens* (Howard Timmins, 1974)

Berman, E., *Toxic Metals and their Analysis* (Heyden, 1980)

Birmingham, G.A., *Murder Most Foul* (Chatto and Windus, 1939)

Bishop, C., *From Information Received* (Hutchinson, 1932)

Bixley, W., *The Guilty and the Innocent* (Souvenir Press, 1957)

Blakiston's Gould Medical Dictionary (McGraw Hill, 1979)

Bland, J., *True Crime Diary* (Futura, 1987)

Block, E.B., *The Chemist of Crime* (Cassell, 1959)

Bosanquet, Sir S.R.C., *The Oxford Circuit* (Hadleigh Thames, 1951)

Boswell, C. & Thompson, S., *The Girl With the Scarlet Brand* (Fawcett, 1955)

Boutet, F., *International Criminals Past and Present* (Hutchinson, 1930) [trans. Walter Mostyn]

Bowker, A.E., *Behind the Bar* (Staples Press, 1947)

Brice, A.H.M., *Look Upon the Prisoner* (Hutchinson, 1933)

Bridges, Y., *How Charles Bravo Died* (Macmillan, 1970)

—— *Poison and Adelaide Bartlett* (Hutchinson, 1962)

Broad, J., *Science and Criminal Detection* (Macmillan Education, 1988)

Browne, D.G. & Tullett, E.V., *Sir Bernard Spilsbury: His Life and Cases* (Harrap, 1951)

Browne, G.L. & Stewart, C.G., *Trials for Murder by Poisoning*

(George G. Harrap, 1883)

Burnaby, E.H., *Memories of Famous Trials* (Sysleys, 1907)

Busch, F.X., *They Escaped the Hangman* (Arco, 1957)

Butler, G.L., *Madeleine Smith* (Duckworth, 1935)

Camp, J., *One Hundred Years of Medical Murder* (The Bodley Head, 1982)

Camps, Dr F.E., *Medical and Scientific Investigations in the Christie Case* (Medical Publications Ltd, 1953)

Christie, T.L., *Etched in Arsenic* (George G. Harrap, 1968)

Christeson, R., *Treatise on Poisons* (A & C Black, 1836)

Cobb, B., *Critical Years at the Yard* (Faber & Faber, 1956)

Devlin, P., *Easing the Passing* (The Bodley Head, 1985)

Dew, W., *I Caught Crippen* (Blackie and Son, 1938)

Dilnot, G., *Celebrated Crimes* (Stanley Paul & Co., 1925)

Dorland, W.A., *Dorland's Illustrated Medical Dictionary* (W.B. Saunders, 1985)

Douthwaite, L.C., *Mass Murder* (John Long, 1928)

Eaton, H., *Famous Poison Trials* (Collins, 1923)

Farrell, M., 'Arsenic Poisoning: The Role of Legal Controls' (*Solicitors Journal*, 133, 35, 1101-2, 1989)

—— 'Arsenic Poisoning and the Armstrong Case' (*Solicitors Journal*, 133, 34, 1074-5, 1989)

—— 'What's Your Poison?' (*Solicitors Journal*, 134, 29, 825, 1990[a])

—— 'Arsenic and the Charlotte Bryant Case' (*Solicitors Journal*, 134, 14, 393-4, 1990[b])

Furneaux, R., *Famous Criminal Cases 1* (Odhams, 1954)

—— *Famous Criminal Cases 4* (Odhams, 1957)

—— *The Medical Murderer* (Elek, 1957)

—— *Famous Criminal Cases 6* (Odhams, 1960)

Gaute, J.H.H. & Odell, R., *Lady Killers* (Granada, 1980)

—— *Lady Killers 2* (Firecrest, 1981)

—— *The New Murderers' Who's Who* (Harrap, 1989)

Goodman, J., *The Country House Murders* (Sphere/Macdonald, 1988)

Goodman, L.S. & Gilman, A.G., *The Pharmacological Basis of Therapeutics* (Collier Macmillan, 1985)

Graves, R., *They Hanged My Saintly Billy* (Xanadu Publications, 1957)

Gribble, L., *Famous Stories of the Murder Squad* (Arthur Barker, 1974)

Griffiths, A., *Mysteries of Police and Crime* (3 volumes) (Cassell, 1898)

Holden, A., *The St Albans Poisoner* (Hodder & Stoughton, 1974)

Holmstedt, B. & Liljestrand, G., *Readings in Pharmacology* (Pergamon Press, 1963)

Honeycombe, G., *The Murders of the Black Museum* (Arrow, 1982)

Huggett, R. & Berry, P., *Daughters of Cain* (Allen & Unwin, 1956)

Humphreys, Sir T., *A Book of Trials* (Heinemann, 1953)

Janaway, J., *Surrey Murderers* (Countryside Books, 1988)

Jesse, T., *Trial of Madeleine Smith* (Notable British Trials) (Hodge, 1927)

Johnson, W.B., *The Age of Arsenic* (Chapman & Hall, 1931)

Kingston, C., *Dramatic Days at the Old Bailey* (John Lane, 1923)

—— *Enemies of Society* (John Lane, 1927)

—— *Law-Breakers* (John Lane, 1930)

Knight, B., *The Post Mortem Technician's Handbook – A Manual of Mortuary Practice* (Blackwell Scientific Publications, 1984)

Lloyd, G., *The Evil That Men Do* (Robert Hale, 1989)

Lustgarten, E., *Verdict in Dispute* (Andre Deutsch, 1949)

—— *Defender's Triumph* (Andre Deutsch, 1951)

—— *The Woman in the Case* (Andre Deutsch, 1955)

—— *The Murder and the Trial* (Andre Deutsch, 1960)

—— *The Judges and the Judged* (Andre Deutsch, 1961)

—— *A Century of Murders* (Andre Deutsch, 1978)

Martindale, W.A., *The Extra Pharmacopea* (The Pharmaceutical Press, 1958)

—— *The Extra Pharmacoeia* (The Pharmaceutical Press, 1982)

Mason, J.K., *Forensic Medicine for Lawyers* [2nd ed.] (Butterworths, 1983)

Maycock, Sir W., *Celebrated Crimes and Criminals* (George Mann, 1973)

Mortimer, J., *Famous Trials* (Viking, 1984)

Odell, R., *Exhumation of a Murder* (George G. Harrap, 1975)

Pearce, C.E., *Unsolved Murder Mysteries* (Stanley Paul, 1924)

Polson, C.J., Green, M.A. & Lee, M.R., *Clinical Toxicology* (Pitman, 1983)

Rowland, J., *Poisoner in the Dock* (Arco Publications, 1960)

Ryan, B. with Havers, Sir M., *The Poisoned Life of Mrs Maybrick* (Penguin, 1989)

Simpson, K., *Forty Years of Murder – An Autobiography* (Harrap, 1978)

Smith, E.H., *Famous American Poison Mysteries* (Hurst & Blackett, 1926)

Solicitors Journal, 133, 34, 1067, 1989, 'Plus ça change ...'

Stevenson, T.W.S., 'The Maybrick Poisoning Report' (*Criminologist*, 4, 11, 30-3)

St Aubin, G., *Infamous Victorians* (Constable, 1971)

Tallant, R., *Murder in New Orleans* (William Kimber, 1953)

Tardieu, A., *L'Empoisonement* (Ballière et files, 1895)

Taylor, F., *The Practice of Medicine* (J.A. Churchill, 1918)

Taylor, A.S., 'Trial for Murder by Poisoning with Arsenic, Berks., Lent Assizes 1845' in Ober, W.B. [ed], (1973), *Great Men at Guys* (Scarecrow Reprint Corporation, New Jersey, USA)

Thompson, C.J.S., *Poison Mysteries in History, Romance and Crime* (Scientific Press, 1925)

—— *Poisons and Poisoners* (Harold Shaylor, 1931)

—— *Poison Mysteries Unsolved* (Hutchinson, 1937)

Thompson, J., *Crime Scientist* (Harrap, 1980)

Thompson, W.A.R., *Black's Medical Dictionary* (A & C Black, 1984)

Thorwald, J., *Dead Men Tell Tales* (Thames & Hudson, 1966)

—— *Proof of Poison* (Thames & Hudson, 1966) [Trans. R. Winston]

Tichy, W., *Poisons: Antidotes and Anecdotes* (Oak Tree Press, 1977)

Tullett, T., *Strictly Murder* (The Bodley Head, 1979)

—— *Famous Cases of Scotland Yard's Murder Squad* (Triad Granada, 1981)

Walbrook, H.M. *Murders and Murder Trials 1812-1912* (Constable, 1932)

Wilson, C. & Pitman, P., *Encyclopedia of Murder* (Pan Books, 1984)

Wilson, C. & Seaman, D., *Encyclopedia of Modern Murder* (Arthur Barker, 1983)

Wilson, J.G., *Not Proven* (Secker & Warburg, 1960)

Wilson, P., *Murderess* (Michael Joseph, 1971)

Young, F., In Mortimer J. (1984), *Famous Trials* (Viking, 1927)